John Gibbons

Tenure and toil; or, Rights and Wrongs of Property and Labor

John Gibbons

Tenure and toil; or, Rights and Wrongs of Property and Labor

ISBN/EAN: 9783744757522

Printed in Europe, USA, Canada, Australia, Japan

Cover: Foto ©Suzi / pixelio.de

More available books at **www.hansebooks.com**

Tenure and Toil;

or,

Rights and Wrongs

of

Property and Labor.

BY

JOHN GIBBONS, LL.D.,

OF THE CHICAGO BAR.

PHILADELPHIA:

J. B. LIPPINCOTT COMPANY.

1888.

INTRODUCTION.

PROPERTY is man's domain, labor the sum of his existence. To own is the passion of life, to do is the necessity of being. The germ and growth of the former are furnished and fostered by the latter. Thus it is that Tenure is the prerogative of Toil, which to abridge would be violence, to abolish, sacrilege. How best to employ the one so as to most fully enjoy the other has been a burden to philanthropy, a foil to statecraft, and a perplexity to human wisdom ever since man received his title-deeds to earth, sealed by the anathema of toil.

The author does not arrogate the ability to solve problems which have eluded the wisdom of philosophers and sages in all the ages, nor does he claim that his are infallible specifics for all the social and political ills which afflict society. The carper and iconoclast are but thorns and stumbling-blocks in the path of social progress and political reform. Where the author seeks to modify or abolish existing conditions and institutions, he proposes plans and furnishes material with which to remodel and replace them. Whether his plans and material shall prove acceptable and effectual thought and time must determine. The weaknesses and wrongs which seem inherent in our system of political

3

economy, as pointed out by the author, are seen and admitted by all ; yet he is aware that the reforms proposed and remedies suggested will provoke opposition in that they comprehend a radical departure from present conditions, but, subjected to the practical analysis of common sense and to the touchstone of actual application, he believes they would prove potent factors in equalizing social conditions and promoting political advancement. It is true, what is proposed may rightly be deemed innovation, and it is also true that innovation is not always reform, yet reformation cannot be had without progression, and progress involves not only change, but advance. Change is the philosophy of life, progress the science of utility.

The time is at hand when America, if she is in any manner to shape and perfect her destiny, must not only determine the true goal of social organization, but also to walk in the best and safest way of attaining that goal ; and every American who feels a concern for the good of his fellow-men, who desires to act intelligently upon the political proposals of the day, who aspires to wield a healthful influence on the moral and material growth of the republic, should make special endeavor to understand the social and industrial problems, beside which all others are but empty queries. A recognition of this duty prompts the writing of this work.

That there is something radically wrong in our national polity cannot be gainsaid. The unrest and discontent felt and heard in every line of social and industrial life are but the protests of a struggling humanity against hardships and oppressions growing out of the inequalities of conditions which are the natural and necessary outgrowth of defective and perverted laws. The murmur of the millions is but a plea for justice. It is the part of wisdom to hearken unto these protests, to inquire as to their cause, and, on finding it, to seek its removal. Humanity demands that this plea should be heard and answered.

It is worse than idle to point to the material wealth abounding on every hand as evidence that peace and plenty are within the reach of all. Wilfully blind is he who does not see want stalking beside wealth at every turn. Within the shadow of the mansion where comfort is forgotten in luxury stands the hut where privation degenerates into want. Upon the boulevards opulent idleness feasts upon tempting viands, while on the back streets and in the alleys industry feeds upon husks.

The soul of popular states is equality; and co-operation is rapidly being recognized as the true social form. This is the basis and inspiration of modern progress, social, industrial, and political. It is the ethics of the advanced thought of to-day,—no romance, but realistic. Labor and Capital must be made sharers in the profits which are the joint product of both. Trusts, capital's conspiracy against the right to live, must be destroyed at whatever cost. As home-owners are seldom malcontents, but are always true safeguards against social disturbances and industrial revolts, the deserving poor in every community should be afforded means to build for themselves homes on the public domain which Providence provided as the common heritage of the people. Speculation in the public lands, which always degenerates into peculation, should be abolished, and ownership itself restrained within such limits that there will be ample acreage for all.

In commercial greatness this republic is destined to exceed the record of all other nations, and, with it perforce allied, all its concomitant evils,—the outgrowth of wealth and luxury enjoyed by the few, and of penury and want suffered by the many. Foster the farm, the mart will maintain its own mastery.

> " Where wealth and freedom reigns, contentment fails ;
> And honor sinks where commerce long prevails."

Build up the home, for it is the centre of love and peace, of harmony and happiness, of social order and patriotic devotion. Make this a nation of homesteaders and peasant proprietors, and our institutions will continue to be in the future, as they have been in the past, the model and marvel of the world.

CONTENTS.

BOOK I.

THE RIGHT OF PROPERTY AND THE HISTORY OF TENURES.

BOOK II.

THE ORIGIN, GROWTH, AND DECADENCE OF FEUDAL TENURES.

BOOK III.

THE RIGHT OF PROPERTY AND THE STABILITY OF TENURES.

BOOK IV.

LABOR; ITS WRONGS AND THEIR REMEDIES.

BOOK V.

LIMITATION OF OWNERSHIP AND PROHIBITION OF TRUSTS.

BOOK VI.

DISTRIBUTION OF POPULATION AND DIVISION OF PROPERTY.

APPENDIX.

TENURE AND TOIL.

BOOK I.

THE RIGHT OF PROPERTY AND THE HISTORY OF TENURES.

CHAPTER I.

THE BASIS OF THE RIGHT OF PROPERTY.

NEXT to the right of life and liberty, there is nothing which so potently and pleasurably impresses the imagination and so interweaves itself in the affections of mankind as the right of property. To know the basis upon which this right is founded, the steps whereby one man acquired that sole and positive authority which he claims and exercises over a certain piece of property to the exclusion of the claim of any other man, it will be necessary to trace the origin of society and the history of property back to the infancy of the world.

In the early ages of the world, before states and kingdoms were formed, the family existed, and was governed by its paternal head, .who was the arbiter

11

and judge of whatever contests and divisions might
arise within it; the natural legislator over his little
society. The laws which paternal wisdom established
for its guidance being dictated by no other motive than
to promote the general welfare, were observed as an
hereditary polity, and the penalty for their breach enforced with paternal tenderness.

Whatever visionary speculations may have been advanced by fanciful writers as to the origin of property
and the mode in which the right to a specific thing became actually vested in one man to the exclusion of all
others, there is no period in the history of civilized nations in which the conditions verify the theory that
property was ever common in the sense that each one
took from the public stock to his own use such things
as his fancy favored or desires demanded. Such a
theory may be deduced from the history of property
and the mode of its enjoyment among savage tribes
whose history is recent as compared with that recorded
in the Pentateuch. In human history, civilization preceded barbarism. The latter is a condition wrought by
the decadence and decomposition of the former.

In the history of the first family (and for all historic
purposes the Pentateuch, or first five books of the Bible,
it is generally conceded, is the most venerable monument of antiquity) we are informed that Abel was a
shepherd and Cain a husbandman : that Cain offered
of the fruits of the earth gifts to the Lord. Abel offered of the firstlings of his flock and of their fat : and
the Lord had respect to Abel and to his offerings. But
to Cain and his offerings he had no regard : and Cain

was exceedingly angry. From this it is reasonable to suppose that there arose, to a certain degree, sole or individual ownership of property, both real and personal, in the person who occupied or possessed it.

When mankind increased in numbers and families multiplied, diverse motives gave rise to different laws. As human society grew more and more refined, comforts and conveniences, such as habitations for shelter and safety and raiment for warmth and decency, were devised to render life more easy and enjoyable; and then it became necessary to entertain conceptions of more permanent dominion over external things than that attaching to the mere right of possession, which existed only so long as the act of possession lasted. No man would be solicitous to provide either shelter or raiment so long as he had only a usufructuary property in them, which ceased the instant that he quitted possession; if, as soon as he walked out of his tent or pulled off his garment, the next stranger who came by would have a right to inhabit the one and to wear the other. "In the case of habitations, in particular, it was natural to observe that even the brute creation, to whom everything else was common, maintained a kind of permanent property in their dwellings, especially for the protection of their young; that the birds of the air had nests, and the beasts of the field had caverns, the invasion of which they esteemed a flagrant injustice, and would sacrifice their lives to preserve them." Whether we admit that "necessity begat property," or contend that the idea of property was the normal resultant of the evolution of natural forces, it would be irrational to assume that any man would till the earth if another might, opportunity offering, seize upon and enjoy the fruits of his industry and labor.

The true theory, grounded in reason and verified by the philosophy of human events, is that the right of property, like the right of liberty, finds its basic principle in the law of natural justice, and its *recognition* and *support* find effective expression in the law of civil society. The family is ordained of God. Civil society in conception and organization is but the expansive application of the family principle. Its multiform and complicate relations are but radiations from the family centre, even when in enlarged combinations constituting the polities of tribes, states, and governments.

In process of time, the family being divided into many branches, each of which had its head, whose various interests and characters might interrupt the general tranquillity, it became necessary to intrust one person with the government of the whole. The person so chosen eventually assumed the title and authority of king. To him a throne was erected and a sceptre given. Homage was paid him, officers assigned him, and guards appointed for the security of his person. Tributes were granted him, and he was invested with full power to maintain the public peace by a uniform administration of justice.

At the dawn of political history each tribe had its chief or king, whose aspirations found full scope within the limits of his own narrow realm. But those inevitable broils which destroy peace between neighbors; envy of rival kings; a lawless and restless spirit; a propensity for war or a desire of conquest; or the ambition to exhibit superior prowess, caused the king of one tribe or country to invade the territory of another. These invasions often resulted in the complete subjugation of the conquered, whose possessions became the spoils of the conqueror and gradually extended the limits of his kingdom. Prompted by diverse propensities, or impelled by different interests, kings utilized their victories in various ways. To some the vanquished were but slaves, and in refraining from taking their lives the conqueror deemed himself generous beyond measure, while he robbed them and their families of their property, their homes, and their freedom; reduced them to servitude; compelled them to perform the most menial and servile drudgery; driving them to dig and delve deep in the earth for the precious minerals simply to gratify his own mercenary greed; hence arose the division of mankind into two classes, masters and slaves, lords and vassals.

Through long centuries warfare between these two classes was waged with varying fortunes and diverse results, the one striving not only to retain but to extend its despotic power, the other struggling to escape from the bondage of tyranny and attain freedom of thought and action. Every effort made for the redress of human wrongs or to gain and defend the sacred rights of person or property, whether, failing, dishonored as rebellion or, succeeding, dignified as revolution, in the world's annals, but lifted humanity a measure higher in the scale of progress and brought it a step nearer universal liberty. Each of these heroic endeavors gathered strength and momentum from the preceding until they culminated in that grand climacteric—the American Revolution—which wrought the political apotheosis of mankind.

While in this nineteenth century we may justly boast of having reached the very climax of political freedom, yet the lord and vassal of mediæval feudalism find their prototypes in the money baron and industrial serf of to-day. The accumulation of vast fortunes by the few, creating corporations with absolute control over the ways and means of doing and living, dictating the enactments of legislative bodies, perverting the administration of justice, prescribing rules of action for executive officials, and, in the arrogance of their plenary powers, ignoring or crushing individual rights and interests, it may be well to ask, Can our loudly-vaunted political freedom much longer endure even as the shadow of the substance so dearly won and once prized so sacredly?

CHAPTER II.

McGLYNN'S BASIC PRINCIPLE.

THE Rev. Edward McGlynn, D.D., in his lecture on "The Cross of the New Crusade," says, "It is the object of this crusade of ours to preach the truth that shall make men see clearly what is the cause of the evident injustice that condemns the mass of men to toil, and in some instances increasingly depriving them of what they produce by their toil. We assert that the one prime reason of the injustice that is done in depriving labor frequently of the opportunity of finding employment, and when it does find employment depriving it of the full equivalent for what it produces, is the constantly-increasing monopoly by a privileged class of the general bounties of nature, which belong by the law of nature, and of nature's God, not to a class but to the whole human family.

"The private ownership of the general bounties of nature is the one supreme cause of all causes of the enslavement of labor, and that condition of things which deprives labor of a full equivalent for what it produces by its exertion.

"That all men have, by the law of nature, and therefore by the law of God, an equal right to these general bounties can be readily demonstrated by a very brief argument. These truths are in consonance with religion and Christian philosophy."

Whether the theories of the reverend doctor "are in consonance with religion and Christian philosophy," it is not my purpose to question. As I am a layman and he a doctor of divinity, I would not presume to question the soundness of his views from the stand-point of "religion or Christian philosophy." I shall simply endeavor to show that his notions of natural justice are inconsistent, illogical, and at variance with reason and common sense.

"The idea of property," he says, "comes only to

men from the idea of making, from the idea of producing. The idea of property among men comes first from the consciousness that men have of owning themselves. Man owns himself, and therefore he owns and controls his own labor. He may work upon this material or that. He is free to choose what he shall do, and where he shall do it, and, out of given materials, what he shall make. And when, by the free choice of his will and the free exercise of his labor, out of the general storehouse of nature, he produces something, that something is his to hold, to own, to use, to give away, to sell, and even to destroy, because he has made it. Thus he acquires the idea and the right of ownership. It is, as it were, a translation of his labor, of his time, his patience, and his skill into the form and the place that he gives to that portion of the general bounties of nature. He is with his cup dipping water from the stream, he is with his line and rod getting fish from the stream, and is with other instruments digging and hewing a block of stone from the quarry. Out of that block with mallet and chisel, if he has the artistic skill and vision to see a sleeping beauty, he makes haste to chisel away the larger parts to reveal the angel that he sees imprisoned there, and that angel is his to give away, to keep, to sell, and even to destroy, because he has made it.

"While he has not made the raw material, he has appropriated that portion of the general bounties of nature legitimately, and no other man can have the right to claim joint ownership in that. If two men should come to the banks of a river, and one should fish all day and the other should sleep all day, the basket of fish would belong to the fisherman, and the reward of the other would be the rest and the refreshment that he had enjoyed. It would be the same with the block of marble. The idea of property comes from *making.*" *

---

* I fail to find in the learned doctor's elegant lecture a thought that is practical or even original. In chapter i., Book VII., of " Progress and Poverty," in answer to a series of interrogatories as to what constitutes the rightful basis of property, George says:

" As a man belongs to himself, so his labor when put in concrete form belongs to him. And for this reason, that which a man makes or produces is his own—as against all the world—to enjoy or to destroy, to use, to exchange, or to give. No one else can rightfully claim it, and his exclusive right to it involves no wrong to any one else. Thus there is to everything produced by human exertion a clear and indisputable title to exclusive possession and enjoyment, which is perfectly consistent with justice, as it descends from the original producer, in whom it vested by natural law. The pen with which I am writing is justly mine. No other human being can rightfully lay claim to it, for in me is the title of the producers who made it. It has become mine because transferred to me by the stationer, to whom it was transferred by the importer, who obtained the exclusive right to it by transfer from the manufacturer, in whom, by the same process of purchase, vested the rights of those who dug the material from the ground and shaped it into a pen. Thus my exclusive right of ownership in the pen springs from the natural right of the individual to the use of his own faculties. . . .

" The equal right of all men to the use of land is as clear as their equal right to breathe the air,—it is a right proclaimed by the fact of their existence. For we cannot suppose that some men have a right to be in this world and others no right.

" If we are all here by the equal permission of the Creator, we are all here with an equal title to the enjoyment of his bounty,— with an equal right to the use of all that nature so impartially

Let us pursue the doctor's fish-story to its logical conclusion, and see what becomes of his theory of the law of natural justice when subjected to the analysis of plain, homely common sense. When the industrious fisherman has filled his basket with fish from the storehouse of nature, the man who had slept all day awakes and demands an equal division of the basket of fish. "This demand," says the doctor, "would be unjust and unreasonable, and to insist upon it would be contrary to the law of natural justice." Right! Now, then, the man who fished all day while the other slept takes his basket of fish to market, sells it, and receives as an equivalent therefor one dollar in cash, and this dollar, the doctor says, he has the right to keep, to use, to enjoy, or destroy, because it is the compensation, the

---

offers. This is a right which is natural and inalienable; it is a right which vests in every human being as he enters the world, and which during his continuance in the world can be limited only by the equal rights of others. There is in nature no such thing as a fee-simple in land. There is on earth no power which can rightfully make a grant of exclusive ownership in land. If all existing men were to unite to grant away their equal rights, they could not grant away the rights of those who follow them. For what are we but tenants for a day? Have we made the earth, that we should determine the rights of those who after us shall tenant it in their turn? The Almighty, who created the earth for man and man for the earth, has entailed it upon all the generations of the children of men by a decree written upon the constitution of all things,—a decree which no human action can bar and no prescription determine. Let the parchments be ever so many, or possession ever so long, natural justice can recognize no right in one man to the possession and enjoyment of land that is not equally the right of all his fellows."

reward of his labor, because "the laborer is worthy of
his hire." The fisherman, therefore, is entitled to his
basket of fish because by his labor he has taken and
appropriated them from the hand of nature. He may
eat them, give them away, or sell them. So far the
doctor construes the law of natural justice correctly.
On the morrow the industrious fisherman and the sluggard return to the river's bank, and again the fisherman
fishes all day while the sluggard sleeps, and at night
the fisherman comes to market with his basket of fish,
sells them, and receives therefor another dollar in cash.
This is repeated from day to day, until the fisherman
has saved up one hundred dollars. These one hundred
dollars, according to the law of natural justice, are as
much his individual property as were the baskets of
fish. The baskets of fish were the reward of his labor,
and the money received as their equivalent was also the
reward of his labor. It was merely an exchange of
fish for money. The fisherman, anxious to secure for
himself and family a home, exchanges the money for a
city lot, when, lo, the sluggard, who had slept and refreshed himself in the shade during all these many days,
comes along, and says, "This lot is ours." "Oh, no,"
says the fisherman, "this lot is mine. While you slept
I fished. The fish which I caught I carried to market,
sold them, and received their equivalent in money, and
with it purchased this lot, therefore it is mine." "The
fish belonged to you," says the sluggard, "because you
caught them. The money which you received for them
was yours also, because it was the reward of your labor,
but this lot is land, and Dr. McGlynn says that all the

men in the universe cannot make one grain of sand ; that God alone can make it, and as God made the land, it belongs to God. So nature has given the perpetual right to use it to all the children of men, and not to one individual more than another. It is true that I slept in the shade and was refreshed while you fished and toiled, but, as I am one of the children of men, I have as much right to this land as you have." "I have always heard," says the fisherman, "and, if I am not mistaken, it is so stated in Holy Writ, that the same God who made the land made the fishes too, and if the fact that I cannot make one grain of sand is to weigh in the balance, and is to be considered as a controlling reason against my right to own this land, suppose you go and tell the learned doctor to try his hand on a little fish."

CHAPTER III.

McGLYNN AND THE ANGEL.

PASSING from the fisherman to the sculptor, who has the vision so refined as to see a sleeping beauty in the rude block of stone taken from the quarry, and who has the artistic skill, with mallet and chisel, to release the angel that he sees imprisoned there, which angel "is his to give away, to keep, to sell, and even to destroy," because he has made it, we find here another illustration of the inconsistency and absurdity of the

learned doctor's conception of the law of natural justice. According to the abstract principles of natural
justice the sculptor has no right to destroy the thing
of beauty which he produced from the rude rock, because the sculptor could not exist separate and apart
from society, and as he is indebted to society for all
that he is and all that he has and all that he enjoys, it
would be a crime against the law of natural justice to
permit him to destroy, to annihilate that which he thus
produced.

The product of the artisan's handiwork *is not* wholly
his own. His ability to transform the unhewn marble
into an image of grace and beauty is a resultant of the
thoughtful toil and aspiring effort of every hand that
has striven with chisel and mallet since the days of
Bezaleel, the son of Hur. In very truth, the civilization of to-day is the crystallization of the human
thought and human effort of all the ages gone before.
But I do not propose to discuss this question, as it is,
at best, a mere side issue, and hardly germane to the
point in controversy, so that whether I admit or deny
the claim that the sculptor has a right to destroy the
angel, I agree with Dr. McGlynn that the angel is his
to give away, to keep, or to sell. If he has the right
to sell it, the money or thing which he receives as its
equivalent is the reward or tribute paid to his genius,
skill, and labor. Some angels sell at a very costly
price. We mean the marble images such as the sculptor formed from the rude rock. But suppose another
man, equally a genius in his way, but not endowed with
the artistic vision and skill to see and free an angel im-

prisoned in the rock, shoulders his pick and shovel, and wends his way to the Rocky Mountains, and his artistic vision reveals to him in the outcroppings of the soil the existence of gold and silver far down amid the strata of the earth. With pick and shovel he makes haste to dig and throw the earth away, that he may secure precious metals hidden there. This gold and silver are his to give away, to keep, or to sell, just as much as was the sculptor's angel, formed out of the rude rock by the mallet and chisel guided by his genius. The gold and silver thus acquired are the rewards of his labor just as much so as the angel was the reward of the sculptor's labor. The gold and silver that he thus appropriated from the storehouse of nature by his perseverance and his toil are his as much as were the fish which the fisherman caught from the stream with his hook and line. The fish in the river equally belonged to the sluggard and the fisherman before they were caught. Both had the same natural right to fish from the stream, which was common property. This much the doctor admits; not only admits but asserts it to be the law of natural justice, and it is because the fisherman appropriated the fish from the storehouse of nature by his toil that they belonged to him in his individual right. It is the same way with the "imprisoned angel." Any other man who has the genius and skill and industry may go to the quarry and appropriate to himself a rock out of which to make something useful or ornamental, just the same as did the sculptor, and what he thus appropriates from the "quarries of the gods" belongs to him because it is the reward of his labor. Any one who has the energy and inclination may shoulder his pick and shovel and wend his way to the Rocky Mountains, and delve and dig until he finds the hidden treasure, and when found, he simply appropriates so much from the storehouse of nature, the thing which he thus appropriates is but the reward of his labor. To say that everybody who pursues this vocation cannot find a mine is no argument against the abstract principle upon which the law of natural justice is based. Two men may fish all day, the one patiently and perseveringly as the other, and one of them may catch fish in abundance, while the other may catch but few or none at all. And so it is in regard to the sculptor, for the thing of beauty which his genius and fancy formed may have a priceless value, while a similar rock may be used by the stone-mason in the construction of a stable. Thus it is that we cannot equalize the value of men's services, nor is there any place in the law of natural justice for the argument that the sculptor should receive no higher reward for his labor than the stone-mason, nor that the successful miner should be limited in his reward to the value of the basket of fish.

After the sculptor had disposed of the "angel," he concluded to go West to settle upon the prairie and grow up with the country. He travelled far out on the plains until he came to a place upon which he decided to locate. There he pitched his tent and fenced in one hundred and sixty acres of land. After years of tireless patience and unremitting toil he transforms the land which he found a wilderness into a garden of beauty and fruitfulness. Other settlers had located near him. At the close of one bright day six seedy tramps, ordained apostles of Dr. McGlynn's new civilization, came along, and without beck or bidding entered the cottage of the whilom sculptor. They remained uninvited guests for the night, and on the morrow, as they stood, with an "at-home" free and easy air, in front of the house, looking over the nicely-cultivated grounds, said to the settler, "Our farm looks fine." "Our farm!" exclaimed the settler. "This is my farm." "Why yours more than ours?" rejoined the tramps. "Is not this *land,* and God made the land? And Henry George has said, and Dr. McGlynn, the Peter of the New Crusade, has echoed his saying, that all things made by God are not of right the property of one man, but belong to all men in common." "Yes, it may be allowed that land in a state of nature belongs to God, but I have appropriated out of nature's wide domain one hundred and sixty acres, which I have entered under the homestead law, fenced and cultivated, and the fruits which it yields are the reward of my labor. No one will deny that it rightfully belongs to me. God ordains it, and the law decrees it. All philosophy teaches it. Adam Smith and all the lesser lights who have written upon politico-economic questions affirm it. Even Henry George—when George is himself— admits it, for he says, 'The man who cultivates the soil for himself receives his wages in its produce, just as, if he uses his own capital and owns his own land, he may also receive interest and rent; the hunter's wages are the game he kills; the fisherman's wages are the fish he takes. The gold washed out by the self-employing gold-digger is as much his wages as the money paid to the hired coal-miner by the purchaser of his labor. In short, whatever is received as the result or reward of exertion is "wages." ' (" Progress and Poverty," ch. ii.) Just beyond you will find broad acres lying in a state of nature, the same as I found the land which I fenced and reclaimed. This you may enter as I have done, reclaim and cultivate it." The new-comers shrugged their shoulders at the very mention of work; having tramped to the frontiers to escape sawing wood, shovelling snow, or carrying coal up-stairs for a breakfast, the idea of toil, so out of harmony with the teachings of the new dispensation, chilled them to the marrow. The spokesman replied, "This land you point out to us is worth nothing. We do not want the untilled plains, we want the cultivated farm. This farm, you understand, has a rental value, and it is the rent we are after, not the farm. We do not ask you to divide the land with us. We have no use for land. You may remain on the farm and cultivate it so long as you pay for that privilege. We would not deprive you of that pleasure for the world. We propose, however, to put it up at auction every year to the highest bidder, and if you do not bid more for it than any other person who wishes to cultivate it, you will have to surrender its possession and give up its enjoyment. Its full rental value, under the new order of things, must be paid into the public treasury, of which *we*, the people, are the trusty guardians. It is true that you display great learning and research and

study in quoting from Moses and the prophets, from
Adam Smith, Henry George, and others, but the world
has made great strides in advance of these fogies.
Even Henry George has advanced since he wrote his
work on 'Progress and Poverty.' He has recently
enlisted in the ranks, and is marching arm in arm with
our clerical Turveydrop, under the banner of the
'Cross of the New Crusade.' This movement that we
would dignify by so honorable a name, in some sense,
may be called a very new one, since it is a new and
a very determined effort to achieve a perfectly clear
and decided end, and yet, in another sense, it may be
called a very old one, since it is to preach and to make
more common the practice among men of a truth that
is as old as man himself, and in some sense may be
said to be as old as God,—the truth that justice must
be the rule of any society that shall be created by God.
Our remedy, then, for the injustice that now exists is
not to dispossess you or drive you out of this farm,
but simply to appropriate to the common treasury its
full rental value through existing forms of taxation, and
thus we shall maintain the absolute equality of man in
the general bounties of nature, without disturbing you
in your possession. Indeed, the chief attraction to
many of us in this crusade is the religion that is in it.
It is founded on the Sermon on the Mount, the Lord's
Prayer, the Brotherhood of Man, and the Fatherhood
of God, which is the soul of all religion. We shall
establish and maintain public victualling-houses and
inns, so that when we invoke the bountiful Giver of all
good things, 'Give us this day our daily bread,' it shall

be given us in fact and in deed. No more shall we be required to saw wood or shovel snow for a breakfast, nor scrub the steps of a bar-room for a drink of poor whiskey, but when the 'bloated but princely tramp' comes along, if you would have him to work for you, it must be at his own price and on his own terms."

Perhaps the writer should crave the intelligent reader's pardon for the apparently trivial diversions of the foregoing pages. Yet I have not been seeking to traverse the imaginary vagaries of a mythical theorist, but in truth to pleasantly dissect the worse than sophisms of the greatest political Don Quixote of the age. For the " New Crusade" is vauntingly proclaimed to be the last evangel that supersedes all others,—a panacea for all ills, social and economic, that afflict the body politic. But a truce to such pleasantry. Let us proceed to a common-sense investigation of the rights of property, and gather a few sheaves of practical justice from the harvests of ages.

CHAPTER IV.

THE DIVINE ORIGIN OF THE RIGHT OF PROPERTY.

" THE inspired sweet singer of Israel tells us," says Dr. McGlynn, "'The heaven of heavens is the Lord's, but the earth he hath given to the children of men;' and again, Moses said, ' The land shall not be sold for-

ever, saith the Lord, for it is mine.' The Scripture
teaches Charles the First and the rest of them that they
shall not give it away or sell it, because it does not belong to them ; it belongs to God." From these quotations he undertakes to assert that any one born into the
world is entitled by divine right to the equal enjoyment
of landed property whether he works or sleeps, and
that, according to the Scriptures, no one has a right to
sell or dispose of land.

Mr. T. E. Cliffe Leslie, in his introduction to Emile de
Laveleye's " Primitive Property," says, " The property
of which M. de Laveleye treats in this volume is property in land ; of all kinds of property that which has
most deeply affected both the economic condition and the
political career of human societies. In one sense, indeed,
land was not primitive property ; it was not man's
earliest possession or wealth. The first forms of property are lost in the mist that surrounds the first infant
steps of the human race. Wild herbs, fruit, berries,
and roots were probably the earliest acquisitions, but
the food thus obtained was doubtless devoured at once.
When at length providence was developed so far as to
lead to the laying by of some sustenance for the future,
the inference to which the earliest developments of
movable wealth, of which we get glimpses, unmistakably point, is that the store which individuals might thus
accumulate would not have been regarded as their own
absolute property, but as part of the common fund of
the community, larger or smaller according to circumstances, of which they were members ;" and he undertakes to prove that movable property in primitive so-

ciety belonged first to individuals. But a close analysis of his introduction will suffice to show that Mr. Leslie confuses terms, and cites, in support of his proposition, certain usages which prevailed alike among civilized and uncivilized races. It is not the purpose of this inquiry to enter into a very elaborate discussion in regard to these matters further than to prove that, according to the Scriptures, the learned doctor's deduction is not warranted, and that Mr. Leslie's assertion, to the effect that " the inference to which the earliest developments of movable wealth, of which we get glimpses, unmistakably point, is that the store which individuals might thus accumulate would not have been regarded as their own absolute property, but as part of the common fund of the community, larger or smaller according to circumstances, of which they were members," is not supported by the history and development of society whether examined in the light of sacred history, profane writers, or the testimony of men, who have devoted much time to researches into the origin of property, and who have given great thought and study to the subject.

In the third chapter of Genesis we read that when Adam disobeyed the injunction of God, the Lord God said to him, " Because thou hast eaten of the tree of which I commanded thee not to eat, cursed is the earth in thy work : with toil shalt thou eat of it all the days of thy life. Thorns and thistles shall it bring forth to thee, and thou shalt eat the herbs of the earth. In the sweat of thy face shalt thou eat bread, till thou return to the earth, out of which thou wast taken. And the Lord God sent him out of the paradise of pleasure to till the earth from which he was taken."

And again, after God had scourged the earth by the deluge, in making a new covenant with Noe, God blessed Noe and his sons, and said to them, "Increase and multiply, and fill the earth. . . . And everything which moveth and liveth shall be food for you: even as the green herbs have I delivered to you all things."

Again, when Abram and Lot went out of Egypt rich in cattle, gold, and silver, so that the land was not able to bear them that they might dwell together, a strife arose between the herdsmen of Abram and Lot, and Abram said to Lot, "Let there be no quarrel, I beseech thee, between me and thee, and between my herdsmen and thy herdsmen; for we are brethren. Behold, the whole land is before thee: depart from me, I pray thee; if thou wilt go to the left hand, I will take to the right: if thou choose the right hand, I will pass to the left. And Lot, lifting up his eyes, saw all the country about the Jordan, which was watered throughout, before the Lord destroyed Sodom and Gomorrah, as the paradise of the Lord. And Lot chose for himself the country about the Jordan, and he departed from the east: and they were separated, one from the other."

Therefore it is evident that the cattle, gold, and silver which Abram and Lot possessed belonged to each of them individually. If the cattle were common property, why was it necessary to have separate herdsmen?

And after Lot was separated from him, the Lord said to Abram, "Lift up thy eyes and look from the place where thou now art, to the north and to the south, to the east and to the west. All the land which thou seest I will give to thee, and to thy seed forever. And I will make thy seed as the dust of the earth: if any man can number the dust of the earth, he shall be able to number thy seed also. Arise and walk through the land in its length and breadth: for to thee I will give it."

As God gave the land absolutely and forever to Abram and his seed, should " Charles the First and the rest of them" show title through Abram or his seed, their titles, from a scriptural stand-point, are indefeasible.

Again, in chapter twenty-third we read that after the death of Sarah in the city of Arba, in the land of Canaan, Abraham came to mourn and to weep for her, and after he rose up from the funeral obsequies he spake to the children of Heth, saying, " A stranger and sojourner am I among you: give me the right of a burying-place with you, that I may bury my dead." And he requested the children of Heth to intercede for him with Ephron, the son of Zohar, to give him the double cave which he had in the end of his field for such money as it was worth for a possession as a burying-place. This field was valued by Ephron at four hundred shekels. And when Abraham had heard this, he weighed out the money which Ephron had asked in the hearing of the children of Heth,—four hundred shekels of silver of common current money. And the field of Ephron, which was the double cave, looking towards Mamre, both it and the cave, and all the trees in all its limits round about, were made sure to

c

Abraham for a possession in the presence of the children
of Heth and of all who went in at the gate of his city.
And so Abraham buried Sarah, his wife, in the double
cave of the field, which looketh towards Mamre; this
is Hebron in the land of Canaan.   And the field was
made sure to Abraham, and the cave which was in it,
for a possession to bury in by the children of Heth. This
probably is the first authentic account we have of the
sale and purchase of land or real property for money.

In the twenty-second chapter of Exodus, in verse
five, God himself, in delivering to Moses the laws by
which the Israelites were to be governed, says that " if
any man commit a trespass on a field or a vineyard by
putting in his beast to feed upon other men's lands"
(*other men's lands*, mark you), " he shall restore the
best of whatever he hath in his own field or in his
vineyard, according to the estimation of the damages."
The book of Numbers abounds with references to
private ownership in land and of the right of inheritance.   In the thirty-second chapter of that book it is
said that the sons of Reuben and Gad, who had many
flocks of cattle, when they saw lands of Gazer and
Gilead fit for feeding cattle they came to Moses and
Eleazar, the priest and the princes of the multitude,
and among other things said to them, " The land which
the Lord smote in the sight of the children of Israel
is rich in pasture, and we, thy servants, have very much
cattle: if we have found favor in thy sight, give it to
us, thy servants, in possession, and make us not pass
over the Jordan."   And in chapter thirty-third, verses
fifty to fifty-six, it is written,—

" The Lord said to Moses : Command the children of Israel, and say to them : When ye shall have passed over the Jordan, entering into the land of Canaan, destroy all the inhabitants of that land, beat down their pillars, and break in pieces their statues, and waste all their high places, cleansing the land and dwelling in it. For I have given it you for an inheritance, and ye shall divide it among you by lot. . To the more numerous ye shall give a larger portion, and to the fewer less. To every one as the lot shall fall the inheritance shall be given. The possession shall be divided by the tribes and families."

In chapter thirty-fourth, after defining the limits of the land of Canaan which he gave to the Israelites, he named and selected men, Eleazar, the priest, and Josu, the son of Nun, and one prince of every tribe, to divide the land. And in chapter thirty-five God speaks to Moses, saying, " Command the children of Israel that they give to the Levites out of their possessions cities to dwell in and their suburbs round about : that they may abide in the towns, and the suburbs may be for their cattle and beasts. . . . And of these cities which shall be given out of the possessions of the children of Israel, from those who have many, many will be taken ; and from those who have less, fewer. Each shall give towns to the Levites according to the extent of their inheritance." And in order that the inheritance might not be alienated from one tribe to another, it is provided in chapter thirty-six that all are to marry within their own tribes.

" And this is the law promulgated by the Lord

touching the daughters of Salphaad : Let them marry
to whom they will, only so that it be to men of their
own tribe : lest the possession of the children of Israel
be mingled from tribe to tribe. For all men shall
marry wives of their own tribe and kindred : and all
women shall take husbands of the same tribe : that the
inheritance may remain in the families, and that the
tribes be not mingled one with another, but remain so
as they were separated by the Lord." . . .

CHAPTER V.

MCGLYNN'S MISTAKE.

THESE chapters explain the meaning of the text
quoted by Dr. McGlynn from the twenty-fifth chapter of Leviticus, twenty-third verse. Dr. McGlynn's
quotation is hardly correct. Dr. McGlynn's version is
as follows : " The land shall not be sold forever, saith
the Lord, for it is mine." The text in King James's
version of the Bible is, " The land shall not be sold
forever : for the land is mine ; for ye are strangers and
sojourners with me." And in Kenrick's* translation
of the Bible it reads : " The land also shall not be sold

------

* Dr. Kenrick's translation of the Bible is recognized among
biblical scholars of every denomination as being a more literal
rendering of the original text than any other, and as there is no
material variance between it and King James's version, the author
has preferred to quote from the former.

forever: because it is mine, and ye are strangers and
sojourners with me." Now, it will be seen that when
Moses made use of this expression he was laying down
the law relative to the feast of the seventh and of the
fiftieth year of jubilee, and it was said also while the
children of Israel were still wanderers and sojourners
in the desert. "The Lord spake to Moses on Mount
Sinai, saying: Speak to the children of Israel, and say
to them: When ye shall have entered into the land
which I give you, keep a sabbath to the Lord. Six
years thou shalt sow thy field, and six years thou shalt
prune thy vineyard, and gather the fruits thereof: But
in the seventh year shall be a sabbath to the land, of
the resting of the Lord." (According to Kenrick
the land was to rest from cultivation for a year.)
"Thou shalt not sow thy field nor prune thy vineyard. . . . And thou shalt sanctify the fiftieth year,
and shalt proclaim release to all the inhabitants of thy
land: for it is the year of jubilee. Every man shall
return to his possessions, and every one shall go back
to his former family: Because it is the jubilee and the
fiftieth year." (The servants in this year were set
free; landed property returned to its original possessors to be again allotted to the members of the
tribe, so that in this manner its permanent accumulation in the hands of others not of the tribe was prevented.) The portion which fell to the lot of the
individual belonged to him to use, enjoy, sell, or give
away until the return of the jubilee year. Every sale
of land, therefore, was limited to the year of jubilee,
and the price varied according to the time which it was

to run from the time of its sale to the year of jubilee, and when the Lord says, through Moses, "The land also shall not be sold forever: because it is mine, and ye are strangers and sojourners with me," he meant that the land should not be sold *forever*, and did not mean that they should never sell it; but rather that it *might* be sold for any term of years not to exceed fifty years. In this chapter, as already stated, he is laying down a law to the Israelites for the observance of the feasts of the jubilee years. In order that the meaning of this quotation may be properly understood and to make it harmonize with the text in which it occurs, it will be necessary to consider the verses preceding and those following it. They are as follows:

"And in the eighth year ye shall sow, and shall eat of the old fruits, until the ninth year: till new grow up, ye shall eat the old store. The land also shall not be sold forever: because it is mine, and ye are strangers and sojourners with me. For which cause all the country of your possession shall be under the condition of redemption. If thy brother, being impoverished, sell his possession, and his kinsman will, he may redeem what he had sold. But if he have no kinsman, and he himself can find the price to redeem it, the value of the fruits shall be counted from the time when he sold it: and the overplus he shall restore to the buyer, and so shall receive his possession again. But if his hands find not the means to repay the price, the buyer shall have what he bought, until the year of the jubilee. For in this year all that is sold shall return to the owner, and to the ancient possessor."

Divine justice seemed to look with peculiar favor upon the tenure by which the title to city property was held, for in this same chapter out of which Dr. Mc-Glynn quotes, and from which he proclaims his communistic doctrine, particularly against the owners of city property, we find it stated as follows:

" He that selleth a house within the walls of a city, shall have the liberty to redeem it, until one year be expired. If he redeem it not, and the whole year be fully out, the buyer shall possess it, and his posterity forever; and it cannot be redeemed, not even in the jubilee."

Kenrick, in a note to this verse, says that the inconveniences likely to arise from temporary and conditional transfers of property in cities caused the right of redemption to be limited to one year, and in order that the Levites, who were dependent upon the children of Israel for their possessions, might not be deprived of their property from inability to redeem the same, the law made a special favor, to the effect that the houses of Levites which are in cities may always be redeemed. If they be not redeemed in the jubilee they shall all return to the owners; because the houses of the cities of the Levites are for their possessions among the childern of Israel. By considering these verses in connection with the book of Numbers, it will be seen that the object of the law was to prevent a sale of property belonging to the individual for a period exceeding fifty years, as in that year all the lands were to return to the original owner, to be again allotted to the members of the tribes.

We also find it written in the book of Ruth that in the days when the judges ruled Israel, a certain man named Elimelech, of Bethlehem, Judea, went to sojourn in the land of Moab with his wife and two sons. The sons of Elimelech married wives of the tribe of Moabites, and after the death of Elimelech and of his sons, the widow of Elimelech, named Naomi, returned to her people, the Israelites, accompanied by her daughter-in-law, Ruth. Elimelech had a kinsman named Boaz, who was rich and powerful, in whose eyes the Moabitess, Ruth, found favor, and Boaz went to the gate of the city, where all solemn and legal acts were performed, and sat there awaiting the coming of the nearest kinsman of Elimelech, and when he saw him he requested him to sit down, in order that they might talk over matters concerning Ruth. And Boaz called as witnesses ten of the ancients of the city, according to the manner of the Israelites, and he spoke to the kinsman of Elimelech, saying, " Naomi, who is returned from the country of Moab, will sell a parcel of land that belonged to our brother Elimelech. I would have thee to understand this, and would tell thee before all that sit *here*, and before the ancients of my people, if thou wilt take possession of it by the right of kindred, buy it and possess it: but if it please thee not, tell me so, that I may know what I have to do: for there is no near kinsman besides thee, who art first, and me, who am second. And he answered: I will buy the field. And Boaz said to him: When thou buyest the field at the woman's hand, thou must take also Ruth, the Moabitess, who was the wife of the deceased: to raise up the name of thy kinsman in his inheritance."

His relative having yielded his right of next of kin, Boaz, taking unto himself Ruth, the gleaner, said to the ancients and to all the people, " Ye are witnesses this day, that I have bought all that was Elimelech's, and Chelion's, and Mahalon's, of the hand of Naomi: And have taken to wife Ruth, the Moabitess, the wife of Mahalon, to raise up the name of the deceased in his inheritance, lest his name be cut off from among his family and his brethren and his people. Ye, I say, are witnesses of this thing. Then all the people that were in the gate and the ancients answered: We are witnesses."

Before the common use of written instruments, transfers of property were publicly made in the presence of witnesses, and something as symbolical of the delivery of the property, such as a twig or a piece of turf, in this case a shoe, according to the custom of the Israelites, was given by the seller to the buyer in the presence of witnesses.

And in the book of Genesis, chapter forty-seven, verses twenty to twenty-two, it is said, " So Joseph bought all the land of Egypt, every man selling his possessions, because of the greatness of the famine. And he brought it into Pharao's hands: And all its people, from one end of the borders of Egypt, even to the other end thereof, except the land of the priests, which had been given them by the king: to whom also a certain allowance of food was given out of the public stores, and therefore they were not forced to sell their possessions."

And in the third book of Kings,* referring to Amri, it is said, " And he bought the hill of Samaria of Semer for two talents of silver, and he built upon it, and he called the city which he built Samaria, after the name of Semer, the owner of the hill."

And in the New Testament we find in the fourth chapter of the Acts, verses thirty-four to thirty-seven, referring to those who had followed the disciples, the following: " For neither was any one among them needy; for as many as were owners of lands or houses, sold them, and brought the prices of the things which they sold, and laid them down at the feet of the apostles: and distribution was made to every one according as he had need. And Joseph, who by the apostles was surnamed Barnabas (which is, by interpretation, the son of consolation), a Levite, a Cyprian born, having land, sold it, and brought the price, and laid it at the feet of the apostles."

These quotations, taken from the Scriptures, and many others which might be found, bear indubitable evidence of the right of individual ownership in land from the beginning of the world down to the time of the apostles.

---

* King James's version, I. Kings xvi., 24.

CHAPTER VI.

PROPERTY RIGHTS RECOGNIZED IN ALL AGES.

HERODOTUS, called by Cicero the Father of History, in speaking of the cause of hostilities between the Phœnicians and the Greeks, says: "This nation [Phœnicians] migrated from the borders of the Red Sea to the place of their present settlement, and soon distinguished themselves by their long and enterprising voyages. They exported to Argos, amongst other places, the produce of Egypt and Assyria. Argos, at that period, was the most famous of all those states which are now comprehended under the general appellation of Greece. On their arrival here, the Phœnicians exposed their merchandise to sale: after remaining about six days, and when they had almost disposed of their different articles of commerce, the king's daughter, whom both nations agree in calling Io, came, among a great number of other women, to visit them at their station. Whilst these females, standing near the stern of the vessel, amused themselves with bargaining for such things as attracted their curiosity, the Phœnicians, in conjunction, made an attempt to seize their persons. The greater part of them escaped; but Io remained a captive with many others. They carried them on board, and directed their course for Egypt." .

Hence it is very reasonable to assume that at this early period the right of private ownership in property was recognized both among the Greeks and Phœnicians. Homer constantly distinguishes the Phœnicians as a commercial and seafaring people. The writers of ancient poetry and ancient history serve alike to confirm the assertion that among the Greeks, Romans, Phœnicians, Persians, Carthaginians, and Egyptians the right of private ownership in property existed from the earliest period of which we have any definite data. In other words, wherever we find a commercial people, we find the right of individual ownership in property recognized.

This is confirmed by reference to the laws of Lycurgus, for in his days, according to the most authentic history, the right of private ownership in property in Sparta existed, and, next to the institution of the senate and the assembly of the people, the new division of the lands instituted by him is by far the most worthy of note.

According to the laws established with respect to the descent of property, the estate of a deceased father descended to his sons; but if no legitimate son survived him, it descended to his daughters, who were compelled to marry their nearest relatives or forfeit their inheritance. Persons who had no lawful issue were allowed to adopt whom they pleased, whether their own natural sons, or, by consent of their parents, the sons of other men. But such as were incapable of making wills were denied this privilege. Adopted children were invested with all the privileges and rights of, and obliged to perform all the duties belonging to, natural children; and, being thus provided for in another family, they ceased to have any claim of inheritance or kindred in the family which they left, unless they first renounced their adoption. This could be done only in cases where children were born to them who would bear the name of the person by whom they were adopted and was intended to prevent the extinguishment of the family name of those who adopted them for the purpose of preserving it. If the adopted person died without lawful issue, the inheritance descended to the relatives of the person who adopted him. Illegitimate children were allowed some share both among the Jews and the Grecians in their father's estate. It was an ancient custom in Greece for legitimate sons to divide their fathers' estates by lots, each taking an equal share without regard to priority of birth, but allowing a small pittance to such as were unlawfully begotten,—the portion allotted being regulated by ancient custom or by law. The Athenian law-giver allowed five hundred drachmas, which was afterwards raised to one thousand. Such as had neither legitimate nor adopted children were succeeded by the next of kin.

The Grecian practice concerning wills was not the same in all places; some states permitted men to dispose of their estates; others wholly deprived them of that privilege. We are told by Plutarch that Solon is much commended for his law concerning wills; for before his time no man was allowed to make one, and all the wealth of deceased persons belonged to their families; but Solon permitted them to bestow it on whom they pleased, esteeming friendship a stronger tie than kindred, and affection than necessity, and thus put every man's estate at his own disposal, yet he allowed not all sorts of wills, but required the following conditions in all persons that made them :

1. That they must be citizens of Athens, not slaves or foreigners; for then their estates were confiscated for the public use.

2. That they must be men who have arrived at twenty years of age; for women, and men under that age, were not permitted to dispose by will of more than one medimnus of barley.

3. That they must not be adopted ; for when adopted persons died without issue, the estates they received by adoption returned to the relations of the man who adopted them.

4. That they should have no male children of their own, for then their estates belonged to them. If they had only daughters, the persons to whom the inheritance was bequeathed were obliged to marry them. Yet men were allowed to appoint heirs to succeed their children, in case these happened to die under twenty years of age.

5. That they should be in their right minds, because testaments extorted through the frenzy of a disease, or dotage of old age, were not in reality the wills of the persons that made them.

6. That they should not be under imprisonment or other constraint, their consent being then only forced, nor in justice to be reputed voluntary.

7. That they should not be induced to it by the charms and insinuations of a wife; for (says Plutarch)

the wise law-giver, with good reason, thought that no difference was to be put between deceit and necessity, flattery and compulsion, since both are equally powerful to persuade a man from reason.

Wills were usually signed and sealed in the presence of several witnesses, and were then placed in the hands of trustees, who were obliged to see them performed. At Athens some of the magistrates, particularly the astynomi (public magistrates) were often present at the making of wills. Sometimes the archons (the chief magistrates) were also present; hence we are told by Harpocration and Suidas, that when anything was given in the presence of the archons, it was termed dosis (gift); for this word though commonly taken for any sort of gift or present, yet was by the Athenian orators peculiarly applied to legacies and things disposed of by will. Sometimes the testator declared his will before sufficient witnesses without committing it to writing. Thus Callias, fearing to be cut off by a wicked conspiracy, is said to have made an open declaration of his will before the popular assembly at Athens. The same was done in the nuncupative wills at Rome.

CHAPTER VII.

THE HEROIC AGE OF GREECE.

LET us return for the moment to the heroic age in Grecian history, and we find the people divided into three distinct classes. The nobles, who were much exalted above the rest of the community in honor, wealth, and power, and being the sole possessors of slaves during this era, were distinguished by their prowess, their large estates, and numerous slaves. But slavery was less prevalent during this period than in republican Greece.

The common freemen, who possessed portions of land as their own property and a class of poor freemen called Thetes, who, though not the possessors of land, were still free and worked for hire on the estates of the others. Among the freemen we find a certain class of professional persons whose acquirements, attainments, and knowledge raised them above those of their class and procured for them the respect of the nobles, such as the seer, the bard, and also the smith and the carpenter, since the knowledge of the mechanical arts in that age was confined to but a few. Still it was not considered derogatory to the dignity of the nobles, or even the kings, to be skilled in the manual arts, for Ulysses is represented as building his own bedchamber and constructing his own raft, and he boasts of being an excellent mower and ploughman.

Agriculture was extensively practised, vineyards carefully cultivated, and property in land was transmitted from father to son.

The third class was that of the slaves, who were vastly more numerous in republican Greece than in former times.

As time passed by and republics rose and fell in Greece, and the poorer classes became deeply involved at the time of Solon, we find two classes, the rich and the poor. The latter ready to rise in open insurrection, for many had been sold into slavery for debt, and their property as well as their persons taken as security for the principal and interest. Solon passed an ordinance which cancelled all contracts by which the land or person had been given as security for a debt; thus the land was relieved from all claims and incumbrances, and all persons were set at liberty who had been reduced to slavery on account of their debts. He provided for the return home of all persons who had been sold into foreign countries. He forbade all loans in which the person of the debtor was pledged as security; thereby releasing the poorer classes from their difficulties. He relieved the debtors by lowering the standard of coinage so that they were saved rather more than one-fourth in every payment. The title of the citizens to the honors and offices of the state was henceforward regulated by their wealth and not by their birth. He divided the people into four classes according to their property, which he caused to be assessed. He instituted courts of judicature wherein the resurrected rights of the private citizen might be vindicated, and consequently many forms of actions suitable to the enforcement of these rights respectively grew into practice. These different forms of action, though rude at first, acquired a high degree of perfection under the system of adjudication inaugurated by Solon, and they became the established means whereby the various wrongs were righted, and it would seem from the well-established system that there was scarcely "a wrong without a remedy."

Whenever daughters inherited the estates of their

parents they were obliged by law to marry their nearest relation, and by a form of action for an inheritance, persons of the same family, each member of whom claimed to be more nearly allied to the heiress than the rest, sought to establish his claim. Among these forms of actions, those used for the recovery of rent and possession, and that in the nature of our ejectment, were very prominent. There was one form of action where the plaintiff laid claim to the house for the rent; another form if he claimed an estate in the land. If the plaintiff cast his adversary in either of the former suits, he then entered a second action against him whereby he laid claim to the house or land as being a part of his estate. And after this, if the person in possession remained obstinate and would not deliver up the estate to the lawful owner, there was a third action commenced, in the form of an action for contempt of court, which was in effect to eject him from the premises and place the lawful owner in possession who had been hindered from entering upon his estate.

CHAPTER VIII.

ROMAN POLITY.

GIVING no credence to the legends of Æneas's escape from the flames of Troy, bearing upon his shoulders his father, Anchises, the punishment of the vestal virgin who gave birth to Remus and Romulus, the miraculous preservation of these two boys, who were ordered to be consigned to the waters of the Tiber, the treachery of Romulus towards his twin-brother, and the founding of the city which was to become famous for all time, history attributes to Romulus the founding of all the early institutions of Rome,—social, political, and military. In the social state the population was divided into two classes, burgesses or citizens on the one hand, and on the other their clients or dependents. The burgesses were called patrons in relation to their clients. These patrons were required by law or custom to defend their clients from all wrong or oppression on the part of others, while the clients were bound to render certain services to their patrons. So that the relation of patron and client in some degree resembled that of lord and vassal in the feudal times. The burgesses alone enjoyed all political rights, and they alone made up what was at this time the body politic of Rome. The citizens or burgesses of the political state were divided into three tribes, the Ramnenses, the Tatienses, and Luceres. The first had its name from Romulus, the second from the Sabine king, and the third from the lucus or grove where the asylum stood, and where the knights of this century had formerly dwelt. Each tribe was divided into ten curias or wards, and each curia had a chief officer or priest called its *curio*. The citizens or burgesses met according to their curiæ in the comitium to vote in all matters of state which the king was bound to lay before them, and their assembly was called the Comitia Curiata or assembly of the curias, and all matters were decided by the majority vote of the curiæ. No law could be made without their consent. Nor was the sovereign power of the king considered legally established until it had been conferred by the curiæ. By virtue of the sovereign power so conferred, the king held the chief command in war, and was supreme judge in matters of life and death, and in token thereof he was attended by twelve lictors, bearing bundles of rods, with sharp axes projecting from the middle of them. Besides this assembly, Romulus nominated one hundred senators as an advisory council, who were styled Fathers from their honorable office, and their descendants Patricians. In every struggle for liberty, in all the revolutions brought about by the various changes of government from Romulus until the decline and fall of the Roman empire, the curiæ exercised a controlling power in the political state. It gradually became the assembly of the people through which the commoners in their respective tribes elected the tribunes and consuls.

That the nature of the tenure by which property was held in Rome under the government of the kings bore a striking resemblance to that which existed under the feudal system will be seen from the institutions established by Servius Tullius. He instituted the census, "an ordinance," says Livy, "of the most salutary consequence in an empire that was to rise to such a pitch of greatness, according to which the several services requisite in war and peace were to be discharged, not by every person indiscriminately, as formerly, but according to the proportion of their several properties.

He then, according to the census, formed the plan of
the classes and centuries, and the arrangement which
subsists at present,* calculated to preserve regularity
and propriety in all transactions either of peace or war."
He divided the Roman citizens into six classes. The
first class consisted of those who possessed at least a
hundred thousand æra (the æra were Roman coins, one
hundred thousand of which would be about equal to
fifteen hundred and seventy dollars), and was composed
of eighty centuries ; forty elder (the elder consisted of
those who had attained to forty-six years of age); and
the same number of younger (the younger from seventeen to forty-six). The business of the elder was to
guard the city, that of the younger to carry on war
abroad. The second, third, fourth, and fifth classes
were established according to their respective wealth.
Then follows minute regulations in regard to the arms
and equipments that they were required to provide,
which show how nearly the feudal system was copied
from these ordinances. The agrarian system was the
cause of continual discontent among the plebeians, and
of incessant dissensions and internal warfare between
them and the landed aristocracy.

And under the third consulship of Spurius Cassius,
an agrarian law was first proposed looking to an adjustment of the difficulties between the classes and the
increase of the political independence of the plebeians.
Liddell, in his " History of Rome," speaking of these

---

* Livy was born fifty-eight years before, and died seventeen
years after, the birth of Christ.

laws, says that "great mistakes formerly prevailed in the nature of the Roman laws familiarly termed agrarian. It was supposed that by these laws all land was declared common property, and that at certain intervals of time the state assumed possession and made a fresh distribution thereof to all citizens, rich and poor. It is needless to make any remarks on the nature and consequences of such a law, sufficient it will be to say, what is now known to all, that at Rome such laws never existed,—never were thought of. The lands which were to be distributed by agrarian laws were not private property, but the property of the state. They were, originally, those public lands which had been the domain of the kings, and which were increased whenever any city or people was conquered by the Romans, because it was an Italian practice to confiscate the lands of the conquered, in whole or in part, to the use and benefit of the conquering people." At this time the patrician burgesses in effect constituted the populus, and they had occupied, the greater part, if not all, of this public land, which consisted of pasturage; and it was manifest that if the plebeians could add to their small farms, which were mostly in tillage, the right of pasturage on the public lands, their means would be much increased, and they were likely to become much less dependent upon the wealthy patricians.

Passing from this general to a more particular view of Roman history with respect to property, we find that the private rights of Roman citizens were first, the right of liberty; second, the right of family; third, the right of marriage; fourth, the right of a father;

fifth, the right of property; sixth, the right of making a will and succeeding to an inheritance; and seventh, the right of tutelage or wardship. As the right of property is the subject of discussion, it is unnecessary to consider the other rights which pertain to the citizen in this connection.

CHAPTER IX.

ROMAN PROPERTY RIGHTS.

THINGS, with respect to property, among the Romans were variously divided. Some things were said to be of divine right, others of human right; the former were called sacred, as altars, temples, or anything publicly consecrated to the gods by the authority of the great pontiff. Things of human right were called profane, and were either public and common, as the air, running water, the sea and its shores, etc., or private, which might be the property of individuals. The things in which a whole society or corporation had the property, and each individual the use, were called the property of the people, as theatres, paths, highways, and the like. Property was also divided, as in the present time, into movable or immovable, corporeal or incorporeal, etc. Property was either *res mancipi* or *nec mancipi*. The locality of the property and not the property itself made the distinction. *Res mancipi* were things which were alienated by *mancipatio*. They included lands, houses, slaves, domestic animals, etc., on Italian soil which might be sold and alienated, or the property of them transferred from one person to another. And it behooved the seller to be answerable for them to the purchaser to secure the possession. *Nec mancipi res* were those things not comprised in the foregoing class, or, more properly speaking, those things which were *extra solum,*—beyond the confines of Rome proper, and not governed by its law and custom. The modes of acquiring property were as follows: The sale and transfer of the property of the *res mancipi* was made by an imaginary sale, in which only Roman citizens could take part. It was effected in the presence of not less than five witnesses, who were Roman citizens of the age of puberty. The civil law fixed the age of puberty at fourteen years in males and twelve in females. At this sale there was also a person of the same condition to hold a pair of scales, the purchaser taking hold of the property or something taken from the property if it was not capable of manual delivery, and affirming it to be purchased by him with the scales and a piece of copper. He then struck the scales with the copper, delivering the copper to the seller by way of earnest money. Cicero commonly uses the word *mancipium* to imply the sale or transfer of property, conferring absolute and indefeasible title, and uses the word *nexus* to imply the deposit or transfer of property by way of pledge. Movable property was also sold or transferred by the parties coming before the prætor or president of the province, who adjudged it to the persons who claimed it, which generally occurred in

the case of debtors, who, when insolvent, gave up their
goods to their creditors. The word *usucaptio* or *usu-
capio* was used to denote the property of a thing obtained by possessing it for a certain time without
interruption: according to the law of the Twelve
Tables, for two years, if it was a farm or immovable
thing, and for one year if the thing was movable; but
afterwards possession for a longer time was necessary
before the right of property accrued by prescription;
in some of the provinces ten, twenty, or in certain cases
a number of years beyond remembrance. Before the
adoption of the Twelve Tables, the Roman law did
not recognize the right of private testamentary disposition. The law prior to this period prescribed the rule
of succession, which a private citizen was not permitted
to alter.

A citizen who was without issue could not constitute
a stranger as his heir or successor without the sanction
of the legislative assembly called the Comitia Calata.
Anciently, wills were made in time of peace in the
Comitia Curiata, which were convened biennially for
the making of wills, but the testament of a soldier
might be made in the presence and hearing of four of
his fellow-soldiers as witnesses before engaging in battle, and these wills were only valid while the expedi-
tion lasted. As the Comitia for making wills convened only once in two years, persons in fear of immi-
nent death mancipated their estates to some friend *per
æs et libram*. (A formality of sale by which the seller,
in token of the bargain being struck, put a weight into
the balance, or more properly the purchaser struck the

scales with a piece of copper and then delivered the
copper to the vendor by way of purchase money.)
These two forms gradually fell into disuse after the
adoption of the Twelve Tables, and thereafter the testator alienated his estate to some friend, who was called
familiæ emptor, whose duties were somewhat analogous
to that of a trustee.   The alienation or imaginary sale
took place in the presence of five witnesses, a *libripens*
and *antestatus*, and the sale having been duly made *per
æs et libram*, the testator holding up the wax tablets
in his hand upon which he had written his will, he
stated orally his wishes and said, *Hæc uti in his tabulis
cerisve scripta sunt ita do, ita lego, ita testor, itaque vos
Quirites testimonium præbitote.*   The antestatus then
stepped forward and touched the ears of the witnesses,
but neither their seals nor signatures were required.

It is said that Servius Tullius was the author of the
first agrarian regulations; that he divided part of the
domain land among the poorer plebeians at the rate of
four-and-a-half acres to the man; but whether these assign-
ments of land had taken effect, and whether the proposal
of Spurius Cassius was merely intended to carry them
into execution, or was an additional law of the same
character, we have no means of judging.   Upon either
supposition the relief of the plebeians would be of the
same kind.   The patrician burgesses did not oppose
the enactment of the law because they thought that it
would be more easy to thwart its execution than to
prevent its adoption.   As soon as Spurius Cassius laid
down his consulship, the patricians, by intrigues and combinations, rendered the law ineffectual, and, as a conse-

quence, whenever Rome was not at war with neighboring nations, a state of civil commotion bordering upon insurrection and rebellion existed among the classes, until at length, under the consulship of Spurius Tarpeius and Alus Æternius, about three hundred years after the foundation of Rome, an embassy was appointed and sent to Athens to procure a copy of the famous laws of Solon, and to make themselves acquainted with the laws, customs, and institutions of the other states of Greece. These ambassadors spent a year in Greece, and upon their return to Rome submitted a report embodying the result of their observations and investigations to the senate, which chose ten of its members to draw up a body of laws based upon the report of the embassy, and then communicate the work to the senate and people for their approbation and confirmation. The decemvirs, having devoted a whole year to this great work, presented, as a result of their labors, the Ten Tables in the open forum, which were afterwards approved by an express decree of the senate and confirmed by the unanimous voice of the Roman people, voting in an assembly of the centuries. These Ten Tables, which are simple maxims or fundamental principles, constituted the basis or ground-work of the Roman civil law. The fifth, sixth, seventh, and eighth tables deal with questions relating to property. They are as follows:

TABLE V.

OF INHERITANCES AND GUARDIANSHIPS.

I. After the death of a father of a family, let the disposition be made of his estate, and his appointment concerning the guardianship of his children be observed.

II. If he dies intestate, and has no children to succeed him, let his nearest relation be his heir; if he has no near relation, let a man of his own name be his heir.

III. When a freedman dies intestate, and without heirs, if his patron be alive, or has left children, let the effects of the freedman go to the family of his patron.

IV. After the death of a debtor, his debts shall be paid by his heirs, in proportion to the share they have in his inheritance. After this they may divide the rest of his effects, if they please, and the Prætor shall appoint three arbitrators to make the division.

V. If a father of a family dies intestate, and leaves an heir under age, let the child's nearest relation be his guardian.

VI. If any one becomes mad, or prodigal, and has nobody to take care of him, let a relation, or, if he has none, a man of his own name, have the care of his person and estate.

TABLE VI.

OF PROPERTY AND POSSESSION.

I. When a man conveys his estate to another, let the terms of the conveyance create the right.

II. If a slave, who was made free on condition of paying a certain sum, be afterwards sold, let him be set at liberty, if he pay the person who has bought him the sum agreed upon.

III. Let not any piece of merchandise, though sold and delivered, belong to the buyer till he has paid for it.

IV. Let two years' possession amount to a prescription for lands, and one for movables.

V. In litigated cases the presumption shall always be on the side of the possessor. And in disputes about liberty or slavery, the presumption shall always be on the side of liberty.

TABLE VII.

OF TRESPASSES AND DAMAGES.

I. If a beast does any damage in a field, let the master of the beast make satisfaction, or give up his beast.

II. If you find a rafter or a pole which belongs to you in another man's house or vineyard, and they are made use of, do not pull down the house, or ruin the vineyard, but make the possessor pay double the value of the thing stolen, and when the house is destroyed, or the pole taken out of the vineyard, then seize what is your own.

III. Whoever shall maliciously set fire to another man's house, or an heap of corn near his house, shall be imprisoned, scourged, and burnt to death. If he did it by accident, let him repair the damage. And if he be a poor man, let him be slightly corrected, etc.

TABLE VIII.

OF ESTATES IN THE COUNTRY.

I. Let the space of two and a half feet of ground be always left between one house and another.

II. Societies may make what by-laws they please among themselves, provided they do not interfere with the public laws.

III. When two neighbors have any disputes about their grounds, the Prætor shall assign them three arbitrators.

IV. When a tree planted in a field does injury to an adjoining field by its shade, let its branches be cut off fifteen feet high.

V. If the fruit of a tree falls into a neighboring field, the owner of the tree may go and pick it up.

VI. If a man would make a drain to carry off the rainwater from his ground to his neighbor's, let the Prætor appoint three arbitrators to judge of the damage the water may do, and prevent it.

VII. Roads shall be eight feet wide where they run straight, and where they turn, sixteen.

VIII. If a road between two fields be bad, the traveller may drive through which field he pleases.

It would be unprofitable in this connection to go over the different changes which took place in the Roman civil law with regard to the right of property, the mode of its transfer, and testamentary disposition, from the adoption of the Twelve Tables to the collection and codification of the Roman civil law under the Emperor Justinian.* From tradition, from history, from legislation, it will be seen that the right of private property in Rome was a right which grew out of immemorial usage, a right sanctioned by custom and held inviolable in law.

CHAPTER X.

A RÉSUMÉ.

FROM the Scriptures, from profane history, and from the writings of men who have given special study to the evolution of the right of property, we learn that among all tribes and peoples, sufficiently civilized to cultivate the lands, that the right of individual ownership in property has been and is recognized, but in each case, so long as they maintained their tribal institutions, the right of the individual to dispose of the land allotted to him was restricted to transfers between the members of the same tribe. He could not alienate his possession and title,—that is to say, he could not dispose of it in such a way as to vest an absolute title in

---

* The most ample provisions are found in the Institutes of Justinian, compiled about the year A.D. 533 by Tribonian and others for the protection and preservation of individual rights of property.

a stranger not of his tribe. This restriction did not destroy the *right* of ownership in land nor the *power* of the individual to sell it for whatever price he could procure. The Mosaic law restricted the sale to a certain number of years, that is, to the fiftieth or Jubilee year, when it returned to its original owner, and under the tribal system the sale was restricted to members of the tribe. The same in effect as if a law of Illinois provided that no citizen of the State shall be permitted to sell his land to an alien for a period to exceed fifty years, and that no alien shall own or inherit lands or tenements in the State of Illinois except for a temporary purpose. Such a law would not be contrary to individual rights of property, but, on the other hand, would be deemed wise and beneficent, preventing the lands from being owned and controlled by aliens who have no interest in the welfare of the State or its people except to collect the rent and tithes from their tenants in possession. Even in newly-discovered countries where there is any evidence of civilization we find individual ownership of land either absolute, qualified, or restricted, but in those countries where there is no approach to civilization, where animal instincts still dominate the mind, where rings dangle from the nose to ornament the face, where pigments and paste besmear the countenance, where figleaf aprons or no aprons at all are worn, the fields lie in a state of nature, unploughed, uncultivated, unfruitful. Here the lands are worthless for agricultural purposes because they produce nothing. These peoples, during long-forgotten centuries, have followed the hunt and the chase, and in many instances we find that they had no more idea of a moral law or moral nature than the beasts of the forest or the fishes of the sea, where the stronger kills and eats the weaker and the larger swallows the smaller. On the contrary, wherever we find a high type of manhood, a tribe, or people plough-ing the fields, cultivating the soil, and living according to the command of God to Adam, "In the sweat of thy face, thou shalt eat bread," we also find individual ownership in land, that the land is valuable, and that every man may sell and receive for it an equivalent in money or goods.

Men of the most profound learning and refined scholarship, whose lives have been spent in the study of books and who know little about the practical affairs of life or the real wants of society, betray an idolatrous veneration for Plato's Republic, the writings of Diogenes, Zeno, and others, who took Minos and Lycurgus for their models. True, it is said that "in the very bosom of corruption, Lycurgus regenerated Sparta and gave her a degree of strength and stability by which for a series of years she was enabled to wield the sceptre of Greece," but can we find in the vaunted laws of Lycurgus one rule of action that is commend-able, practicable, or grounded in the principles of natural justice? We are informed that Lycurgus found a greater part of the people so poor that they had not one inch of land of their own, while a smaller number of individuals were possessed of all the lands and wealth of the country, and in order to punish indolence, envy, fraud, luxury, and to prevent

extreme poverty and excessive wealth, he persuaded
the citizens to give up all their lands to the commonwealth and to make a new division of them that they
might all live together in perfect equality, and that
no preferences or honors should be given save to virtue
and merit.   This scheme Lycurgus put into execution
partly by persuasion, partly by force, by dividing the
lands of Laconia into thirty thousand parts, which he
distributed among the inhabitants of the country, and
the territories of Sparta into nine thousand parts, which
he distributed among an equal number of citizens, and
having met with great opposition in effecting a division
of all their movable goods and chattels, he resorted to
the expediency of demonetizing gold and silver, and
made iron alone current money, so that it required a
cart and two oxen to carry home a sum of money
equivalent to twenty pounds sterling or to one hundred
dollars.   In accomplishing these ends, Lycurgus converted Sparta into a military camp, armed his fellow-
citizens, and made them a nation of warriors and
soldiers.   He destroyed her commerce, prohibited the
cultivation of the arts and sciences, demonetized her cur-
rency, and made her a nation of slaves and Helots over
whom the privileged few might domineer as though they
were cattle and shoot them down as dogs.   Let those
who may laud the laws and institutions of the mythical Lycurgus.   It occurs to the writer that they should
be considered fit only for Hottentots or Tartars.

Rollin, the scholar, the thinker, the historian, in his
reflections upon the government of Sparta and the laws
of Lycurgus, says, "The design formed by Lycurgus

of making equal distribution of the lands among the citizens, and of entirely banishing from Sparta all luxury, avarice, lawsuits, and dissensions, by abolishing the use of gold and silver, would appear to us a scheme of a commonwealth finely conceived in speculation, but utterly impracticable in execution, did not history assure us that Sparta actually subsisted in that condition for many ages.

"When I place the transaction I am now speaking of among the laudable part of Lycurgus's laws, I do not pretend it to be absolutely unexceptionable; for I think it can scarce be reconciled with that general law of nature which forbids the taking away one man's property to give it to another; and yet this is what was really done upon this occasion. Therefore, in this affair of dividing the lands, I consider only so much of it as was truly commendable in itself and worthy of admiration.

"Can we possibly conceive that a man could persuade the richest and most opulent inhabitants of a city to resign all their revenues and estates, to level and confound themselves with the poorest of the people, to subject themselves to a new way of living, both severe in itself and full of restraint; in a word, to debar themselves of the use of everything wherein the happiness and comfort of life is thought to consist? And yet this is what Lycurgus actually effected in Sparta."

Imagine to yourself the people of a city composed of a million inhabitants depending upon public caterers to prepare and serve their morning coffee, noon luncheon, and evening meal. Yet historians, commentators, and philosophers extol as not among the least of his laws that which compelled all the citizens, their wives and children, to eat at public tables. Such a custom might do in a small community clustered together, sheltered from the rays of a tropical sun, but how would it succeed in New York or Chicago where the thermometer touches 30° below zero?

> " But who, to feed a jaunty coxcomb,
>   Would have an Abyssinian ox come ?
>   Or serve a dish of fricassees,
>   To clodpoles in a coat of frieze ?"

Lycurgus before establishing his institutions journeyed into Crete, Egypt, and Asia Minor to study the manners, customs, and laws of those peoples. He persuaded Thales, the Cretan poet, to proceed to Athens, where, by the influence of his poetry upon the understandings and hearts of his countrymen, they might be gradually prepared for those alterations in government and manners which he was then contemplating. Notwithstanding the great wisdom, learning, and foresight of the law-giver, he was convinced that he could accomplish but little by appealing to the understanding alone. He therefore availed himself of whatever the temper, the prejudices, and superstitions of the times afforded to insure the success of his undertaking. He journeyed to Delphi to consult the oracle, and armed with the decree of divine sanction he unfolded his plans and established his laws among a superstitious people. Minos had persuaded the Cretans that his laws were delivered to him from Jupiter. Moses persuaded the

Hebrews that the laws written by him on the tables of stone were traced there by the finger of God on Mount Sinai. Instances of other ancient legislators might be given in which they found it convenient to declare that their institutions were direct from the gods. For that self-love in human nature, which would but illy have borne with the superiority of genius acknowledged in an unaided law-giver, found an case and satisfaction in adopting and submitting to his new regulations when presented as a gift from heaven. Among every people we discover an awe and reverence of the Divinity; an homage and honor paid to him; and an open profession of an entire dependence upon him in all their undertakings, in all their necessities, in all their dangers and adversities. Incapable of themselves to penetrate into futurity and to compel success, we find them careful to consult the Divinity by oracles, and by other methods of a like nature; and to merit his protection by vows, prayers, and offerings. It is by the same supreme authority they believe the most solemn treaties are rendered inviolable. It is that which gives sanction to their oaths; and to it by imprecations is referred the punishment of such crimes and enormities as escape the knowledge and power of men. In all their concerns, voyages, journeys, marriages, diseases, the Divinity is ever invoked.

The main design of Lycurgus in establishing his laws, and especially that one which prohibited the use of gold and silver, was to curb and restrain the ambition of his citizens; to disable them from making conquests, and to force them to confine themselves within the narrow bounds of their own country without carrying their views and pretensions further. So long as the Spartans worshipped at the shrine of the law-giver with a superstitious veneration little less than that accorded to the Delphian god, they obeyed his laws and observed his ordinances. While this little republic which he founded remained in seclusion from the rest of mankind, its people were comparatively happy and contented.

> "Though poor the peasant's hut, his feasts though small,
> He sees his little lot the lot of all."

No gloomier picture than that presented by the miserable condition of the Helots of Sparta can be found in the world's history. Every mean device was adopted to reduce them below the level of beasts. They were even forced into a condition of drunkenness for the purpose of exhibiting them in sportive mockery to the Spartan youth, so that he might the more keenly detest their contemptible condition. It was customary for the most active and intelligent of the Spartan braves to go into the country and lie in ambush, armed with spear and dagger, and rush out from their hiding-places to murder the unoffending Helots, and those in whom any superiority of spirit or genius had been observed were singled out as the special objects of these fiendish and murderous attacks. Differing from Burn's conception of the cruelty of devils where he says,—

> "I'm sure sma' pleasure it can gie,
> Ev'n to a *deil*,
> To skelp an' scaud poor dogs like me,
> An' hear us squeel!"

the Spartans seemed to take pleasure in such devilish work, and Spartan institutions seemed to encourage it on the pretence that the Helots might revolt and fight for their freedom. The ambition of Spartan warriors could not long be confined to practising their lances upon the unoffending Helots. Like Rasselas, the prince of Abyssinia, confined in the happy valley, they longed to go beyond the confines of Spartan territory, to go abroad in the great world and measure spears and daggers and lances with foemen more worthy of their steel, with Messenians, Persians, and Athenians. Ambition stimulated valor, and with valor came the love of conquest and its inseparable attendants, avarice and luxury. Sparta soon became intoxicated over the wealth which flowed into her from the plunder of surrounding states, and the institutions of Lycurgus vanished as her wealth and commerce increased. Perished the institutions of this lauded law-giver,—institutions more detestable than feudalism, which no one can contemplate without feelings of scorn and indignation.

Rollin pertinently observes that, " In order to perceive more clearly the defects in the laws of Lycurgus, we have only to compare them with those of Moses, which we know were dictated by more than human wisdom. . . . To begin, for instance, with that ordinance relating to the choice they made of their children, which of them were to be brought up, and which exposed to perish ; who would not be shocked at the unjust and inhuman custom of pronouncing sentence of death upon all such infants as had the misfortune to be born with a constitution that appeared too weak and delicate to undergo the fatigues and exercises to which the commonwealth destined all her subjects ?"

The puny infant who developed into the giant intellect of a Sir Isaac Newton, under the tender care, fond solicitude, and endearing love which our Christian civilization inculcates in the mother, would have been consigned, when born, to undergo the sentence of death under the laws and institutions of Lycurgus, because he had the misfortune to be born possessed of a feeble constitution. I will not refer to those other model republics and political utopias of which we read, because they would be deemed as barren of utility for this age and these times, as the laws and institutions of Lycurgus would be considered inhuman and barbarous.

BOOK II.

THE ORIGIN, GROWTH, AND DECADENCE OF FEUDAL TENURES.

CHAPTER I.

THE VILLAGE-MARK.

I HAVE no disposition to question the theories advanced by men of learning and research who contend that no vestige of the Roman laws and customs can be found in the existing laws of the Anglo-Saxons. I simply declare that the history of Rome is the history of "The Western Empire," the empire of Charlemagne. Wipe out Roman history, Roman laws, Roman customs, and Roman civilization, and what remains to guide us in our investigations? Nothing. In ancient, differing from modern, times, the country was cultivated by the inhabitants of towns and villages. That Rome which became the seat of empire, the centre of civilization, was, in its infancy, but a walled town on the Palatine Hill. The government of Rome was merely a confederation of towns or villages. Ancient Italy is said to have contained over eleven hundred towns. Teutons, Franks, Gauls, and Britons, although regarded as barbarians, lived in towns and villages. Gaul and Spain

72

could boast of towns and cities of some pretensions connected with each other and the capital of Rome by the imperial high-ways,—those marvels of Roman enterprise and monuments of Roman civilization. The Teutonic towns were merely the aggregate of individuals of each tribe or community held together by the ties of kinship or the necessity of mutual defence. Their edifices built of rough timber, thatched with straw and pierced at the top to leave a free passage for smoke, were not even contiguous. Men dwelt together in communities; it was their normal condition, and when they wished to migrate or change their place of habitation they moved in communities. These communities were governed by well-known and, in some respects, salutary laws and customs. It would be an interesting but unprofitable undertaking to trace the history and recount the laws, customs, and manners prevailing in these village communities. Each tribe or community occupied a district or mark divided into three parts.

First, The town or village, in which the dwelling-house and space surrounding was held by the heads of families in individual proprietorship. This was the estate that descended to the sons, or went in the male line. It was called Salic land, because the mansion of a German was called *sal*, and the space enclosing it *salbac*,—the homestead. When the Franks issued from their own country, and gained possession in Gaul, they still continued to give to their new settlements the name of Salic land ; and hence, the law of the Franks that regulated the course of descent was called the Salic law.

Secondly, There was the arable portion, or the district of cultivated land, in which separate plots were held, for a time, at all events, in severalty, by individual members of the tribe or community, subject to certain established regulations as to common, cultivation, enjoyment, and the like.

Thirdly, There was the common or waste land not appropriated to individuals at all, on which the whole community had rights of pasturage; and also, varying in different localities according to the nature of their surroundings, there was the right of fishing in the waters and of hunting in the forests, and also the right of turbary,—the right to dig turf for fuel on the bog-land. The peasantry in European countries can find evidences of these ancient village-marks in every community, I am told, without the aid of learned treatises upon the subject. In Ireland, where the Feudal system never gained a footing, we can trace the village-mark to an absolute certainty. True, the worst agrarian system to be found anywhere exists there, but neither the invasion and settlement of the Danes, the plunder and rapacity of the Normans, nor the cruel, devastating wars of Elizabeth and Cromwell, could eradicate it. In the town-land of Springfield,* parish of Clondavadog,† Barony of Kilmacrenan, Diocese of Raphoe, County of Donegal, Province of Ulster, Ireland, a Morier, a Laveleye, or a Sir Henry Maine could find in the attendant vestiges of collective property materials

---

* The birthplace of the writer.
† Commonly called Fanad.

for an interesting essay on early institutions or village communities. In that township, and no doubt in every township among the wild and picturesque mountains and valleys of Donegal, the village-mark has defied the mutations in the law of property, has withstood the changes introduced by conquerors and taskmasters, and resisted the ravages of time. The hut or straw-roofed cabin and the plot of ground surrounding, the long and narrow strips of arable land, the right of pasturage and the right to dig a certain quantity of turf, regulated by the amount of rent paid by the tenant, —these all remain as evidences of the village-mark, but the person in possession, and to whom the priliveges attach, has in them no vested or proprietary rights. Everything is held at the will or caprice of an absentee landlord. But this state of affairs does not add strength to the argument in favor of a community of property. Before the Norman invasion, Ireland had a well-defined code of laws known as the Brehon laws. According to these laws, each occupant of land belonged to a tribe, and he was liable in common with other members of his tribe to certain obligations, such, for example, as the support of aged members of the tribe, who had no children to support them; he was also subject to discharge his proportionate liability of contracts entered into by others, when made with the consent of the tribe. As his property was considered, to a certain extent, tribal property, he could not dispose of his individual interest therein until he first offered it to his nearest kinsman or some other member of the tribe. Similar restrictions are found attached to the enjoyment and transfer of tribal property wherever found. These restrictions might depreciate the value, but did not materially interfere with the beneficial use and enjoyment of property.

There was a time when the Roman empire included within its limits the fairest part of the earth, and the most civilized portion of mankind,—when the gentle but powerful influence of her laws and manners had gradually cemented the union of the provinces, and the public administration was conducted by the virtue and abilities of her emperors, who were content with maintaining the dignity of the realm without attempting to enlarge its limits. Guided by prudence and moderation, they invited the friendship of the surrounding nations, and for a time succeeded in convincing mankind that the Roman power, raised above the temptation of conquest, was actuated only by the love of order and justice. Public virtue and patriotism guided the councils of the republic, and inspired the Roman troops to deeds of valor and renown. The golden eagle which glittered in front of the legion was the object of their fondest devotion ; nor was it deemed less impious than ignoble to abandon that sacred ensign in the hour of danger.

Until the privileges of the Romans had been progressively extended to all the inhabitants of the empire, an important distinction was preserved between Italy and the. provinces. The former was considered the centre of public unity and the firm basis of the constitution. Italy claimed the birth or at least the residence of the emperors and the senate. From the foot of the

Alps to the extremity of Calabria, all the natives of
Italy were born citizens of Rome. Their partial distinctions were obliterated, and they became moulded into
one great nation, unified by language, manners, and
civil institutions. The republic gloried in her generous
policy, and was frequently repaid by the merit and services of her adopted sons. Some of the most illustrious
names which make up the galaxy of her fame may be
traced to the provinces.

CHAPTER II.

DISINTEGRATION OF THE ROMAN EMPIRE.

WHILE the nations of the empire were almost imperceptibly absorbed by the Roman name and Roman
people, there still remained, in the centre of every
province and of every family, a servile class who endured the burdens without sharing the benefits of society.
The greater number of this class were barbarians, taken
captive by thousands in war or purchased at a vile price.
It was a maxim of ancient jurisprudence that a slave
had no country of his own, although he acquired with
his liberty an admission into that political society of
which his patron was a member. The honorable distinction of freedman was confined to those slaves only,
who for just causes, and with the approbation of the
magistrate should receive a solemn and legal manu-

mission. Even they obtained no more than the private
rights of citizens, and were rigorously excluded from
civil or military honors. Whatever the merit or fortune of their sons, they likewise were regarded unworthy of a seat in the senate; nor were the traces of
a servile origin allowed to be completely obliterated
until the third or fourth generation. It is said that
four hundred slaves were maintained in a single palace
at Rome, and also that a freedman during the reign of
Augustus left behind him three thousand six hundred
yoke of oxen, two hundred and fifty thousand head
of smaller cattle, and four thousand one hundred and
sixteen slaves.

Slavery and democracy cannot long exist side by side.
True democracy like true religion destroys castes and
levels conditions. The abuse of the one leads to disorder and anarchy, of the other to fanaticism and
superstition. While true democracy was unknown to
the Roman people and Roman institutions, nevertheless it was through the spirit of democracy, however
base, the slaves were enabled to make some advance-
ments in their social and political conditions. Their
grievances, long stifled by the voice of authority, at
length found a responsive echo in the discontent of the
soldier who became insubordinate from excessive indolence and contemptuous of power from excessive in-
dulgence. As the civil authority was gradually
usurped by the military, disintegration of the empire
became manifest not only at Rome but in the provinces. Pomp and splendor sharpened the avarice,
while luxury and sensuality dulled the genius of the

people. Personal valor, no longer nourished by the love of conquest or the pride of independence, became emasculated and the military spirit languished. Public patriotism became an article of bargain and sale, corruption and bribery stalked at will through all avenues to justice, and ministers of the state became subservient tools in the hands of military marplots. Without a violation of the principles of the constitution, the general of the Roman armies might receive and exercise an authority almost despotic over the soldiers and the subjects, as well as over the enemies of the republic. The dictator or consul had the right to command the service of the Roman youth, and to punish disobedience by the most severe and ignominious penalties, by confiscating his property and by selling his person into slavery. The right to declare war or to negotiate terms of peace was usually decided by legislative authority; but when the arms of the legions were carried a great distance from Italy these responsibilities devolved upon the generals who were the accredited representatives of the emperor.

When the crafty Augustus played the comedy of refusing the purple in order that its glory might be thrust upon him, he was authorized to retain his military command, supported by a numerous body of guards, even in time of peace, and in the heart of the capital. By thus introducing the Prætorian guards, as it were, into the palace and the senate, Augustus and his successors inspired them with a confidence in their own strength, and encouraged them to despise the weakness of the civil government; to view the vices of

their masters with familiar contempt, and to lay aside
that reverential awe which only distance and mystery
can inspire for imaginary power. In the luxurious
idleness of an opulent city, their pride was nourished
by a consciousness of irresistible weight, nor was it
possible to conceal from them that the person of the
sovereign, the authority of the senate, the public treasury, and the seat of empire were all in their hands.
To divert the Prætorian bands from these dangerous
reflections, the firmest and best-established princes were
obliged to mix blandishments with commands, rewards
with punishments, to flatter their pride, indulge their
pleasures, connive at their irregularities, and to purchase their precarious allegiance by liberal donations
which, after the elevation of Claudius, was exacted as
a legal claim on the accession of every new emperor.
They maintained, and who was to resist their pretensions, that according to a proper construction of the
constitution their consent was necessary to the appointment of an emperor. Incited by an insatiable greed
for gain they violated the sanctity of the throne in the
atrocious murder of Pertinax, and dishonored its majesty by negotiating with Sulpicianus, the price to be
paid for the imperial dignity. Apprehensive that, by
private contract they would not obtain a just price for
so valuable a commodity, the Prætorians ran out upon
the ramparts, and with a loud voice proclaimed that
the Roman world was for sale to the highest bidder at
public auction. The vain old Didius Julianus, a
wealthy senator, at the bidding of his family and para-
sites, hastened to the Prætorian camp, and from the

foot of the rampart openly bid against Sulpicianus, and became the successful purchaser by offering to each soldier a sum equal to about one thousand dollars. The Prætorian guard conducted the new emperor to the throne, and the senate, which though inclined, dared not to oppose, ratified his election, and conferred upon him all the several branches of the imperial power. The empire for a time survived, but never recovered from this, the crowning insult of a long category of abasements heaped upon Roman valor and Roman virtue. Tyranny and murder, bribery and corruption, usurpation and rebellion, civil war and sedition convulsed the empire from centre to circumference. The emperors, eager to uphold the tottering dynasty and to render more secure their own precarious title to the throne, had received into their service entire battalions from the ranks of the barbarians, and to recompense their services had assigned them large tracts of land in the frontier provinces. These mercenaries, devoid of those virtues which made the legions of the commonwealth models of discipline and valor, regarded the provinces as their property and the people as their prey. The ancient proprietors, deprived of the use of arms, overawed by the military, plundered by rapacious governors, and drained of their wealth by hordes of ruthless tax-gatherers, had neither the ability nor the inclination to resist the invaders from whom they had little to fear, because it would be difficult to render their condition more wretched. The strength of the empire, which had always consisted in arms rather than in fortifications, was insensibly undermined, and

f

the fairest provinces were exposed to the rapaciousness or ambition of the barbarians who swarmed around the Roman world like vultures around their prey.

CHAPTER III.

GERMANIC FEUDALISM.

ALMOST the whole of Northern Germany, Denmark, Norway, Sweden, Finland, Lavonia, Prussia, and the greater part of Poland, were peopled by the various tribes of one great nation whose complexion, manners, and language denoted a common origin and preserved a striking resemblance. In the rude institutions of these barbarians, and especially those of the German tribes, we may still discover some traces of our present laws and manners. They were unacquainted with the use of letters and had no knowledge of those arts and sciences which gave to Greece and Rome immortal fame. They lived in camps or rude fortifications constructed in the centre of the wood. The game of various sorts with which the forests were plentifully stocked, supplied them with food and exercise. Numerous herds of cattle constituted their principal source of wealth. Corn (oats) and barley were the principal products which the land yielded. The care of the house and family, the management of the lands and cattle, were assigned to the old and the infirm, to women and slaves. The assembly of the warriors or freemen of the tribe was convened at stated times or on sudden emergencies. The trial of public offences, the election of magistrates, and the great business of peace and war were determined by its independent voice. A general of the tribe was elected on occasions of danger, and if the danger was great or pressing, several tribes concurred in the choice of the same general. The bravest warrior was chosen to lead his countrymen to battle by his example rather than by his command. But his power, however limited, was still invidious. For they were so jealous of any encroachment upon their liberties that the authority which they conferred upon a chief, intended to meet a given emergency, terminated with the occasion which gave rise to it. Princes were appointed in a general assembly to administer justice, or rather to compromise differences in their respective districts, to dispose of the landed property therein, and to distribute it every year according to a new division. At the same time they were not authorized to punish with death, to imprison, or even to strike a citizen.

When the youths attained the age of manhood they were introduced as equals in the general council, and it was their pride to be numbered among the faithful companions of some renowned chief to whom they devoted their arms and services. To be ever surrounded by them was the pride and strength of the chiefs, their ornament in peace, their defence in war. In the hour of danger it was shameful for a chief to be surpassed in valor by his companions; shameful for the companion not to equal the valor of his chief. To survive the chieftain's fall in battle brought lasting infamy to his chosen adherents. To protect his person, and to adorn his glory with the trophies of their own exploits were the most sacred of their duties. The chief fought for victory, the companions for the chief.

Such were the characteristics and institutions of the barbarous tribes who in a few centuries overthrew the throne of the Cæsars, caused a total change in the geography of the Roman provinces, reduced into feudal dynasties the Western Empire, and gave to every nation of Europe a new race of kings. Various causes had contributed to accelerate the downfall of the Roman empire, which it is unnecessary to discuss here. Suffice it to say that towards the close of the fourth century commenced that famous invasion which resulted in the downfall of the Western Empire. From the extremity of Scandinavia to the frontiers of China, nation after nation appeared, and although often repulsed and driven back beyond the confines of the empire, they returned in increased numbers and with renewed energy until the whole empire was dismembered, the older inhabitants plundered of their movable property, their estates confiscated, and themselves reduced to slavery. The barbarians who established themselves in the provinces, introduced the political institutions by which they had been governed in their native countries. These institutions partook of the nature of military democracies under a king or chief, generals and subordinate officers, who were elected or chosen to fill these offices by the freemen of the tribes. In the distribution of the spoils taken and in the division of the estates confiscated, the king himself could claim nothing but what fell to his lot. While he received a quantity proportioned to the dignity of his rank, he held it by no higher or different tenure than that by which the soldier in the ranks held the quantity allotted to him. The property so acquired by allotment is known in law as *allodial,*—that is, he to whom it was allotted was not only entitled to its possession and enjoyment, but he could dispose of it at pleasure or transmit it as an inheritance to his children. In this respect the warriors who followed the fortunes of their king not by constraint but from choice were his equals. It is quite difficult to determine whether the lands allotted to them were held according to the Roman laws or the laws and customs prevailing in their tribes. But as the land-laws of a country become, as it were, stamped upon its soil, it is reasonable to assume that the Roman laws regulating the sale, transfer, and descent of real property, obtained for a time, at least, after her other institutions had perished.

It was a rule among all ancient nations and tribes that the victor became the lawful owner of the enemy whom he had subdued, and over whom he had the power of life and death. As the vanquished inhabitants of the Roman provinces were reduced to a state of slavery in the allotment of the confiscated estates, the slaves residing upon them became the property of him to whom the land was allotted. The soldier who was always a freeman of the tribe took possession of his allotment as his own, and was under no obligation to take an oath of fealty to his king or chief as a condition upon which to receive it. Nor was such an oath exacted of him. We must look to a later period to find this peculiar investiture accompanying grants of real property. As the original proprietors were not all reduced to slavery, these allotments and distributions of property were confined to those districts subdued and peopled by the invaders. In many districts of the provinces the original inhabitants joined the invaders in their warfare against the empire, or capitulated on satisfactory terms, and were permitted to retain their possessions upon rendering to the conquerors the tribute agreed upon. The incursions of the barbarians did not resemble the conquests of the Roman legions during the commonwealth. The latter, when they conquered a province, established therein Roman laws and institutions, but the raids of the former were made, in many instances, in quest of spoils and not of homes and habitations. The tribes who first settled in adjacent territories were connected by ties of consanguinity, affinity, or hospitality with the provincials, officials, and former proprietors, and by treaties and agreements. A portion of the lands were left in the possession of their owners; and, although this portion was abridged by each successive nation of invaders, yet it was many centuries before the whole transfer was completely effected. As states, like individuals, retain their identity though changed in their constituent elements, neither the manners nor customs of tribes which inhabited the provinces prior to their conquest by the Romans, nor the Roman laws and jurisprudence ingrafted upon them, were entirely superseded by those of the invaders. From these combined elements and the necessities of the times a new institution was evolved, which in process of time became known to the world as the Feudal System.

CHAPTER IV.

ANGLO-SAXON FEUDALISM.

AMONG the states which rose on the ruins of the Roman empire, that of the Franks attained the most imperial greatness, and for several ages it sustained the character of being the most powerful kingdom in Europe. This monarchy, founded by Clovis, and extended still more by his successors, embraced nearly all of Gaul and the greater part of Germany. The kingdom of Clovis was divided into a number of districts, each under the government of a count or duke whose duty it was to administer justice, preserve tranquillity, collect the royal revenues, and to lead when required the free proprietors into the field. These offices, conferred during pleasure or for a limited period, gradually became hereditary and proprietary. While the distinction of birth was not entirely disregarded in those times, yet the aristocracy of wealth or of official position preceded it. A Frank of large estate was given the title of noble. If he wasted or was despoiled of his wealth his descendants fell into the mass of the people and the new possessor became noble in his stead. Only they whose parents were rich in possessions were considered noble by descent. In those times a pecuniary compensation was paid to the relatives of persons killed or murdered which was estimated according to the rank to which the deceased belonged, and from the differences made in the prices or amounts paid according to rank we must conclude that there existed the elements of aristocratic privileges. Wealth and possessions being the essential prerequisites connecting eminent privileges with posterity, an ambitious prince could find little difficulty in supplying his favorites and sycophants with them by the grant of hereditary benefices. Besides the confiscated estates distributed in the general public allotments, already described, great tracts of country remained uncultivated and uninhabited. These lands, which in process of time became known as "crown lands" or "royal domains," became the property of the government whether a monarchy, a democracy, or a commonwealth.

These lands, located in different parts of the kingdom, not only formed the most regular source of the king's revenue but supplied him with the means of rewarding the services of favorites and of purchasing the friendship of those whose enmity he had reason to fear. The recipients of these royal bounties were more closely connected with the crown than were the allodial proprietors. The possessor of a benefice was bound to serve his sovereign in the field, but, of allodial proprietors, only those whose property was of certain value were called upon for personal services. The owners of these benefices carved out portions of them which they gave to their own favorites and retainers, and in this manner the custom best known by the name of "Subinfeudation" became universal. The oath of fidelity which favorites of royalty had taken, and the homage which they had paid to the sovereign, they in turn exacted from their vassals. The essence of the compact between the lord and vassal was the reciprocity of service and protection. The abuse of benefices or fiefs was carried to such an extent by the Franks that almost all property had become feudal before the end of the tenth century. Not only grants of land and portions of large estates, but governments, dukedoms, and counties, were conferred and held by this species of tenure. The consequence of this was that the great, by the allurement of fiefs or benefices, became devoted followers of the king, while the body of the nation sold themselves as retainers of the great. In the descending line of feudal bondage, a condition of servitude existed which resembled, in some degree, the serfs of Russia or the negroes of the Southern States of the American Union about fifty years ago. These bondmen of the same race as their masters were called serfs and villeins.* No rest-

---

* At a very early period after the Norman Conquest the name of slave disappears, and the lowest ranks in the rural districts were called villeins. There was a legal difference between the villein in gross, whose bondage was to the person of the lord, and who could be sold and transferred from one to another the same as the American slaves before the war of the Rebellion, and the villeins regardant whose bondage was to the land and who could be sold

ing-place can be found in the depths of human degradation at which to fix the status of the serf, and as to the villein it seems that the lord could seize whatever he acquired or collected, or remove him from the soil at pleasure. The tenure bound him to what were called villein services, ignoble in nature and indeterminate in degree; the felling of timber, the carrying of manure, the repairing of roads for his master, who seems to have possessed an equally unbounded right over his labors and its fruits. Against his master he had no right of action; because his indemnity in damages, if he should have recovered, might have been immediately taken away. If he fled from his master's service, or the land which he held, a writ issued for his apprehension, and his master pursued and recovered his fugitive slave. His children were born to the same state of slavery. The same causes which led to the overthrow of feudal institutions brought about the freedom of these bondmen, and their condition up to this period need not be further discussed.

The mode of warfare then universally practised rendered the lord independent of aid from his vassals and slaves. Battles were decided by steel-clad knights, who rode through the unprotected infantry as a modern reaper or mower sweeps through the wheat-field. It was their brother knights alone who either attracted

---

only with the land which they held in villeinage. The one probably represented a class taken in battle, carried away and reduced to slavery by their captors, the other a class of persons also conquered but permitted to remain with their families upon the land to cultivate it for the benefit of their captors.

their notice or were deemed worthy of their hostility. The incursions of invaders, the ravages and rapacity of neighboring chiefs, provoked but little resentment while their victims were only the slaves of the country; and the baron, secure in his well-fortified castle, beheld with indifference his villages in flames, and the long files of weeping captives who were carried off from beneath his ramparts. "Liberty, Equality, and Tranquillity," says Guizot, " were all alike wanting, from the tenth to the thirteenth century, to the inhabitants of each lord's domains; their sovereign was at their very doors, and none of them was hidden from him or beyond reach of his mighty arm. Of all tyrannies, the worst is that which can thus keep account of its subjects, and which sees from its seat the limits of its empire. The caprices of the human will then show themselves in all their intolerable extravagance, and, moreover, with irresistible promptness. It is then, too, that inequality of conditions makes itself more rudely felt; riches, might, independence, every advantage and every right present themselves every instant to the gaze of misery, weakness, and servitude. The inhabitants of fiefs could not find consolation in the bosom of tranquillity; incessantly mixed up in the quarrels of their lord, a prey to his neighbors' devastations, they led a life still more precarious and still more restless than that of the lords themselves, and they had to put up at one and the same time with the presence of war, privilege, and absolute power."

Although slavery had existed in England prior to the Conquest, this species of feudal servitude was first

introduced by William the Conqueror, and enforced in
all its rigor and barbarity among the people. Within
twenty years from the accession of William, almost
the whole soil of England was parcelled out among his
retainers and followers. The native proprietors who
escaped with their lives from the scenes of rapine and
tyranny which attended the conquest were reduced to
serfs, villeins, and vassals. The name of Englishman
became a reproach even in his own country, and none
of the race was raised to any office of dignity for over
a century. The native tongue was rejected as barbarous; children were instructed in the French language, and even the cruel laws made for the persecu-
tion of the Saxon were not understood by him as they
were enacted and enforced in the language of the
stranger. The detestable game-laws, the depopulating
of whole districts to serve as hunting-grounds for royal
pastime, were first enacted by William the Conqueror,
who made the penalty for killing a stag or a wild boar
—the loss of eyes—a greater crime than the killing of
an Englishman ; "for William loved the great game,"
says the Saxon chronicle, "as if he had been their
father." The intolerable exactions of tribute, the
rapine of purveyance, the inequality of the nobility,
the sale of wardships, the right to interdict the marriage of the daughters of vassals or to compel them to
marry those who paid the highest sum into the royal
exchequer, the forest laws, wager of battle, the extinguishment of fires at the sound of curfew,—all these
may be traced to Norman rule and Norman feudalism
as established in England. This state of affairs which

the people long endured, might have riveted their chains for centuries, had not the Norman barons upon finding that the penalties of the rigid laws enacted for the punishment of the Saxon were visited upon themselves, hoisted the standard of revolt, and on the plains of Runnymede wrung from King John, Magna Charta, —the boast and pride of Englishmen, and the great bulwark of English liberty.

CHAPTER V.

DECLINE AND OVERTHROW OF FEUDAL SERVITUDE IN ENGLAND.

THE contest which resulted in the concessions contained in Magna Charta was a contest between an unscrupulous, tyrannical, and grasping monarch on the one side, and haughty barons, jealous of any infringement of their ancient rights, on the other. The serfs and villeins composed probably nine-tenths of the population of England, but their rights were not taken into consideration, and were not directly benefited by Magna Charta. These degraded human beings were beneath the notice of legislation, except in so far as it was concerned in defining their crimes and fixing their punishments. "No freeman shall be disseized nor imprisoned," etc., is the language of Magna Charta; yet long centuries elapsed ere the word "freeman" was construed to include every British subject. Indeed, it would seem that the last case of villeinage to be found in the law-books is as late as the fifteenth year of the reign of James I. I shall not attempt to follow villeinage in the several steps of its decline, it being sufficient here to note a few of the controlling causes which happily concurred, first, to check its progress, and finally, to suppress it in England. The first of these was the influence of the Christian religion. After it became established, Christian princes bestowed large tracts of land upon religious houses in the division of conquered provinces. The prelates and abbots of these houses swore allegiance to the king or other superior, received the homage of their vassals, enjoyed the same immunities, exercised the same jurisdiction, and maintained the same authority as the lay lords among whom they dwelt. In these grants, the same as in grants of land made to the laity, villeins regardant, as they were called (meaning those who had been attached to a certain manor from time immemorial), together with their families and all the goods and chattels which they possessed, were conveyed and passed with the grant of the land. The religious houses were not only the first to emancipate the slaves which in this manner became their property, but " when the dying slaveholder asked for the last sacraments, his spiritual attendants regularly adjured him, as he loved his soul, to emancipate his brethren for whom Christ had died."*

---

* Macaulay's History of England.

Many of the freedmen voluntarily remained under the shadow and protection of the monastery to which they had been attached in preference to facing the world on their own account, just as many southern slaves would not leave their kind masters though emancipated by the proclamation of President Lincoln. And it was upon the ecclesiastical estates to which they thus became attached that the first germs of industry and freedom began to spring. "While the vassals of the military proprietors were sunk in slavery, or lost in the sloth which follows so degraded a state, industry was reviving under the shadow of the monastic walls, and the free vassals of the religious establishments were flourishing in the comparative security of their protection."† The cruel custom of enslaving captives taken in war was also abolished through the influence of the Christian religion, which proclaimed the universal equality of mankind in the sight of heaven. Haughty barons, who would not agree to the absolute release of their slaves, might consider it mutually advantageous to enter into an undertaking with them that, after a stated time, in consideration of faithful service, they should receive their manumission. These undertakings were usually recorded in the lord's book or rolls of the manorial court. These and other obligations of a like nature, in process of time, developed into certain customary rights out of which immediately grew a species of land-tenure known as copyhold estates. Lords of generous dispositions granted indul-

---

† Alison's History of Europe.

gences which were either intended to be or readily became perpetual. Having time out of mind permitted their villeins and children to enjoy their possessions without interruption, in a regular course of descent, the common law, of which custom is the life, now gave them title to prescribe against their lords; and, on performance of the same services, to hold their lands in spite of any determination of their lord's will. While great numbers of the villeins crept into freedom under the name of copyholders, many more became enfranchised in a different manner. In many instances those whom the lord could not provide with labor, or supply with food and raiment, were permitted to go from place to place in search of employment. Such of them as were bound to cruel or unkind masters were not slow to make good their escape. If captured, the courts of justice took advantage of the slightest technicality, and indulged every presumption in favor of the fugitive, so that his lord had little hope of carrying to a successful issue a suit for his recovery.

Many causes and circumstances, both moral and physical, contributed to bring about a change in the manners of the governing classes as well as in the mode of government, so that the disorders of feudal anarchy gradually disappeared. Religion, politics, civil commotion, the black plague, the wars of the Roses, and many other causes which might be mentioned, redounded to the advantage of the inferior classes, and by a succession of fortuitous circumstances occurring during several generations before the middle of the fifteenth century, the serfs and villeins had gradually worked out their own freedom through their relation to the lands. So that when James I. succeeded to the throne the whole system of personal and territorial servitude had virtually expired, and that able, daring, unscrupulous, and grasping prince hastened the downfall of feudalism, already tottering to decay. He deprived the feudal lords of the crown lands which they had usurped from his predecessors, confiscated the estates of some of the most audacious, whom he condemned to execution, and strengthened the royal authority by humbling the power of the grandees and nobles.

CHAPTER VI.

EXTIRPATION OF FEUDALISM IN FRANCE.

THERE is no period in the world's history which furnishes so much food for intelligent thought and profitable investigation as do the three centuries preceding the French Revolution. What great and salutary lessons may be drawn from a study of the lives of the men and the philosophy of the events which that period produced! It was the dawn of a new era,— the advent of a new civilization. If proof be wanting to convince mankind that to establish a free and stable government, the subordinate holder of power must have a durable interest in the soil, it will be only necessary to study the relative conditions of the people

E   g   9

of France and England during this period. The death of feudalism in England was so gradual, and its effects upon the people were apparently of such slow growth that it requires the closest researches of the historian to be able to fix the date of its complete extinction. But not so in France. The fires of discontent that had smouldered for centuries among the feudal slaves in France, now burst forth into a great conflagration which lighted the country from the Channel to the Pyrenees, and spread ruin and devastation all around. The desolation which it wrought in its expiring moments is its lasting monument. The best blood of France enriched the ashes of its pyre.

The circumstances which contributed to the enfranchisement of the serfs in England not only conferred upon them personal liberty, but attached to that liberty proprietary rights, which, if not valuable as a merchantable commodity, possessed a certain durability of which they could not be deprived on a moment's notice. Customary laws and usages added privileges to these proprietary rights which in process of time developed into hereditary tenures, at first transmissible from father to son, and subsequently transferable by gift or sale. The result was that the great body of the English people became comparatively contented with their condition, and strongly attached to the principles of a government which afforded them not only personal freedom but the means of acquiring and enjoying property. And while we find occasional attempts at insurrection, induced by the arbitrary exactions and cruel oppressions of the feudal lords, the great revolutions of this period in England cannot be attributed to popular discontent arising from agrarian causes.

If we look to France during the same period, no social or political advancement is discernible in the condition of her feudal vassals. Consigned to the abasement of feudal bondage, no prolonged and resolute effort was made by church or State to elevate or disenthrall them. No privileges were here sanctioned by usage or sanctified by law to ripen into personal or proprietary rights. The hounded fugitive found here no Asylæan or sanctuary, ancient borough or walled city, where he might halt with safety or tarry in security. The seal of servitude here was seldom broken through Christian love or human compassion. In his flight for freedom the weary slave here, as elsewhere, found refreshment and repose within monastic walls, but even there he was not beyond reach of his pitiless, powerful, and persistent pursuer. For many centuries these human beings were deprived of civil and political rights, without morals, without religion, without property ; beings more than cattle but less than men ; beings who had everything to gain but nothing to lose in the overthrow of order and the destruction of power ; beings who knew how to hate because never taught to love ; beings in whose breasts rankled the scorn of power, the disdain of religion to whom king and prince, baron and priest, were alike the subjects of attack, the objects of revenge. When the supreme moment arrived which gave license to their pent-up fury, what could have been expected to follow but that

vandalism of anarchy, that reign of terror, that night-
mare of horror, that carnival of diabolism memorably
and forever known as "The French Revolution."

The morning of the seventeenth century saw a new
era dawn for France when the giant intellect and
mighty arm of Armand de Richelieu gave a new
impetus to the world of thought, aroused anew the
love of chivalry in the people, and restored to France
her national fame and military glory. But it was not
until the American Revolution, "When was fired the
shot heard around the world," that the Sun of Freedom rose to set no more on a land of feudal slaves.

The people of France clamored long and incessantly
to be restored to liberty and to be relieved from the
thraldom and oppressions of their cruel and pitiless
taskmasters. They were answered by the minions of
power, in the name of the law,—driven to the galleys
and consigned to the Bastile. The peasantry now
formed leagues and societies in every election district,
met in club-rooms and halls to discuss their grievances
and organize in defence of their rights. Their protests
and remonstrances but served to excite the ridicule of
the nobility and clergy, who deemed themselves secure
in the support of the military.

A general election took place amid the greatest ex-
citement. Mirabeau, rejected by the nobility, was the
chosen representative of the commonalty. The states-
general assembled at Versailles. The nobility and
clergy refused to meet with the representatives of the
people. Refused admittance to the legislative hall by
a cordon of soldiers, the tiers-état repaired without a

murmur to Tennis-Court. Those brave and determined men assembled by the will of the people to do battle for constitutional government and the rights of man, endured with silent patience every affront offered by the nobility, remained firm, unwavering, immovable in their purpose and betrayed not a trust. In the historic hall of Tennis-Court, with its dark and gloomy walls and rude floor, with no useless ornaments or costly furniture, the deputies of the people stood around a bench to deliberate on the affairs of state, found a new government for France, a charter of liberty for her people. No dilatory motions or puerile points of order were interposed to retard the progress of that solemn, thoughtful assembly of great and patriotic men, bound together by the sacred tie of love of country, determined never to separate " till the Constitution of the kingdom is established and founded on a solid basis."

Induced by the intrigues of the nobility, the weak but well-meaning Louis XVI. undertook to dissolve the assembly. When the Marquis de Brézé made known to the tiers-état the mandate of the king, Mirabeau—brave, fearless, daring—rose up, and addressing the Marquis, said, " Go, tell your master that we are here by the power of the people, and that nothing but the power of bayonets shall drive us away." Danger threatened on every side. Alarm was pictured on every face as the National Guards surrounded the capital, and all communication with Paris was cut off.

The Assembly demanded a withdrawal of the military, but Louis hesitated, vacillated between the prompting of his own better judgment and the pressure brought to bear upon him through the machinations of the nobility.

Wild rumors of the dismissal of Necker, the Minister of Finance, and of the imprisonment of the Assembly reached Paris. Consternation seized the populace. They wildly hurried to the Palais-Royal, where the mob was assembled, listening to the most inflammatory speeches. A young republican mounted the table, held up a pair of pistols, shouting, "To arms!" The hour arrived, the signal given, the pent-up fury of a nation long in chains wildly broke the seal of feudal bondage. "To the Bastile!" "Storm the Bastile!" was heard above the deafening noise and confusion of the frantic rabble. Onward they pressed amid showers of fiery hail from guards and pickets, from post and garrison.

"On, then, all Frenchmen that have hearts in their bodies! Roar, with all your throats of cartilage and metal, ye sons of liberty! Stir spasmodically whatsoever of utmost faculty is in you,—soul, body, or spirit! Smite, thou Louis Tournay, cartwright of the Marais, old soldier of the regiment Dauphine! smite at that outer drawbridge chain, though the fiery hail whistles around thee! Never, over nave or felloe, did thy axe strike such a stroke. Down with it man; down with it to Orcus; let the whole accursed edifice sink thither, and tyranny be swallowed up forever!" Fell that frowning monument of feudal barbarism which stood for ages a menace to French liberty, —fell the Bastile, which the mighty Condé besieged in vain,—fell that blood-stained tower, black with the crimes of centuries, before the frantic fury of the Revolutionists! French vassals became citizens and peasant proprietors. France was free. Revolution made her free.

CHAPTER VII.

EXTINCTION OF FEUDALISM IN PRUSSIA.

THAT period which marks the wane of the eighteenth and the dawn of the nineteenth centuries is a remarkable era in the world's history,—remarkable alike in the history of nations and in the progress of events. It is a period full of life, full of thought, full of social and political reforms, full of religious bitterness, full of warfare, full of commotion. At such a period, when the old landmarks had been overthrown by the bitterness of the Reformation, and when all Europe was torn asunder by the wild passions engendered by the French Revolution, if we turn to Prussia we find the whole monarchy suffering from the devastating wars of Napoleon, whole villages laid waste, and whole districts depopulated. Agitation for land-reform, for civil and political liberty, and for relief from the exactions of the crown and the grasping avarice of the nobility received a peaceful impetus from the political and social revolutions now transpiring. Even the German serf dreamed of his

long-lost possessions, and thought of the happy days
long past when each bauer was a freeman. He too
had now the hardihood to assert his rights, the nerve
and will to fight for and maintain them.

At this period the entire land of Prussia was distributed among three classes of society,—nobles, peasants, and burghers. These classes were distinct castes,
their personal status was reflected in the land held by
them, and conversely, the land held determined the
status of the holder. The noble could follow no avocation but that of his caste. The burgher had a
monopoly of trades and industries, which, with some
very limited exceptions were confined to the towns, and
could not be exercised in the country. The military
profession was closed to him as well as the higher civil
employments. The condition of the peasant differed
widely in the different provinces, but there was this
feature common to all peasant-holdings that they were
not isolated farms but united in a "commonalty," and
these "commonalties" stood under the jurisdiction of
the manor. The rural area of Prussia was divided
into three districts,—the manorial district, consisting
of demesne lands, cultivated by the manorial proprietor, and in which he exercised the functions of a
police magistrate; the township of the peasant community, with its arable mark and common mark, in
which a schultze, usually an hereditary office, exercised the police authority in the name and under the
authority of the lord of the manor and the different
communities held by different kinds of tenure, varying
in an ascending scale from those in which the allottees

were in a state of personal villeinage with unlimited services, to those in which they were free settlers, who, though under the jurisdiction of the manor, and paying dues to it by virtue of that jurisdiction, were yet owners of their lots. The allottees were originally slaves, who settled upon the demesne lands, and had gradually emerged to the higher level of villeinage, and the free settlers were originally allodial owners of the land held by them, but who had surrendered their rights of full ownership to the manorial lords, but which they again received upon taking the oath of allegiance.

As the nature of these tenures are elsewhere described it is unnecessary to go into further details here. Suffice it to say that the battles of Jena and Friedland, which led to the humiliating peace of Tilsit, hastened the consummation of events which led to the Edict of October 9, 1807, that struck the shackles from the slave and broke forever the yoke of feudal bondage in Prussia. While this edict removed the distinctions of castes, rent the fetters which bound them, allowed such rights as existed to be freely used, and broke down the barriers which separated from each other the different classes of society, it created no new forms of property. It proclaimed freedom of exchange, but did not point out the manner nor provide the means therefor. Peasants' lands could now be held indiscriminately by all the citizens of the state, but they were still held under the old forms of tenure; there were still two kinds of property. The lord was still owner of the peasant's land without the right of possessing it. The peasant was free, but was not master of his labors.

The legislation of 1811 was intended to remedy this state of affairs, and undertook to substitute allodial ownership for feudal tenures.

The legislation of 1811 consisted mainly of two edicts, one entitled an "Edict for the Regulation of the Relations between the Lords of the Manor and their Peasants," the other, an "Edict for the Better Cultivation of the Land." The first is concerned with the new title-deeds for the peasant holders and the commutation of the services rendered in virtue of the old tenures. This had in view the adjusting of the equities between the lord of the manor and the peasant, and substituting allodial for feudal tenures. It would enlarge the scope of this work to too great an extent to discuss in detail all its provisions, and hence we will pass to the Act of 1850. This latter law abrogated the direct dominion or suzerainty of the lords of the manor without compensation; so that from the day of its publication all hereditary holders throughout Prussia, irrespective of the size of their holdings, became proprietors, subject, however, to the customary services and dues which, by the future provisions of the law, were commuted into fixed money rents, calculated on the average money value of the services and dues rendered and paid during a certain number of years preceding. By a further provision these rent-charges were made compulsorily redeemable, either by the immediate payment of a capital equal to an eighteen-years' purchase of the rent-charge, or by a payment of four and a half or five per cent. for fifty-six and a twelfth or forty-one and a twelfth years on a capital equivalent to twenty-years' purchase of the rent-charge.

The law for the establishment of rent-banks provided the machinery by which the peasants might redeem their property.

The state, through the instrumentality of the rent-banks, constituted itself the broker between the peasants, by whom the rents had to be paid, and the landlords who received them. The bank established in each district advanced to the landlord in rent debentures, paying four-per-cent interest, a capital sum equal to twenty-years' purchase of the rent. The peasant, besides his ordinary rates and taxes, paid into the hands of the district tax-collector each month one-twelfth part of a rent calculated at five or four and a half per cent. on this capital sum, as he elected to free his property from encumbrance in forty-one and a twelfth or fifty-six and a twelfth years, the respective terms within which, at compound interest, the one or the half per cent. paid in addition to the four-per-cent. interest on the debenture, would extinguish the capital. This one per cent. and half per cent., when so utilized and hoarded by the government through these instrumentalities constituted a kind of sinking-fund for the redemption of the debenture or bond which the peasant gave to the landlord as the purchase-price of his property. Thus, by a wise and far-seeing policy engrafted by legislation upon German tenures, the peasantry secured their freedom, obtained an interest in the soil which they cultivated, and were transformed into loving and devoted citizens of a common fatherland. German wisdom, through masterly statesmanship, averted the danger which threatened the monarchy, and saved the country from the horrors which were brought about by the French Revolution.

CHAPTER VIII.

DECREMENT OF FEUDALISM IN RUSSIA.

RUSSIAN noblemen were not great landed proprietors like the feudal barons of Western Europe. The lands which they held were usually allotted to them from the crown lands, and were cultivated by their slaves. To those noblemen who did not own slaves, the czar not unfrequently awarded the yield of the taxes due him from the peasants of one or more villages. The peasants of the villages, like the nobles to whom they paid tribute in taxes, were the servants of the czar. The village, not the family, was the social unit. Movable property alone belonged to the individual. The land was the common property of the villagers. During the reigns of the Emperors Ivan III. and IV. a petty nobility fashioned after the feudal order was created in Russia. This nobility consisted partly of the courtiers or nobles whom the czars left in possession of the yield of taxes above alluded to, the servants of the czar who were in part taken from among the villagers themselves, likewise endowed with the yield of taxes of one or more villages, and the proprietors of such villages. It was not until the reign of Boris Godunow, the usurper, that the full weight of the mailed power of feudalism was felt by the peasants residing in villages, who uniformly hitherto enjoyed many political privileges. By a series of decrees issued by this emperor, from the year 1592 to the year 1606, the peasant was forbidden to quit his village without permission and passport from the village authorities. Any peasant found abroad without such permission was taken into custody, and sent back in irons and punished for his disobedience.

During the seventeenth century the condition of peasant and slave was alike pitiful and degrading, and while, as early as the year 1797, the Emperor Paul restored to the peasants the right of electing their village heads, little progress was made towards improvement in their condition until the reign of the Emperor Nicholas, who in the year 1842 issued his ukase permitting the proprietors of private estates to confer, by treaties, upon their serfs the rights and political privileges of farmers, the government vouching for the farmer-serfs fulfilling the conditions undertaken by them. The idea being to ascertain what form of treaties would prove the most acceptable and beneficial to both parties, before framing a general compulsory measure embodying the contents of a popular form of contract. He further re-enforced the law interdicting the sale of peasants without land by forbidding the transforming of peasants, first, into household slaves, in which menial condition it was per-

mitted to buy and sell them, and second, forbade the
sale of land without peasants, if by such sale the village
acre was curtailed in such a way as to amount to less
than twelve acres for every male villager. Finally,
he issued regulations defining more specifically than
before, how much labor, or how much payment in lieu
of labor, in a variety of places, the peasant serf owed
to his master. All measures hitherto adopted for the
purpose of initiating and stimulating a voluntary
abandonment of the serf-system on the part of the
masters having proved ineffective, Alexander II., upon
his accession to the throne, determined to eradicate
serfdom from agrarian legislation. In striking contrast
with the improvident policy pursued by the United
States in emancipating the slaves of the South, turning
them adrift, helpless and purposeless, abolishing their
servile dependence upon their masters but failing to
provide means or methods for their exercise or enjoyment of their independence, the Russian emperor
incorporated in his proclamation abolishing serfdom
measures dictated by wisdom and humanity, which
enabled the disenthralled serf to make for himself a
home in the land of his birth, and become owner of
the soil he tilled. The legislation of Russia in 1861,
which so happily and successfully solved this great
problem,—at once social, industrial, and political,—
reflects the highest credit upon Russian statesmanship.

The Act of 1861 was based upon the assumption
that a sudden and radical transition in the matter of
compulsory rent payable in labor to the same payable
in money was inadmissible even if it were possible for

each of the villagers to discharge their liabilities, and also that the preservation intact of a numerous peasantry could be best assured by an acquiescence not only in a fragment of coercion in general but also in a remnant of compulsory labor, the law fixing its money equivalent. In adjusting the relative proportions of labor-rent and money-rent, and the time and manner of working out the former and of paying the latter, due care was taken not to do violence to the interests of the lord nor infringe upon the newly-vested rights of the liberated serf, or render him powerless to enjoy the benefits of the change of his condition. The transition from labor-rent to money-rent was made optional with the peasants, with the whole community, or with every single family, only two years after the law became valid, provided they were not in arrears for labor-rent. The money-rent to be paid by each male head of the population was determined not by the size or fertility of the land-share he was entitled to so much as by its location relative to distance from a market, the place of exchange.

The most important, however, of the main provisions of the Act of 1861 is that which refers to the *right* of the peasants to purchase the copyhold on which they are living. They are *compelled* to accept the copyhold; but, in compensation, the proprietor of the *estate* is *compelled* to accept their money, if they are able and willing to buy either each his own share, dissolving the community, or together the whole of the grant, continuing the community. This option left to them has been the subject of much controversy. The proprietors would have preferred to see the whole village do either the one or the other. Where the community is not dissolved, and not inclined to purchase the land in common, each single peasant may yet assert his right of purchasing his own share, but on condition that he pays one-fifth more than the purchase-money otherwise would amount to.

" Government has undertaken to assist the peasantry in purchasing the land by advancing, on the security of the 'obrok' collected by their agents, part of the necessary sum, amounting to four-fifths where the whole grant is purchased, and to three-quarters where a part of it of certain size is purchased, in form of bonds of the Imperial Bank bearing five-per-cent. interest, or titles to rent, guaranteed by government which afterwards are to be taken in exchange for such bonds of the bank. They are to be paid over at once to the proprietor of the estate or to his creditors. Only such peasants, of course, can receive the benefit of governmental assistance who have already turned the labor-rent into 'obrok.' But government, always zealous in the interest of securing the existence of a numerous order of peasants, has placed another condition on their assistance. The purchase-money is only advanced in behalf of such peasants as consent to purchase the dwelling-houses and farm-yards *with* the land. This also will tend to lessen the number of cases—apprehended by the proprietors—of a part of the peasants in a village purchasing the houses and farm-yards *with* the land, and a part *without* it."

BOOK III.

THE RIGHT OF PROPERTY AND THE STABILITY OF TENURES.

CHAPTER I.

THE RIGHT OF PROPERTY DEFINED.

THE right of property is not an absolute right which belongs to man as a natural being but a relative and restricted right, which arises from his social relations. Austin, treating of *jus in rem* (ownership) uses the terms "ownership" or "property" as synonymous, and, referring to this term, he says that it is of such complex or various meaning that he does not undertake to accurately define it, but for his present purpose gives the following definition: "The right to use or deal with some given subject in a manner and to an extent which though not unlimited is indefinite." After discussing the subject as thus defined, he says, "Ownership or property is therefore a species of *jus in rem*. It is a right residing in a person, over or to a person or thing and availing against other persons universally or generally." It will be perceived that this definition, as the author concedes, does not fully answer the purpose even in a technical sense, and it would but increase the difficulty to undertake to give a definition against which no objection can be urged. For all practical purposes, however, I may say that the right of property is a right which belongs to man as a member of society, and correlative to it, is the right in every man to use and enjoy that which is his, in such manner as he pleases, so that in the use and enjoyment thereof he does nothing that is hurtful to himself or to another. This right of property is a private right, a natural right, and a legal right. It is a private right because confined to the owner; it is a natural right because every member of society may enjoy it, and it is a legal right because it grows out of the common compact, and is sanctioned by universal usage at all times among all civilized nations and peoples.

Dr. Wm. Paley, in his "Moral and Political Philosophy," speaking of property rights, very aptly says that "The real foundation of our right is the law of the land. It is the intention of God that the produce of the earth be applied to the use of man. This intention cannot be fulfilled without establishing property; it is consistent therefore with his will that property be established. The land cannot be divided into separate property without leaving it to the law of the country to regulate that division. It is consistent therefore with the same will that the law should regulate the division, and, consequently, 'consistent with the will of God,' or 'right,' that I should possess that share which these regulations assign me.

"By whatever circuitous train of reasoning you attempt to derive this right, it must terminate at last in

the will of God. The straightest, therefore, and short-
est way of arriving at his will, is the best.

"Hence it appears that my right to an estate does
not at all depend upon the manner or justice of the
original acquisition, nor upon the justice of each subsequent change of possession. It is not, for instance,
the less, nor ought it to be impeached, because the
estate was taken possession of at first by a family of
aboriginal Britons, who happened to be stronger than
their neighbors; nor because the British possessor was
turned out by a Roman, or the Roman by a Saxon
invader; nor because it was seized without color of
right or reason, by a follower of the Norman adven-
turer, from whom, after many interruptions of fraud
and violence, it has at length devolved to me.

"Nor does the owner's right depend upon the *expediency* of the law which gives it to him. On one
side of a brook an estate descends to the eldest son,
on the other side to all the children alike. The right
of the claimants under both laws of inheritance is
equal, though the expediency of such opposite rules
must necessarily be different."

In chapter ii., Book VI., "Progress and Poverty,"
Henry George says:

"To extirpate poverty, to make wages what justice
commands, they should be the full earnings of the
laborer, we must therefore substitute for the individual
ownership of land a common ownership. Nothing
else will go to the cause of the evil,—in nothing else
is there the slightest hope.

"This, then, is the remedy for the unjust and un-

equal distribution of wealth apparent in modern civilization, and for all the evils which flow from it. We
must make land common property."

This is the panacea which George would offer for all
our social and political woes. "We have reached this
conclusion," he says, "by an examination in which
every step has been proved and secured. In the chain
of reasoning no link is wanting and no link is weak.
Deduction and induction have brought us to the same
truth,—that the unequal ownership of land necessitates
the unequal distribution of wealth." Evidently the
links in the chain of reasoning by which George
reached his conclusion were composed of sand and
fashioned by the ocean's waves. Before establishing
the truth by induction that the unequal ownership of
land necessitates the unequal distribution of wealth, he
infers by deduction that the remedy for this "and for
all the evils which flow from it" is "to make land
common property." The assumption that unequal
distribution of land is of itself the cause of these
evils is untrue, and any deduction drawn or conclusion
reached from such an assumption must necessarily be
false. What has the unequal distribution of land to
do with stock-, grain-, and provision-corners which demoralize trade and bankrupt individuals; with railroad pools which rob both producer and consumer;
with sugar trusts, coffee trusts, oil trusts, and coal
trusts which filch the last penny from the pocket of
the workman every Saturday night? What has it to
do with the monstrous iniquity of the law which deprives the workman, who is injured through defective

machinery or who is not paid his wages, of a speedy remedy? And what has it to do with a thousand other wrongs which it is unnecessary here to mention. George wields such a facile pen that his writings are well calculated to decoy and ensnare those who have little practical knowledge of wordly affairs, or who do not penetrate beneath the surface to discover and detect his fallacious reasoning. That the monopoly and combination of wealth (and by wealth I mean cash, bonds, stocks, real and personal property), and the inefficiency of the law to prevent this monopoly and combination, are the *real causes* of the discontent and unrest of the toiling millions, every man who investigates and thinks must admit. But as these views will be found more fully expressed in subsequent chapters of this volume, I will not enlarge upon them here, further than to assert that the right of property is best regulated and enjoyed when each individual owns, controls, and possesses that which is his absolutely and of right. That this mode of owning and enjoying property is more advantageous to the individual, and more beneficial to society because promotive of thrift, progress, and prosperity, is established by the testimony of men whose opinions ought to have great weight with every thoughtful man.

CHAPTER II.

HOW THIS RIGHT IS BEST REGULATED AND ENJOYED.

EMILE DE LAVELEYE, whose researches into the history of institutions and the mode of enjoying property, comprehending nearly every country of the world, almost unconsciously, as it were, draws the line of demarcation in the progress of civilization where community property ends and individual property begins, demonstrating the advantages of the latter mode of enjoyment over the former. Any argument advanced or conclusions drawn by him to the contrary are hardly sustained by the evidence which he produces. The social development and progress which mark the evolutions in the form of landed property, so minutely and ably presented in his valuable work on the "Origin of Property," furnish indubitable evidence of the surperior advantages of individual ownership over communal property. Speaking of the inroads which this social development are producing in Russia, he says:

"Since the emancipation the old patriarchal family has tended to fall asunder. The sentiment of individual independence is weakening and destroying it. The young people no longer obey the 'ancient.' The women quarrel about the task they have to perform. The married son longs to have his own dwelling. He can claim his share of the land; and, as the Russian peasant soon builds himself a house of wood which he shapes, axe in hand, with marvellous facility, each couple sets up a separate establishment for itself. . . .

"How marked is the contrast between the Russian and the American! The latter, eager for change and action, athirst for gain, always discontented with his position, always in search of novelty, freed from parental authority in his earliest years, accustomed to count on no one but himself and to obey nothing but the law, which he has himself helped to make, is a finished type of individualism."

After describing the characteristics and family life of the communities among the southern Slavs he says:

"The flourishing appearance of Bulgaria shows decisively that the system is not antagonistic to good cultivation. And yet this organization, in spite of its many advantages, is falling to ruin, and disappearing wherever it comes in contact with modern ideas. The reason is that these institutions are suited to the stationary condition of a primitive age; but cannot easily withstand the conditions of a state of society in which men are striving to improve their own lot as well as the political and social organization under which they live. I know not whether the nations who have lived tranquilly under the shelter of these patriarchal institutions will ever arrive at a happier or more brilliant destiny; but this much appears inevitable, that they will desire, like Adam in 'Paradise Lost,' to enter on a new career, and to taste the charm of independent life despite its perils and responsibilities."

M. de Sismondi, comparing the conditions of tenant farmers and peasant proprietors, says:

"Wherever we find peasant proprietorship we also find comfort, security, confidence in the future, and independence, which assures at once happiness and virtue."

In a carefully-prepared treatise on Flemish husbandry, in the "Farmers' Series of the Society for the Diffusion of Useful Knowledge," the writer states that the Flemish agriculturists seem to want nothing but a space to work upon. "It is highly interesting," he says, "to follow, step by step, the progress of improvement. Here you see a cottage and rude cow-shed erected on a spot of the most unpromising aspect, the loose white sand blown into irregular mounds is only kept together by the roots of the heath; a small spot only is levelled and surrounded by a ditch; part of this is covered with young broom, part is planted with potatoes, and, perhaps, a small patch of diminutive clover may show itself; and this is the nucleus from which in a few years, a little farm will spread around. If there is no manure at hand, the only thing that can be sown, on pure sand, at first, is broom; this grows in the most barren soils; in three years it is fit to cut, and produces some return in fagots for the bakers and brickmakers. The leaves which have fallen have somewhat enriched the soil, and the fibres of the roots have given a certain degree of compactness. It may now be ploughed and sown with buckwheat, or even with rye without manure. By the time this is reaped, some manure may have collected, and a regular course of cropping may begin."

Step by step the improvement goes on, the soil under-
goes a complete change; it becomes mellow and reten-
tive of moisture, and is enriched by the decomposition
of vegetable matter, and made fertile by the hand of
industry, and patient and intelligent husbandry. The
people labor constantly and industriously, and wait
patiently for returns, because the land which they cultivate belongs to them. "The magic of property turns
sand into gold."

Joseph Kay, A.M., of Cambridge University, speaking of the division of land in foreign countries, referring to Germany, says: "In Saxony it is a notorious
fact, that during the last thirty years, and since the
peasants became the proprietors of the land, there has
been a rapid and continual improvement in the condition of the houses, in the manner of living, in the
dress of the peasant, and particularly in the culture of
land. The peasants endeavor to outstrip one another
in the quantity and quality of the produce, in the preparation of the ground, and in the general cultivation
of their respective portions. All the little proprietors
are eager to find out how to farm so as to produce the
greatest results; they diligently seek after improvements; they send their children to the agricultural
schools in order to fit them to assist their fathers, and
each proprietor soon adopts a new improvement introduced by any of his neighbors."

Mr. Howitt, writing on the Rural and Domestic
Life of Germany, says: "The peasants are the great
and ever-present objects of country life. They are the
great population of the country, because they them-

selves are the possessors. This country is, in fact, for
the most part, in the hands of the people. It is parcelled out among the multitude,—the peasants are not,
as with us, for the most part, totally cut off from property in the soil they cultivate, totally dependent on
labor afforded by others,—they are themselves the proprietors. It is, perhaps, from this cause that they are
probably the most industrious peasantry in the world.
They labor busily, early and late, because they find that
they are laboring for themselves. The English peasant
is so cut off from the idea of property that he comes
habitually to look upon it as a thing from which he is
warned by the laws of the large proprietors, and becomes, in consequence, spiritless, purposeless. The
German farmer, on the contrary, looks on the country
as made for him and his fellow-men. He feels himself
a man; he has a stake in the country, as good as that
of the bulk of his neighbors; no man can threaten
him with ejectment or the work-house, as long as he is
active and economical; he walks, therefore, with a bold
step; he looks you in the face with the air of a free
man, but of a respectful air."

CHAPTER III.

THE SUBJECT CONTINUED.

St. Thomas Aquinas, the great doctor and theolo-
gian of the Roman Catholic Church, says: "It is
lawful that man should possess things as his own.

For this is necessary to human life for three reasons : First, because every one is more solicitous to procure what belongs exclusively to himself than that which is common to all or many, since each one, evading work, leaves to another what is the business of all, as it happens where there is a number of servants. Besides, there will be better order in the management of human affairs if to each citizen is laid the burden and care of acquiring certain things ; moreover, there would be confusion if each one promiscuously procured every kind of thing. Thirdly, the community is kept in greater peace while each one is satisfied with his own property. Hence we see that, among those who possess something in common and indivisibly, contentions arise more frequently."

The master-spirit of Catholicity in England, Cardinal Manning, in his recent admirable exposition of the Law of Nature, Divine and Supreme, regarding the rights of the poor, says :

" By the law of nature all men have a common right to the use of things which were created for them and for their sustenance.

" But this common right does not exclude the possession of anything which becomes proper to each. The common right is by natural law, the right of property is by human and positive law, and the positive law of property is expedient for three reasons : (1) What is our own is more carefully used than what is common. (2) Human affairs are better ordered by recognized private rights. (3) Human society is more peaceful when each has his own protected by the law of justice.

" Theft is therefore always a sin,—for two reasons: (1) It is contrary to justice. (2) It is committed either by stealth or by violence.

" But the human and positive law cannot derogate from the natural and Divine law. According to the Divine law all things are ordained to sustain the life of man, and, therefore, the division and appropriation of things cannot hinder the sustenance of man in case of necessity. Therefore the possessions of those who have food superabundantly are due by the natural law for the sustenance of the poor. . . . This doctrine lies at the foundation of the positive law of property in all Christendom. It exists as an unwritten law in all Catholic countries. . . . The obligation to feed the hungry springs from the natural right of every man to life, and to the food necessary for the sustenance of life. So strict is this natural right that it prevails over all positive laws of property. Necessity has no law, and a starving man has a natural right to his neighbor's meal. I am afraid that those who speak so confidently about rights, obligations, and laws have not studied, or have forgotten, the first principles of all human positive law. If the law of property did not rest upon a natural right it could not long exist. . . . Before the natural right to live all human laws must give way."

Aristotle, in his efforts to find what is the best government, briefly outlines the first principles of man's social nature, and of domestic life in its various relations, showing how these relations naturally combine into that form of social existence which is called a state, and after demonstrating that, the community of women and children, as advocated by Socrates and Plato, is not beneficial to the state, speaking of the community of property, says:

"We proceed next to consider, as to property, in what way it should be regulated among those who are to live under a state formed after the most perfect mode of government, whether it should be common or not; I mean, whether it is better (although these should be held separate, as is now the case everywhere), that not only the possessions but also the produce of them should be in common; or that the soil should belong to a particular owner, but that its produce should be brought together and used as one common stock, as some nations at present do; or, on the contrary, that the soil should be common and be cultivated in common, while the produce is divided among individuals for their special use, as is said to be the practice among some of the barbarians; or whether both the soil and the fruit should be in common? When the husbandman and the citizen are distinct, there is another and easier method; but when they each labor at their possessions for themselves, this may occasion several difficulties; for if there be not an equal proportion between their labor and what they consume, those who labor hard and have but a small proportion of the produce, will of necessity complain against those who take a large share and do but little labor. Upon the whole, it is difficult to live together as a community, and thus to have all things that man can possess in common, especially this is the case with respect to such property. This is evident from the partnerships of those who go out to settle a colony; for nearly all of them have disputes with each other upon the most common matters, and come to blows upon trifles: we find, too, that we oftenest disagree with those slaves who are generally employed in the common offices of a family. A community of property, then, has these and other inconveniences attending it: but the manner of life which is now established, more particularly when embellished with good morals and a system of upright laws, is far superior to it, for it will embrace the advantages of both; by 'both' we mean, the advantage arising from properties being common, and from being divided also; for in some respects it ought to be common, but upon the whole private. For the fact that every man's attention is employed on his own particular concerns will prevent mutual complaints; and property will increase as each person labors to improve his own private property; and it will then happen that, from a principle of virtue, they will perform good offices to each other, according to the proverb, 'All things are common among friends.' . . .

"This system of polity does, indeed, recommend itself by its good appearance, and specious pretences to humanity; and the man who hears it proposed will receive it gladly, concluding that there will be a wonderful bond of friendship between all its members, particularly when any one censures the evils which are now to be found in society, as arising from property not being common; as, for example, the disputes which happen between man and man, upon their contracts with each other; the judgments passed to punish perjury, and the flattering of the rich; none of which arise from properties being private, but from the corruption of mankind. For we see those who live in one community and have all things in common, disputing with each other oftener than those who have their property separate; but we observe fewer instances of strife, because of the very small number of those who have property in common compared with those where it is appropriated. It is also but right to mention not only the evils from which they who share property in common will be preserved, but also the advantages which they will lose, for, viewed as a whole, this manner of life will be found impracticable.

" We must suppose, then, that the error of Socrates arose from the fact that his first principle was false; for we admit that both a family and a state ought to be one in some particulars, but not entirely so, for there is a point beyond which, if a state proceeds towards oneness, it will be no longer a state."

In speaking of the manners and customs of the Germans, Tacitus says: " To the rest of the Germans we display camps and legions, but to the Hermundurians we grant the exclusive privilege of seeing our houses and our elegant villas. They behold the splendor of the Romans, but without avarice or a wish to enjoy it." Rome had her houses and elegant villas when the Germans " neither knew the use of mortar nor of tiles. They built with rude materials, regardless of beauty, order, and proportion." Rome was civilized,—Germany barbarian. The Romans owned houses, built imperial highways, engaged in commerce,—the Germans lived in communities, shifting from place to place, "dispersed up and down as a grove, a meadow, or a fountain happened to invite." These distinctions in the conditions of the social life of the peoples are not peculiar to Rome and Germany. The same may be said of Rome and Britain in the days of Cæsar, and generally wherever it is possible to place civilization and progress side by side with a nation which has not emerged from barbarism, we meet with similar contrasts.

CHAPTER IV.

RIGHTS, VESTED AND PROSPECTIVE.

THE right of property embraces not only the exclusive privilege to use and enjoy the thing owned, but also the exclusive power to sell, transfer, and dispose of the same upon such terms, at such times, and to such persons as may be agreeable to the owner, provided that in so doing he violates none of the laws or customs established by the society of which he is a member, and to which he is indebted for the protection, preservation, and enjoyment of that which is his. Nor does the right of property end here. There are rights beyond these which are as absolutely his, and which are as sacred and inviolable as those already mentioned. The right to which I now refer follows as the direct and necessary consequence of the law or custom upon which all other rights are based. It follows as certainly and logically as effect follows cause.

So long as society exists for the protection, preservation, and perpetuation of personal liberty, of personal security, and of the inviolability of private property, a man ought not only to be protected in his right to things tangible and possessory, but should also be protected in his just expectations as to things intangible, such as the fruits of his labors which *become* valuable rights of property. For example, if I plant a vineyard, the vines which I plant are things tangible and possessory, they are vested rights of property of which I cannot be deprived under the law without just compensation. While my vines have ripened into a vested and possessory right of property, they are of no real present value until vintage, no more than the wheat which I sow is of any real present value until harvest. But I may as justly and as reasonably expect my vines to yield fruit, and that I will gather the vintage, as I have to expect my wheat to grow and that I will reap the harvest. When I planted my vineyard, and during all the years that I trimmed and tended my vines, it was just as lawful for me to expect that I might gather my grapes and convert them into wine, as it was for me to expect that I might reap my wheat and convert it into flour. The yield of my vineyard is but the reward of my skill and labor, just the same as the yield of my wheat-field. It was just as harmless and as innocent and as lawful for me to

i

plant my vineyard and trim the vines as it was for me to sow my wheat-field and gather the harvest.* It was just as lawful for me to make wine from grapes, when I planted and tended my vineyard, as it was to convert wheat into flour. The vines which I planted were as surely my property, and as securely protected under the law, as the growing wheat. In fact, the laws and customs of the society, of which I was a member, encouraged the cultivation of the vine, and, relying upon the faith of these laws and customs, I expended my labor in its cultivation. This labor was my capital, my property, my all. The law declared in no uncertain terms that my property could not be taken for public purposes without just compensation. This was the solemn assurance held out to me, and upon the faith of which I expended my labor. As vintage-time drew near, and when about to reap the reward of my labor,—when my just expectations with regard to my rights of property were about to be realized,—the society of which I was a member, if not in the letter in the spirit, violated the solemn assurance which it held out to me under the law, for although it did not actually *take* from me my property, it did that which was virtually the same. It passed a law which deprived me of the reward of my labor,—a law which

---

* M. de Lavergne, in a letter to Cliffe Leslie, in 1869, written from Toulouse, France, says: " You could not believe what wealth the cultivation of the vine has spread through that country, and the peasantry have gotten no small share of it. The market price of land has quadrupled in ten years.'' So that the cultivation of the vine is not only a legitimate but a profitable rural industry.

declared the manufacture or sale of wine from grapes unlawful. My vineyard was so far removed from market that my grapes could not be sold or utilized for any purpose but for the manufacture of wine. In consequence of this unjust law my grapes were left to wither on the stem, my vineyard was consigned to waste, and thereby my labor was robbed of its just reward. I appealed to the law through the regularly constituted tribunals for redress, but was answered that my grapes were not actually *taken*, that, as they *might* be used for any purpose other than the only purpose for which, under the circumstances, they could be used, I was not entitled to compensation. That the State could not in *fact take* my property without making just compensation therefor, but that it might play dog in the manger, and in this way deprive me of its use. And this process of reasoning, of legal subterfuge and of judicial robbery, is based upon the theory that individual rights must yield and be set aside whenever the public good requires that such a sacrifice shall be made. If by this process of reasoning the property of any individual may be destroyed, where is the line to be drawn? Upon the same theory and with as much semblance of justice I may be compelled to give up my fallow and pasturage, my unimproved and un-occupied city lots, to any one who will plough and sow the one, or improve and occupy the other, whenever it shall be decreed that it is necessary for the public good, provided I am not absolutely deprived of my naked legal title. It may as plausibly be said that in author-izing a farmer to plough and sow my fallow and pasturage, or a manufacturer or merchant to improve and occupy my city lot, I am not deprived of my property but of its use only, as to say that I am not deprived of my vintage. Legislative sophistry and judicial legerdemain cannot convince the common mind that this system of robbery is more consonant with the principles of natural justice than that which is advocated by Henry George and his followers. Indeed, Georgeism is the more commendable because to him what is equal seems just, and in founding his republic individual rights would be sacrificed only upon the theory of equality. Georgeism has this merit at least to commend it, that the individual who gives up his property for the common good may hope to receive back an equal proportion of his own in the general distribution as one of the community, while the prohibitory liquor laws recently passed in Kansas and Iowa deprive individuals of their property without even distributing it among the community, or awarding to the owners the poor privilege of participating in the benefits which would arise from its general distribution. Men in those States invested hundreds of thousands of dollars in constructing beer-cellars and breweries under the sanction of law, and with the assurance held out to them that private property should not be taken for the public use without just compensation. Upon the security of these properties large sums of money were advanced and credit given because it was just as innocent, just as harmless, and just as lawful to build a beer-cellar and erect a brewery as it was to settle upon the prairie and pre-empt a homestead.

As the law offered to the lender and borrower full assurance that capital invested in this kind of property would be protected, it was the solemn duty of the State to keep its faith with those who invested their capital in, and gave credit upon, this kind of security. There is no principle of natural justice which exempts a State from fulfilling its moral and legal obligations any more than an individual. The property in these beer-cellars and breweries is of no more real value, of no more utility for any purpose, other than that for which they were built and constructed, than are the hollow caves which yawn back the roar of the dashing waves along the sea-shore. Yet, because the law did not actually *take* from its owner his naked legal title, because the property in them may be used for some purpose,—that is, the stone and mortar and wood, of which they are constructed, may be carted off or shipped to some other point and there converted into use,—there has not been a *taking* within the meaning of the fundamental law, and, therefore, the owners are not entitled to compensation.

CHAPTER V.

SUBVERSION OF LAW IS INVASION OF RIGHT.

A NATION may outlive civil commotion, rebellion, and even anarchy, provided the body politic has not become so corrupt as to be unable to distinguish between the first principles of right and wrong, of justice and injustice. I admit, as Aristotle says, that all men have some natural inclination to justice, " but they proceed therein only to a certain degree, nor can they universally point out what is absolutely just." But the universal voice of mankind will unite in one acclaim in saying, that if I am encourged by society (and by society I mean the State) to invest money in a certain kind of property, or to build up a certain industry at a time when the fundamental law of that society declares my right of property therein inviolable, and thereafter that society should change the law so as to deprive me of the use of my property, and render it valueless to me, it should make compensation for the injury done. This would be but natural justice, anything less is flagrant injustice. If the public safety or the public morals require the discontinuance of any business or manufacture, the legislature of a State has the undoubted right to provide for its discontinuance, but where this business or manufacture grew into vested rights of property under the sanction of the law and under the assurance of the public policy of the State, its discontinuance can only be justly and *legally* commanded upon making due compensation for the loss which necessarily and inevitably will accrue to the individual.* I designed writ-

---

* Edmund Burke, the statesman, legislator, and philosopher, in proposing "a plan of reform in the constitution of several parts of the public economy," in the British House of Commons, speaking of the uneasiness of the people in regard to the abuse of sinecures, said : " I think with the public, that the profits of these places are grown enormously ; the magnitude of those

ing this book with a view of combating communistic doctrine, but I am met at the threshold with the anomaly of legislative acts and judicial decrees which, if sound law, are more dangerous to society, because evincing a corrupt state of public morals, than all the wild vaporings of the wildest anarchists from the beginning of the French Revolution down to the execution of

---

profits, and the nature of them, both call for reformation. The nature of their profits which grow out of the public distress is itself invidious and grievous. But I fear that reform cannot be immediate. I find myself under a restriction. These places, and others of the same kind, which are held for life, have been considered as property. They have been given as a provision for children, they have been the subject of family settlements; they have been the security of creditors. If the barriers of law should be broken down, upon ideas of convenience, even of public convenience, we shall have no longer anything certain among us. If the discretion of power is once let loose upon property, we can be at no loss to determine whose power, and what discretion it is that will prevail at last. It would be wise to attend upon the order of things, and not attempt to outrun the slow, but smooth and even course of nature. There are occasions, I admit, of public necessity, so vast, so clear, so evident, that they supersede all laws. Law, being only made for the benefit of the community, cannot in any one of its parts resist a demand which may comprehend the total of the public interest. To be sure, no law can set itself up against the cause and reason of all law. But such a case very rarely happens, and this most certainly is not such a case. The mere time of the reform is by no means worth the sacrifice of a principle of law. Individuals pass like shadows, but the commonwealth is fixed and stable. The difference, therefore, of to-day and to-morrow, which to private people is immense, to the State is nothing. At any rate it is better, if possible, to reconcile our economy with our laws than to set them at variance; a quarrel which in the end must be destructive of both.''

August Spies and his associates. If the acts and decisions already alluded to be law, there is no legal security, there is no constitutional safeguard for the protection of individual rights and the inviolability of private property which may not be overthrown, and trampled upon by State legislation.

In one of the latest decisions prepared by that able jurist, Mr. Justice Cooley, when on the Supreme bench of the State of Michigan he took occasion to say : "Personally, I have little care how this case shall be decided. But it seems to me that in constitutional questions the court is drifting to this position : that these statutes are constitutional which suit us, and those are void which do not." This severe comment upon judicial morals, I fear, is but too true.

Ordinarily it is of little consequence to society how the cause of any particular individual may be decided when there is no principle involved other than the question with whom the merits of the case lie; but the recent acts of Iowa and Kansas, and the decisions of the courts with reference thereto, involve a principle of no little importance to the whole American people, and that is, whether the language employed in the fourteenth amendment to the constitution means what it says, or is but a mere idle play of words. No man who observes the assaults upon corporate property and encroachments upon vested rights occurring almost daily in crowded cities and legislative halls can but realize that between the conspiracies of the commune and the fanaticism of well-meaning but ill-guided zealots, our institutions are not only threatened, but are enduring a crucial test. Judges and statesmen ought not to pause too long, but should wisely contemplate and calmly consider the limits within which every invasion of property and personal rights, under whatever guise, should be confined.

Every lawyer who has given thought to the subject of legislation for the suppression of intemperance, and who has carefully examined and analyzed the decisions of courts, will admit that more uncertainty and doubt have crept into the administration of the law through hasty and ill-guarded dicta and decisions bearing upon this class of statutory crimes than through all other agencies. It is not my purpose to assail the motive of courts that would give sanction to laws of this nature, for, whatever views I may entertain on the subject, I agree with the author of the " Rights of Man," that " it is better to obey a bad law, making use at the same time of every argument to show its errors and procure its repeal, than to forcibly violate it, because the precedent of breaking a bad law might weaken the force and lead to a discretionary violation of those which are good." From this text courts and judges may learn salutary lessons. To ascertain what the law is and to decide whether or not it conflicts with the constitution is the alpha and omega, the beginning and the end, of a judge's duty. A penal statute of doubtful meaning ought always to be construed in favor of the liberty of the citizen rather than against it, and when a law falls within the ban of the constitution, courts ought to place their seal of condemnation upon it regardless of their personal feelings, predilections, or prejudices. In this way only can courts uphold the dignity and maintain the supremacy of the law under the constitution. Under our political system, we ignore the " divine right" of kings and the "infallibility" of parliament,—the court alone is the final arbiter between the citizen and the State, and the law its " golden met-wand and measure." In war and in peace, at all times and under all circumstances, our courts should be ready to guard and protect the rights and liberties of the citizen under the constitution. At their bidding legislative enactments made in contravention of the constitution are held inoperative and void. Executive decrees, functions, and prerogatives exercised and performed by the President, whether in the capacity of civil magistrate or as commander-in-chief of the land and naval forces of the nation, when not sanctioned by that instrument, are stayed, modified, or annulled. From the moment, therefore, that any judge who is called upon to decide a question involving the rights or liberties of the citizen permits himself to be swayed by personal prejudices, however honest, our constitutional guarantees are as nothing, and the liberties of the people are at an end. It is aptly said by the learned historian who wrote " The Decline and Fall of the Roman Empire" that " the principles of a free constitution are irrecoverably lost when the legislative power is dominated by the executive." And, with equal force may it be said that when a man is elected to fill a judicial position because of his predilections in favor of a particular law, or, when he is set aside and defeated for the office because he has the manhood to do right, the boast of freedom under a written constitution becomes a "tinkling cymbal," the cant of hypocrites, and sooner or later, in such case, the structure of our institutions must fall with crushing force upon the heads of those who are slowly but surely weakening and impairing its foundations. If judges, who are the creatures of the people, are to be swayed by the clamor of the majority and to hold that those statutes are constitutional which suit them, and those void which do not, what difference can there be in this particular between a republican form of government under a written constitution and an absolute monarchy, such as that despicable despot, James the First of England, sought to establish?

CHAPTER VI.

SECURITY UNDER THE CONSTITUTION.

THE fifth amendment to the Constitution of the United States provides that "no person shall be held to answer for a capital or otherwise infamous crime, unless on a presentment or indictment of a grand jury. . . . nor shall any person be subject, for the same offence, to be twice put in jeopardy of life or limb; nor shall be compelled in any criminal case to be a witness against himself; nor be deprived of life, liberty, or property, without due process of law; nor shall private property be taken for public use without just compensation." But, notwithstanding this constitutional guarantee of personal rights and of private property, the State might deprive its own citizen, or any person within its jurisdiction, of life, liberty or property in any mode or by any form of law enacted by its legislature and sanctioned by its courts, and, however tyrannical, cruel and unusual the punishment, or unjust the decree which deprived him of his life or liberty or despoiled him of his property, he was without the protection of the Federal Constitution.

"Congress shall make no law respecting an establishment of religion, or prohibiting the free exercise thereof," is the language of the first article of the constitution; and broad and beneficent as this language may seem, if Utah were a member of the sisterhood of States his polygamic majesty, by edict from his temple or by rescript of his legislature, might compel every citizen within the jurisdictional limits of the State to bow in reverence before the shrine of Mormonism and lay yearly tithe at the foot of a Mormon altar. Can any man who fought to uphold the Union and sustain the supremacy of the nation be convinced that all the lives which were sacrificed and all the treasure which was expended to establish a principle and consummate a fact are to go for naught, and that, after all, he is but the serf of a provincial baron instead of a proud citizen of the United States under the protection of the Constitution? "If I were to ask you, gentlemen of the jury," said Erskine in one of his noted speeches in defence of liberty, "what is the choicest fruit that grows upon the tree of English liberty, you would answer, security under the law. If I were to ask the whole people of England, the return they look for at the hands of government, for the burdens under which they bend to support it, I should still be answered, security under the law; or, in other words, an impartial administration of justice." There is no such thing as security under the law if the legislature can, without compensation, destroy vested rights of property acquired under the existing law. Judicial refinements may strip constitutional guarantees of their common sense and every-day meaning, may tax the art of sophistry, and throw around their decisions a glamour of pedantry, but, after all, the fact remains indelible, unchanged, and unchangeable that the individual has been wrongfully deprived of that which was legally and rightfully his.

When rights are acquired by the citizen under the existing law, there is no authority vested in any branch of the government to take them away without just compensation.* But where they are held contrary to the

---

* I agree with the Supreme Court of the United States in the Mugler case (123 U. S., 623), that the right of every citizen to manufacture intoxicating liquors for his own use, or as a beverage, " does not inhere in citizenship." Indeed, I go further, and hold it to be the law that every member of society is bound by the rules of civil conduct prescribed for the guidance, government, and well-being of all, and when he transgresses those rules he thereby forfeits his right to the enjoyment of liberty and the pursuit of happiness. While under our system of government sovereignty remains with the people, by whom and for whom all government exists and acts, yet here, as elsewhere, the individual

existing law, or are forfeited by its violation, then they may be taken from him,—not by an act of the legislature, but in the due administration of the law itself

---

does not enjoy personal liberty, exercise inherent sovereignty, or possess absolute rights which are separate and apart from the society of which he is a member. I do not contend, therefore, that the State cannot, through its legislature, prohibit the manufacture, sale, and consumption of an article of commerce which is believed to be pernicious in its effects, and the cause of disease, pauperism, and crime. At the time the legislature of the State encouraged and sanctioned the building of breweries, statistics similar to those accessible to every one tended to prove, then as now, "that the idleness, disorder, pauperism, and crime existing in the country are, in some degree at least, traceable to the evils of intemperance." Yet the States of Kansas and Iowa, when they were anxious to have their lands settled and cultivated, made large appropriations for the printing and distribution of documents, in the German and Scandinavian languages, setting forth the advantages of these States, the peculiar nature of the soil, and the splendid facilities for growing and producing hops, were not the least of the inducements held out to allure these frugal and thrifty peoples to settle upon their lands. The persons who built breweries built them not only under the tacit sanction of the law, but under its direct and positive assurance that they might do so with entire safety. There are no statistics accessible to any one to prove that the German and Scandinavian peoples are not among our best, law-abiding, temperate, and industrious citizens.

The distinction which I draw in regard to the power of the State and the rights of those whose properties have been invaded and destroyed by legislation is very simple,—the mere distinction between right and wrong. The State has the power to prohibit the manufacture, sale, and consumption of intoxicating liquors, —that is the right of the State; but to do so by destroying the use of the property in which the manufacture and sale had been conducted under the sanction of State law, without making just compensation therefor, is morally and legally wrong.

before the judicial tribunals of the State. The cause or occasion for depriving the citizen of his supposed rights must be found in the law as it is, or, at least, it cannot be *created* by a legislative act which aims at their destruction. " Where rights of property are admitted to exist the legislature cannot say they shall exist no longer, nor will it make any difference that a process and a tribunal are appointed to execute the sentence. If this is the 'law of the land,' and 'due process of law,' within the meaning of the constitution, then the legislature is omnipotent. It may, under the same interpretation, pass a law to take away liberty or life without a pre-existing cause, appointing judicial and executive agencies to execute its will."†

" The right of property has no foundation or security but the law, and when the legislature shall successfully attempt to overturn it, even in a single instance, the liberty of the citizen is no more."‡

Sir William Blackstone, in his classification of fundamental rights, says: " The third absolute right, inherent in every Englishman, is that of property, which consists in the free use, enjoyment, and disposal of all his acquisitions, without any control or diminution, save only by the laws of the land. . . . The laws of England are, therefore, in point of honor and justice, extremely watchful in ascertaining and protecting this right. Upon this principle the great charter has declared that no free man shall be disseized or divested

---

† Comstock, J., in Winehamer *vs.* The People, 13 N. Y., 392.
‡ Mr. Chief Justice Gibson in Nooman *vs.* Heist, 5 Watt's and Sergeant (Pa.), 193.

of his freehold, or of his liberties or free customs, but by the judgment of his peers or the law of the land. . . . So great, moreover, is the regard of the law for private property that it will not authorize the least violation of it; no, not even for the general good of the whole community. . . . In vain may it be urged that the good of the individual ought to yield to that of the community, for it would be dangerous to allow any private man, or even any public tribunal, to be the judge of this common good, and to decide whether it would be expedient or no. Besides, the public is in nothing more essentially interested than in the protection of every individual's private rights, as modelled by the municipal law. In this and similar cases the legislature alone can, and indeed frequently does, interpose, and compel the individual to acquiesce. But how does it interpose and compel? Not by absolutely stripping the subject of his property in an arbitrary manner, but by giving him a full indemnification and equivalent for the injury thereby sustained."

So that, according to Blackstone, the right of private property, in England, under a government founded upon the feudal principle, is more secure to the subject than it is to the citizen of the United States under a republican form of government. If this be the case, then away with the boasted guarantees of the American constitution!

CHAPTER VII.

THE STABILITY OF TENURE.

In chapter i., Book VIII., "Progress and Poverty," Henry George says: "What is necessary for the use of land is not its private ownership but the security of improvements. It is not necessary to say to a man 'this land is yours' in order to induce him to cultivate or improve it. It is only necessary to say to him 'whatever your labor or capital produces on this land shall be yours.' Give a man security that he may reap, and he will sow; assure him of the possession of the house he wants to build, and he will build it. These are the natural rewards of labor." And again, in chapter ii., he says: "We should satisfy the law of justice, we should meet all economic requirements, by at one stroke abolishing all private titles, declaring all land public property, and letting it out to the highest bidders in lots to suit under such conditions as would sacredly guard the private right to improvements." . . . "I do not propose either to purchase or to confiscate private property in land. The first would be unjust; the second, needless. Let the individuals who now hold it still retain, if they want to, possession of what they are pleased to call *their* land. Let them continue to call it *their* land. Let them buy and sell, and bequeath and devise it. We may safely leave them the shell if we take the kernel.

It is not necessary to confiscate land ; it is only necessary to confiscate rent." The impracticability and injustice of this method will be readily seen and appreciated by the most casual observer. It must be inferred from his statements that Henry George is willing to let land to whomsoever would improve the same, and for any term of years or for all time, provided the fee to the land remained in the government. By no sophistry could he convince even the most simple-minded that he might invest his earnings in improving a vacant lot without affording him some assurance of a fixity of tenure, and hence he is willing that in his republic any man who will improve his property shall be guaranteed protection in the nature of a lease for years, for life, or in perpetuity. But is this any protection to him who invests his means in the improvement of vacant property? Such men now hold the absolute title to their property under the guarantee of the constitution, and under that instrument there is no power in a municipality, a State, or in the Federal Government to take it away from them or to deprive them of it without just compensation. Yet Henry George and his disciples maintain that the paper titles, by and through which they claim title, are but old and musty documents, and that the titles which they evidence were acquired by fraud and force, by usurpation and confiscation, and therefore unworthy of protection. Granting these premises for the sake of argument, would the titles which *they* propose be more sacred or more durable? After George and his followers shall have overthrown our institutions and consigned these musty documents to the flames, and when new institutions are established, new compacts adopted, and new contracts entered into between the citizen and the State, and the industrious and frugal citizen improves his vacant property and feels secure in the protection of the law, a new *doctrinaire* writes a book on " Progress and Poverty" to show that the bane of society is the monopoly of land, that the preceding government had no power to grant leases so as to bind succeeding generations, and that the panacea for all the ills of life is in the destruction of existing tenures; that instead of giving leases for years, for life, or in perpetuity, the owners of land must pay their rent in taxes to the full rental value of their holdings, the value to be determined by the assessor and collected by the tax-gatherer. Here again we are brought face to face with the same order of things and the same condition of society existing in India, China, and unhappy Ireland. Not only so, but the affairs of the government would be placed in the hands and under the control of unscrupulous and corrupt officials who would hedge themselves around by political rings controlled by rum-sellers, fine workers, and pot-house politicians to such an extent that it would be impossible to remove them from office either through an election or by conviction in the criminal courts. The owners of property now try to control and manage it themselves or through their authorized agents, and nothing is left for public officials to do but to attend to the improvement of public highways, the distribution of public charities, the keeping and confinement of criminals and the like,

yet the country is cursed with boodlers and boodlerism.
What would be the condition of affairs and the state
of society if the powers of these public officials were
enlarged and extended to the extent contemplated in
Mr. George's paper republic?

It is conceded that before men will improve property
they must be assured protection for improvements,
permanent possession of the houses which they build,
and without such assurance they will not make improvements.   What difference could it make to future
generations whether George M. Pullman purchased
absolutely the title to the property upon which he has
built a city or agreed to give ten dollars an acre rent
to the government for the use of the property in
perpetuity?   Ten dollars an acre was infinitely more
than the land was worth by way of rental at the time
Mr. Pullman took possession of it; but because he had
the means and ability to improve it, he has made it
valuable.   It is no answer to assert that it would
have been valuable in any event, because it would not
but for the improvements made upon it.   It might
have lain there for a million years and all the speculations of philosophers that now live or who may here-
after live, during all that time, could not by any
subtlety of reasoning or any adroit application of the
argument in regard to unearned increment add one
dollar to its value, unless they could induce some
capitalist to invest who had sufficient means and ability
to establish factories and build up a city for the accommodation of the men and families employed in
these factories.   Mr. Pullman might have reclaimed a

part of Lake Michigan, might have gone down to
"Hoop Pole" Township in Indiana, if you please, and
have made that property as valuable as now is the
beautiful city of Pullman, which he found an unprofitable and unproductive marsh. His capital is what
made his own property valuable, and the improvements
which he placed thereon increased the value of surrounding property. The public and not the individual owner
of the surrounding property are entitled to this increase. It is unnecessary to overthrow our institutions
or to destroy existing tenures in order that the public
may derive the benefit of the increase in value to the
surrounding property. This may be accomplished by
legislation in the manner proposed in the chapter on
Unearned Increment.

Suppose that fifty years ago Mr. Pullman made a
contract with the government by which he was to pay
ten dollars a year rent in perpetuity for a lot on the
corner of State and Madison Streets, Chicago, which at
that time would not have been deemed a very profitable investment or promising speculation on the part of
Mr. Pullman; that he improved the lot by erecting
thereon a dry-goods store which he has occupied ever
since; and supposing the lot adjoining had not been
improved, but, owing to the increase in the value of
the property, the annual rental value of the adjoining
lot is now worth a thousand dollars, note the advantage
Mr. Pullman would have in business competition over
the man who is now compelled to pay a yearly rental
of a thousand dollars for the adjoining lot. Mr. Pullman is a gainer to the extent of nine hundred and

ninety dollars per year by virtue of the improvements placed alongside of him by his neighbor,—a gainer to this extent without any effort on his part,—just as if he had bought the lot absolutely in the first place. Had he purchased the lot in the first instance, he would have been compelled to pay taxes in proportion to its increase in value, but as he rented the lot from the government at a fixed annual rent of ten dollars a year in perpetuity, this rent is the only tax which the government can exact from him in the future, so that the nine hundred and ninety dollars a year is his individual gain. The government, therefore, is not only deprived of its just proportion of taxes incident to the increase in the value of the property, but the neighbors and competitors of the lot-owner are placed at a disadvantage by virtue of the monopoly acquired through his contract with the government. And thus it will be seen how impracticable and unjust is Mr. George's theory when subjected to the test of a common-sense analysis.

CHAPTER VIII.

THE FALLACIES OF GEORGE'S LAND-TAX THEORY.

In Book IX. chapter i., Henry George says:

"THE advantages which would be gained by substituting for the numerous taxes by which the public revenues are now raised a single tax levied upon the value of land will appear more and more important the more they are considered. This is the secret which would transform the little village into the great city. With all the burdens removed which now oppress industry and hamper exchange, the production of wealth would go on with a rapidity now undreamed of. This, in its turn, would lead to an increase in the value of land,—a new surplus which society might take for general purposes."

This doctrine is laid down by its author as the remedy for unequal taxation. It is based upon the claim that ground values in the centres of the great marts of trade represent an immense "unearned increment" and constitute the larger portion of investments in business real estate. This is also accompanied by its correlative that ground values in rural districts and in the outlying parts of towns and cities are so small, compared with the value of property in the heart of cities, that a single land-tax would rest easily on the farmer and the owners of lots in the cheaper residence portions of the city, while the capitalistic owners of lots and blocks in the business centres would have to bear the great burden. Subjecting this claim to a practical test will at once expose its fallacy, and demonstrate that this method of shifting tax-burdens, instead of relieving the farmer and small property owner and placing the heavier burden on the millionaire, will produce just opposite results.

The properties listed below are located in the business centre of Chicago; the assessment given being only about twenty per cent. of the true value:

Structure.	Ground.	Building.
Board of Trade	$110,000	$300,000
Palmer House	190,000	300,000
Royal Insurance Company	40,000	116,000
Sherman House	75,000	85,000
Chicago Opera House	77,000	87,000
Merchants' National Bank	9,000	32,000
Times Building	20,000	25,000
Pullman Building	18,000	90,000
J. V. Farwell	100,000	160,000
Marshall Field	109,000	129,000
Insurance Exchange	50,000	75,000
Chicago Deposit Vault	75,000	120,000
Phœnix Insurance Company	80,000	125,000
Lakeside Building	32,000	50,000
Home Insurance Company	50,000	130,000
Montauk Building	12,000	55,000

It is seen that the immense " unearned increment" is invariably less than the improvement, and in some cases equals only one-third or one-fourth of it. The above figures reveal the utter fallacy of exempting immense business structures from taxation and laying the entire tax on the ground, not one foot of which may belong to the owners of the buildings. This condition obtains still more strongly in the case of residence property. The properties of this kind in the following list have dwellings which occupy in width nearly the entire lot frontage, and, of course, belong to the capitalist, upon whose shoulders Mr. George proposes to lay the burden of taxation :

	Ground.	Building.
No. 1	$5,500	$25,000
No. 2	16,600	25,000
No. 3	7,500	13,000
No. 4	3,000	20,000
No. 5	2,500	12,000
No. 6	5,000	10,000

In exceptional instances, where the ground is un-usually valuable or a larger area is reserved for the dwelling, the above ratio may be reversed. Improve-ments depreciate, and it is true that ground values usually appreciate, but it may be laid down as a rule that on the most desirable residence streets in all our cities first-class houses are valued higher than the ground upon which they stand. This being the actual relative condition of grounds and improvements, it is at once seen that the dweller in the humble cottage, if the land alone is to be taxed, will have proportionately heavier taxes to pay than owners of palatial residences. And more, many of the money barons do not possess a foot of land. Which is true also of the thousands of speculators who gamble and grow rich upon the stock and grain exchanges, in running corners on breadstuffs and provisions, and whose mercenary schemings and combinations frequently produce financial panics which, with other disturbances, cause depression of land values and increase the cost of living. And yet these men, according to George's theory of taxation, would be un-disturbed by the tax-gatherer, while the small home-steader, whose possessions they have depreciated and whose expenses they have increased, would have to pay tribute not only for himself but for his oppressors.

Applying the theory of Mr. George to farm lands, its utter failure to produce the result claimed is still more apparent. The valuation of farm property in Massachusetts, as shown by the most reliable census ever taken in this country, gives the following re-sults :

Land	$116,629,849
Buildings	66,033,291
Land and Buildings	$182,663,140

Here we see that in a State of small land-holders, possessing many and costly improvements, but a poor soil, the ground value is nearly three-fourths of the total. This disproportion would be still greater in the vast farming districts of the West, where farms are larger, soil more fertile, and improvements meagre and inexpensive. The total value of town and city grounds and improvements in the United States, as shown by the last Federal census, is $10,000,000,000. Not more than three-tenths of this is naked ground value. George would extinguish rents by taxing this value at six per cent. Admitting that the farmers hold seven-tenths of the naked ground value of the country, they then would have to pay, following out George's theory, six per cent. on $7,000,000,000 or $420,000,000 yearly, which would be $108,000,000 more than is paid in State, county, township, and municipal taxes in the United States. In brief, the farmers, who (at a true valuation) own scarce one-half of the real estate of the country, would pay seven-tenths of all the taxes, and $100,000,000 more than is now paid on all real and personal property of every description. While the farmers would be groaning under this burden of taxation, the owners of town and city real estate, whose properties equal the farmers' in value, would pay taxes only on three-tenths of a true valuation. The city capitalists paying only $180,000,000 while $420,000,000 is exacted from the farmers. Would not this vaunted theory of Mr. George's work the most ruthless spoliation of the agricultural class? Let George himself answer.

CHAPTER IX.

GEORGE'S SELF-REFUTATION.

IN Book IX., chapter i., of " Progress and Poverty," Mr. George exposes the fallacy of his own theory in these words :

" For the simple device of placing all taxes on the value of land would be in effect putting up the land at auction to whoever would pay the highest rent to the State. The demand for land fixes its value, and hence, if taxes were placed so as to very nearly consume that value, the man who wished to hold land without using it would have to pay very nearly what it would be worth to any one who wanted to use it."

This mode of taxation would instigate the same tyranny, the same causes for rack-renting, which Henry George describes and denounces in a previous part of his work in commenting upon the condition of the people of Ireland and India. In Book II., chapter ii., " Progress and Poverty," he says :

"In India, from time immemorial, the working classes have been ground down by exactions and oppressions into a condition of helpless and hopeless degradation. For ages and ages the cultivator of the soil has esteemed himself happy if, of his produce, the extor-

tion of the strong hand left him enough to support life
and furnish seed ; capital could nowhere be safely
accumulated or to any considerable extent be used to
assist production ; all wealth that could be wrung from
the people was in the possession of princes who were
little better than robber chiefs quartered on the country,
or in that of their farmers or favorites, and was wasted
in useless or worse than useless luxury, while religion,
sunken into an elaborate and terrible superstition,
tyrannized over the mind as physical force did over
the bodies of men.   Under these conditions the only
arts that could advance were those that ministered to
the ostentation and luxury of the great.   The elephants
of the rajah blazed with gold of exquisite workman-
ship, and the umbrellas that symbolized his regal power
glittered with gems; but the plough of the ryot was only
a sharpened stick.   The ladies of the rajah's harem
wrapped themselves in muslins so fine as to take the
name of woven wind, but the tools of the artisan were
of the poorest and rudest description, and commerce
could only be carried on as it were by stealth.

" Is it not clear that this tyranny and insecurity have
produced the want and starvation of India, and not, as
according to Buckle, the pressure of population upon
subsistence that has produced the want, and the want
the tyranny ?   The Rev. William Tennant, a chaplain
in the service of the East India Company, writing in
1796, two years before the publication of the ' Essay
on Population,' says : ' When we reflect upon the great
fertility of Hindostan, it is amazing to consider the
frequency of famine.   It is evidently not owing to any

sterility of soil or climate; the evil must be traced to some political cause, and it requires but little penetration to discover it in the avarice and extortion of the various governments. The great spur to industry, that of security, is taken away. Hence no man raises more grain than is barely sufficient for · himself, and the first unfavorable season produces a famine.

" 'The Mogul government at no period offered full security to the prince, still less to his vassals, and to peasants the most scanty protection of all. It was a continued tissue of violence and insurrection, treachery and punishment, under which neither commerce nor the arts could prosper, nor agriculture assume the appearance of a system. Its downfall gave rise to a state more afflictive, since anarchy is worse than misrule. . . . The rents to government were, and, where natives rule, still are, levied twice a year by a merciless banditti, under the semblance of an army, who wantonly destroy or carry off whatever part of the produce may satisfy their caprice or satiate their avidity, after having hunted the ill-fated peasants from the villages to the woods. Any attempt of the peasants to defend their persons or property within the mud walls of their villages, only calls for the more signal vengeance on those useful but ill-fated mortals. They are then surrounded and attacked by musketry and field-pieces till resistance ceases, when the survivors are sold, and their habitations burnt and levelled with the ground. Hence you will frequently meet with ryots gathering up the scattered remnants of what had yesterday been their habitation, if fear has permitted them to return, but

14

oftener the ruins are seen smoking, after a second visitation of this kind, without the appearance of a human being to interrupt the awful silence of desolation. This description does not apply to the Mohammedan chieftains alone, it is equally applicable to the rajahs in the districts governed by Hindoos.'"

In speaking of Ireland Mr. George says:

" It is difficult for one who has been looking over the literature of Irish misery, as while writing this chapter I have been doing, to speak in decorous terms of the complacent attribution of Irish want and suffering to over population which are to be found even in the works of such high-minded men as Mill and Buckle. I know of nothing better calculated to make the blood boil than the cold accounts of the grasping, grinding tyranny to which the Irish people have been subjected, and to which, and not to any inability of the land to support its population, Irish pauperism and Irish famine are to be attributed; and were it not for the enervating effect which the history of the world proves to be everywhere the result of abject poverty, it would be difficult to resist something like a feeling of contempt for a race who, stung by such wrongs, have only occasionally murdered a landlord ! . . . How could there fail to be pauperism and famine in a country where rack-rents wrested from the cultivator of the soil all the produce of his labor except just enough to maintain life in good seasons ; where tenure at will forbade improvements, and removed incentive to any but the most wasteful and poverty-stricken culture ; where the tenant dared not accumulate capital, even if he could get it, for fear the landlord would demand it in the rent; where, in fact, he was an abject slave, who, at the nod of a human being like himself, might at any time be driven from his miserable mud cabin, a houseless, homeless, starving wanderer, forbidden even to pluck the spontaneous fruits of the earth, or to trap a wild hare to satisfy his hunger? No matter how sparse the population, no matter what the natural resources, are not pauperism and starvation necessary consequences in a land where the producers of wealth are compelled to work under conditions which deprive them of hope, of self-respect, of energy, of thrift; where absentee landlords drain away without return, at least a fourth of the net produce of the soil, and when, besides them, a starving industry must support resident landlords, with their horses and hounds, agents, jobbers, middlemen, and bailiffs, an alien state church to insult religious prejudices, and an army of policemen and soldiers to overawe and hunt down any opposition to the iniquitous system? Is it not impiety far worse than atheism to charge upon natural laws misery so caused? . . .

" At the period of her greatest population (1840–45), Ireland contained something over eight millions of people. But a very large proportion of them managed merely to exist,—lodging in miserable cabins, clothed with miserable rags, and with but potatoes for their staple food. When the potato blight came they died by thousands. But was it the inability of the soil to support so large a population that compelled so many to live in this miserable way, and exposed them to starvation on the failure of a single root crop? On the contrary, it was the same remorseless rapacity that robbed the Indian ryot of the fruits of his toil, and left him to starve where nature offered plenty. A merciless banditti of tax-gatherers did not march through the land plundering and torturing, but the laborer was just as effectively stripped by as merciless a horde of landlords, among whom the soil had been divided as their absolute possession, regardless of any rights of those who lived upon it.

"Consider the conditions of production under which this eight millions managed to live until the potato blight came. It was a condition to which the words used by Mr. Tennant in reference to India may as appropriately be applied, 'the great spur to industry, that of security, was taken away.' Cultivation was for the most part carried on by tenants-at-will, who, even if the rack-rents which they were forced to pay had permitted them, did not dare to make improvements which would have been but the signal for an increase of rent. Labor was thus applied in the most inefficient and wasteful manner, and labor was dissipated in aimless idleness, that, with any security for its fruits, would have been applied unremittingly."

Further comment becomes unnecessary. Mr. George's argument is the refutation of his own theory. By "putting up the land at auction, to whoever would pay the highest rent to the State," no man would be secure in his possessions. An army of tax-gatherers, rivals in rapacity of the "merciless banditti" of India, who carry off whatever part of the produce might satiate their avidity, or of the crow-bar militia who raze to the ground the houses of the Irish peasantry, would infest the land, despoiling the peasantry of all the fruits of their labor, and crushing every inducement to industry.

The feudal serf was bound to the soil and ordinarily had the right to live and die upon it, but no legal tie binds George's tenant of the commonwealth to the land which he improves. The civilizing influences and endearing charms of home can never find lodgement in the mind and affections of an unsettled and restless peasantry.

14*

BOOK IV.

CHAPTER I.

LABOR.

LABOR is the life of the world. Labor ministers to the wants of the body, and awakens the tenderest emotions of the soul. Labor is the creator of wealth, the employer of capital. Labor, not gold or silver, is the true standard of values. What can a pair of hands produce? Crœsus views with alarm a depreciation of values, but witnesses with indifference the debasement of labor. Pauperism has become a constitutional vice, immorality a chronic disease. The savage, in his untutored freedom, claims ownership in the forest, and is a patriot in the desert. The laborer of to-day is a slave,—an alien to the soil he tills, without home or country. His vote elects the law-maker, but the voice of capital dictates the law. Labor advances, marches, but makes no progress. Its progress is another's. The accumulation of wealth is not progress. The decline of Rome began when it was gorged with the riches of the provinces. We are to-day a national anomaly,— a marvel of wealth and a prodigy of want. While our

162

national progress is the wonder of the world, the wretchedness of our millions portends degeneracy and decay. We subordinate the spiritual to the physical, and in crowning the material we dethrone the divine. Labor is a slave to wealth. A slave is not a patriot. Labor builds palaces for its master, but has not even a hovel which it can call its own. Labor is without motives to courage, without incentives to industry. Labor has no ideals to give it dignity beyond its immediate wants and circumstances.

In advocating the elevation of labor, I offer no premium upon indolence. Labor is free from the dross of idleness. Labor seeks nothing but its just reward. Labor has no "yearnings for an equal division of unequal earnings." This is a libel upon labor. The unequal division of equal earnings enervates and enslaves labor. It defaces and destroys the family altar, it severs the most sacred ties, and works the ruin of home. It draws the veil of hypocrisy over the face of the moral teacher, and transforms trusted officials into defaulters and embezzlers. It fills the poor-house, and crowds the prison. It makes anarchists of men that have enriched others by their toil, but who see their own wives and children without shelter or bread. "Work," not "charity," is the demand of labor. The equal division of equal earnings is the right of labor. Out of the nettle of toil we pluck the flower of progress.

Justice to labor is a conservation of the equity of the nation, redounding to the preservation and perpetuity of the republic. "Justice to Labor" must

become our watchword and battle-cry, for labor is the
mode of man. The Author of life wills and commands it,—"In the sweat of thy face shalt thou eat
bread till thou return to the earth out of which thou
wast taken." Nature ordains and proclaims it. Labor
is typified in God and personified in all His works. The
earth and the sea, not less than the beasts and the fishes,
labor. Without labor, man cannot exist. Labor is
the song of the fields and the anthem of the heavens.
Labor is the sunshine and the shower. There is
motion, there is labor, in all things. Wisely, Virgil
wrote "*Labor omnia vincit,*" for labor overcomes, sub-
dues, and conquers all things. Labor makes and builds
up the physical man, the moral man, and the intellect-
ual man,—"There is nothing better for a man than
that he should eat and drink, and that he should make
his soul enjoy good in his labor." The troubled heart
finds rest in labor, for "man is born to labor as the
young birds take up their flight." It is meet that man
should labor, for labor is the sum of his existence.
"Whatsoever thy hand is able to do, do it earnestly,
for neither work, nor reason, nor wisdom, nor knowledge shall be in hell." Rest and repose are added to
the reward of him that labors,—"Sleep is sweet to a
laboring man, whether he eat little or much; but the
fulness of the rich will not suffer him to sleep." The
earth is the field and the workshop where all is life and
all is labor. The rivers run to the sea, and "unto the
place from whence the rivers come, whither they return
again," ascending in myriads of rays reflected from the
sun, descending in the sparkling dew-drop and in the

life-giving shower, shedding heaven's benediction upon
the labor of man's hands. "He that tilleth the land
shall be filled with bread," but "an idle soul shall
suffer hunger." By labor we found cities; "by
slothfulness, a building is brought down." Solomon
says, "I passed by the field of the slothful man, and
by the vineyard of the foolish man : and, behold, it
was all filled with nettles ; and thorns had covered the
face thereof; and the stone wall was broken down.
Which, when I had seen, I laid it up in my heart :
and by the example I received instruction. Thou wilt
sleep a little, said I : thou wilt slumber a little; thou
wilt fold thy hands a little to rest : and poverty shall
come to thee as a runner, and beggary as an armed
man."

Labor inspires the imagination, elevates the thought,
and ennobles the mind. "He that gathereth by labor
shall increase," but "wealth gotten in haste shall be
diminished." Labor is the harbinger of civilization ;
idleness and envy and covetousness and sloth disappear
before labor as snow disappears before the summer sun.
Labor is the condition of man, the harmony of nature,
the apostrophe to God. Labor is the song of David,
the voice of the prophets, the parable of the sower, the
lesson of the talents, the Lord's Prayer, the Sermon on
the Mount, the life of the body, the harmony of the
soul, the religion of heaven.

Any system of religion, philosophy, or political
economy that discourages honest labor by teaching that
the land which other men reclaim, cultivate, and make
fruitful belongs as much to him that sleeps as to him

that toils is contrary to the laws of natural justice, inimical to civilization, and blasphemous as against things sacred and essential to the welfare of society. Sublimely moral is the lesson which Hesiod * taught :

> " But thou, O Perses! what my words impart
> Let memory bind forever on thy heart.
> O son of Dios! labor evermore,
> That hunger turn abhorrent from thy door;
> That Ceres bless'd, with spiky garland crown'd,
> Greet thee with love, and bid thy barns abound.
> Still on the sluggard hungry want attends;
> The scorn of man, the hate of Heaven impends;
> While he, averse from labor, drags his days,
> Yet greedy on the gains of others preys;
> E'en as the stingless drones, devouring seize,
> With glutted sloth, the harvest of the bees.
> Love every seemly toil, that so the store
> Of foodful seasons heap thy garner's floor.
> From labor, men returns of wealth behold,
> Flocks in their fields, and in their coffers, gold :
> From labor shalt thou with the love be bless'd
> Of men and gods; the slothful they detest.
> Not toil, but sloth, shall ignominious be;
> Toil, and the slothful man shall envy thee ;
> Shall view thy growing wealth with alter'd sense
> For glory, virtue, walk with opulence.
> Thou, like a god, since labor still is found
> The better part, shalt live beloved, renown'd ;
> If, as I counsel, thou thy witless mind,
> Though weak and empty as the veering wind,
> From others' coveted possessions turn'd,
> To thrift compel, and food by labor earn'd.
>   *   *   *   *   *   *   *   *   *

* Herodotus says that Hesiod was born about 884 years before Christ, and Pliny speaks of him as the earliest writer who laid down precepts of agriculture.

With thy best means perform the ritual part,
Outwardly pure, and spotless at the heart;
Now burn choice portions to the gods; dispense
Wine-offerings now, and smoke of frankincense;
When on the nightly couch thy limbs repose,
Or sacred light from far its coming shows:
So shall they yearn to thee with soul benign,
And thou buy others' lands, not others thine."

CHAPTER II.

CAPITAL SHOULD SHARE PROFITS WITH LABOR.

THE wide gulf which separates labor and capital may be bridged and the bitter differences which are fostering a dangerous antagonism between them may be harmonized in a simple and practical manner, viz.: By allowing the laborer to participate in the profits of his employer's business,— profits which are the joint products of his labor and his employer's capital. For example, I have one million dollars, which I desire to invest in a manufacturing, railway, or other business venture, but, to inaugurate the enterprise and carry it on successfully, I must enlist the services and co-operation of one hundred men. Unless I can do so, my million dollars is an unproductive encumbrance upon my hands, since it, in and of itself, can yield no profit. I find one hundred men who are anxious and willing to work, but are unable for want of capital to engage in business for themselves. The capital represented by the labor of these men is virtually lost to them, since they cannot utilize it. I approach these men and I say to A, "Your labor is worth five hundred dollars a year; now if you give your time and labor to a business enterprise which I desire to establish, I will pay you five hundred dollars a year as wages, and, in addition thereto, I will give you an interest in the concern equal to double the amount of your annual salary, so that, if the investment prove profitable, you will be entitled to a dividend from the profits at the end of every year on a sum equal to one thousand dollars of the capital stock." To B, who is a skilled laborer, I say, " I will pay you one thousand dollars a year for your services, and I will give you an interest in the concern equal to one and three-fourths as much as your annual salary." To C, whom I wish to place in charge of a department, I say, " I will pay you two thousand dollars a year for your services, and give you an interest in the concern equal to one and one-half times your annual salary." And so on, decreasing the amount of the interest given each employé in the concern in relative proportion to the increase of salary, so that the common laborer or person who receives the smallest pay for his services will have the largest relative interest in the welfare of the enterprise, and to that extent he will be the more careful and vigilant in promoting and protecting its interests. The million dollars cash actually invested and the whole amount represented as the equivalent of labor would constitute the capital stock for the purpose of participating in the profits. The men employed would, in this way, receive the same pay for their services, or nearly so, as they do now, and the capital represented as the equivalent of labor would simply be a working interest given to the men, in one sense, as an inducement in order to incite them to a greater vigilance and more effective industry, and, in another sense, as a more just and equitable mode of compensating labor. It may be urged that after the men are paid reasonable wages as the reward of their labor I ought to be allowed a certain percentage of the earnings before the employés would be allowed to participate in profits. But when it is considered that labor and not money is the basis of all values, no injustice can be done the capitalist in permitting the laborer to stand upon equality with him in the division of profits. The amount I pay the laborer is not the real value of his labor, as the real value should be the net profits arising from the sale of the thing or article produced by him, but it is simply an approximate value which barely enables him to live and support himself while performing the labor. The amount which I pay him, therefore, is paid him upon the same basis that I pay for a tie or rail, a locomotive or car. It is as necessary to purchase his labor in order to build the road as it is to purchase the right of way and the materials used in its construction. The right of way, the tie, the rail, the locomotive engine, the car, and the labor which produced and brought together these several parts may be sold and converted into money, and thereby I receive back the equivalent which I paid for the labor just the same as I receive back, with accrued profits, that which I paid for the right of way and the materials out of which the road is built and equipped. So that the cash which I invest I may receive back at any time, while the capital which represents the labor of the workman is lost to him. He has invested his labor in my enterprise, and it has become wholly merged therein, lost to him; but as long as the industry endures, the profit-producing power of that labor is contributing to the enhancement of my business and the increase of my revenue. Hence, as the representative value of the workman's labor operates as an ever-present and positive investment in the enterprise just the same as my million dollars, and which, like the right of way and materials, contributes to the growth and consequent increase of its value, it is not unjust to me that he should participate in the net profits produced as the combined result of his labor and my capital. The fact that the ratio between the profit-producing power of a million dollars and that of a thousand is so much greater than the ratio between the two amounts themselves, is an important element for consideration, and should be recognized in passing judgment upon the equity of the plan of co-operation here proposed. All men in their exercise of watchful care and industrious skill are largely actuated by selfish motives, and when interested in and part owners, as it were, of a business, will not be apt to unite with or enter into combinations, strikes, or boycotts that would injure or destroy their own interests. If I should devote my time and energy in attending to the concerns of business, I ought to be paid reasonable compensation for my services, the same as any other employé capable of attending to similar duties, but there ought not to be any sinecures attached to it, or relatives or favorites connected with it receiving compensation for services never performed. After salaries of employés and other legitimate expenses of the business are paid, the net profit should be divided upon the basis already stated, in the same way as stock dividends are now divided among stockholders. A scheme of this kind could be adapted to railroad, manufacturing, and business ventures of every kind, where labor and capital are mutually dependent upon one another, each indispensable to the success of the other. The only difficulty to overcome arises in adjusting matters so that there can be no evasion or fraud practised by employers upon the employés on the one hand, and that upon no trivial or flimsy pretext can the employés involve the concern in litigation on the other. An intelligent, broad-gauge attention to details will obviate any difficulty which can arise between employé and employer under wise legislation, defining and limiting their relative rights and duties. When one estimates the magnitude of loss to capital and labor, the inconvenience to the public and detriment to business which have been occasioned by strikes, boycotts, and lock-outs during the past few years, he must conclude that some remedy ought to be adopted to prevent their recurrence. What better preventive measure can be devised or suggested than to make every man a joint participator with his employer in the profits arising from his vigilant and skilful labor, and to hold both parties to a strict observance and performance of their mutual rights and duties?

CHAPTER III.

STRIKES AND LOCK-OUTS PREVENTED BY ARBITRATION.

THE third annual report of the Commissioner of Labor to the Secretary of Interior, submitted December, 1887, covering the six years ending December 31, 1886, is a startling exhibit of the strained conditions existing between Labor and Capital, and a pregnant portrayal of the great losses to both factors of industry in strikes and lock-outs, which are the legitimate resultants of these strained conditions. The strike is the unintelligent effort of the workman to remedy his wrongs, and the lock-out is the venal resort of the employer to reduce wages or limit production.

The report exhibits simply the facts belonging to each industrial trouble, and the bare statement of these frozen facts is sufficient,—it carries with it its own commentary.

Figures speak, and there are voicings in the following table it were wise for the money-masters and law-makers to hearken to and heed:

Year.	Strikes.	Establishments involved.	Average No. of Establishments involved in each Strike.
1881..........	471	2,928	6.2
1882..........	454	2,105	4.6
1883..........	478	2,759	5.8
1884..........	443	2,367	5.3
1885..........	645	2,284	3.5
1886	1411	9,861	7.0
Total Average...	3902	22,304	Gen. Av. 5.7

New York and Chicago, the two great trade centres of our country, had the largest number of establishments affected. The total number of employés involved in the whole number of strikes was 1,323,203,—a number equal to the entire population of bread-winners in the State of New York. The number of employés originating the strikes was 1,020,156. Is it rational to assert that no just cause for complaint exists when over one million of men unite to obtain one common end? The number of employés in all establishments prior to the strikes was 1,660,835, while the whole number employed after the strikes was 1,635,047, a loss of 25,788. This decrease in the number employed is a witness, that can neither be bribed nor intimidated, to the truth of the charge that strikes are sometimes provoked by employers themselves when they desire to curtail their working force and wish to shirk the responsibility of turning men out of work. During the period named there were 2214 establishments in which lock-outs were ordered, employing 175,270 men before the lock-outs, and 170,747 after,—another loss to labor caused by the rapacity of capital. 74.84 per cent. of the whole number of establishments affected by the strikes, and 89.48 per cent. of the lock-outs, were in New York, Pennsylvania, Massachusetts, Ohio, and Illinois, which five States contain 49 per cent. of all the manufacturing establishments, and employ 58 per cent. of the capital invested in mechanical industries in the United States. Of the 22,304 establishments in which strikes occurred, 18,342, or 82.24 per cent., of them were ordered by labor organizations, while of the 2214 lock-outs, 79.18 per cent. were ordered by combinations of managers.

The results of the strikes, so far as gaining the objects sought, were as follows: Successful, 10,375, or 46.52 per cent.; partially successful, 3004, or 13.47 per cent.; and failure followed in 8910 cases, or 39.95 per cent. By lock-outs, 564 establishments, or 25.47 per cent., succeeded in gaining their points; 190, or 8.58 per cent., partially succeeded; and 1339, or 60.48 per cent., failed. As to causes or objects of strikes, the report referred to shows that an increase of wages was the principal one,—42.32 per cent. The other leading causes: reduction of hours, 19.48 per cent.; against reduction of wages, 7.77 per cent.; for increase of wages and reduction of hours, 7.59 per cent.; against increase of hours, 0.62 per cent.

The losses to strikers and employers is given as follows: Losses to strikers, $51,814,723, and loss to employés through lock-outs, $8,157,717, making a total wage-loss of $59,972,440. The assistance given to strikers and to those suffering from lock-outs was $4,430,595. The employers' losses through strikes amounted to $30,701,553; through lock-outs, $3,362,261; or a total loss of $34,163,814.

These strikes and lock-outs—the conflict between labor and capital—are rendered possible by the inadequacy of our legislation to provide for the former and control the latter. Whether these forces shall continue in conflict until labor destroys capital, or capital reduces labor to a vassalage worse than African slavery, or whether they shall be brought into perfect harmony with each other, depends upon the capacity of those who frame the laws to meet the exigencies of present conditions. Every conflict between labor and capital finds its primal cause in bad statutes, and is a natural resultant of the perversion of justice which finds expression in the enforcement of rights that are legal but unjust.

The State may, and ought to, make provision for the speedy adjustment of the differences which give rise to strikes and lock-outs. This might be done without creating new tribunals or officers. We have a superabundance of officers now. The law should provide that the parties considering themselves aggrieved, whether locomotive engineers, moulders, bakers, or brewers, on the one hand, or the employers on the other, shall present to the Chief Justice of the Supreme Court of their State, a petition setting forth in full and detail their grievances; that notice shall thereupon be given to the parties complained of, who shall within a certain day, to be fixed by the Chief Justice, answer the charges in full, after which an opportunity may be given petitioners to reply. Should it be claimed that the issues thus made up do not present the matter fairly, the counsel or persons representing the respective parties shall set forth the points upon which they disagree, and thereupon the Chief Justice shall refer the matter to some person to be named by him to take testimony upon the points of disagreement. The person so named shall be clothed with all the powers of a chancellor, who shall issue subpœnas and cause witnesses to come before him to testify to such matters. In order to avoid delay and to prevent unnecessary expenses, no more than two witnesses on each side should be allowed on any one point, as the merits or demerits of the claims of the respective parties will be as readily comprehended from a very few as from a great number of witnesses, the main question for determination being which party is at fault in the matter,— differing in this respect from a contest over rights of property. After the issues are thus settled and the testimony taken, the Chief Justice shall name three Circuit Court judges, to meet at a time and place to be designated by him, to examine into and determine the questions involved. The decision of the judges so named, or any two of them, shall be final and conclusive, and binding upon the parties interested. Until after the announcement of said decision it shall be unlawful for the leader of any combination of men to order a strike, and any person offending shall be guilty of misdemeanor and liable to fine or imprisonment, or both, in the discretion of the Court; and it shall also be unlawful for any corporation or individual to order a lock-out, the penalty for so doing to be the payment of full wages to the men affected by such lock-out, and one thousand dollars to be recovered in an action of debt for the use of the school fund.

The next question for serious consideration arises as to how the decision of this tribunal should be enforced. This is a difficulty of the utmost magnitude, for of what value, it may be asked, is the decision of a tribunal unless that decision can be enforced. " Of all the parts of a law," says Blackstone, " the most effectual is the *vindicatory.* For it is but lost labor to say, ' do this,' or 'avoid that,' unless we also declare, 'this shall be the consequence of your non-compliance.' We must, therefore, observe that the main strength and force of a law consists in the penalty annexed to it." No one will question the force of this assertion as applied to municipal laws prescribing rules of civil conduct. Nevertheless, the object of the law proposed is not so much to prescribe a rule of civil conduct as it is to ascertain the causes which give rise to certain difficulties and adjust these difficulties by amicable arbitration. The object is to create a tribunal, which shall stand impartial and indifferent between the parties, whose decision will be relieved of the rancor and bitterness which invariably follow an arbitration arrived at by the parties interested, and which is usually characterized as a victory or back-down by the one party or the other. Which party in fault could bear up and sustain itself with the public against a judicial finding that it is in the wrong? Besides, I should deprecate the wisdom of legislation which would seek to compulsorily enforce a decree of this nature upon either party to the controversy. Even the Statute of Laborers of Edward III. of England soon became a dead letter, and if such legislation became inoperative and ineffectual in the days of feudal bondage, it were folly to attempt similar experiments in this day and generation. Let us simply create a tribunal to take the place of the opinionated laborer on the one side, and the haughty employer on the other, and in the legislation creating it provide a penalty somewhat similar to that suggested herein, so as to prevent the one or the other party from precipitating a strike or lock-out

m

until the question as to who is in fault shall be judicially ascertained and determined.

When Anacharsis visited Solon, and knew the nature of the institutions which that sage law-giver designed to establish at Athens, he laughed at his undertaking and at the absurdity of imagining he could restrain the avarice and injustice of his citizens by written laws. These laws, he said, resembled, in all respects, spiders' webs, and would, like them, only entangle and hold the poor and weak, while the rich and powerful easily broke through them. To this Solon replied, "Men keep their agreements when it is an advantage to both parties not to break them ; and he would so frame his laws as to make it evident to the Athenians that it would be more for their interest to observe than to transgress them." The same may be said in the case proposed. It would be to the mutual advantage of both parties to observe rather than transgress the decree.

CHAPTER IV.

THE GLARIS ARTISAN AN INDEPENDENT COMMONER.

THESE strikes are but the physical manifestation of a deep-seated discontent with things as they are in the industrial world,—a discontent while protesting at times violently against wrongs unquestioned, yet dreads

in the righting of these wrongs to go to the extreme
length which outraged humanity prompts, for the
reason that man will endure oppressions grievous to be
borne rather than involve himself in turbulence. The
political utopia,—the fairy-land of political dreamers,—
in which a perfect natural order of things should obtain
through the untrammelled action of social forces, has,
like the fabled Atlantis, vanished from sight. It has
been superseded on the one hand by pessimism, on the
other, and more generally, it has given way to a determination not to let things go on themselves, but to
make them go in such manner as may be desired. The
conviction is growing that, in the divine economy, it
was never proposed that a social and industrial world
should be left to itself. The material is given out of
which man may construct a social order and formulate
a political system consistent with right, justice, and the
well-being of society. This is the basis of modern
progress, social, industrial, and political. Acting upon
this basis, and imbued with these principles, the
founders of our institutions aimed to construct a system
of government which should keep pace with the progress of events and endure for ages. It seems they
have but led us to the verge of a precipice unless we
are able, in some measure, to equalize the inequality of
social conditions which, in this country, exist side by
side with political equality. Laveleye's words of
timely warning are: "Either you must establish a
more equitable division of property and produce, or
the fatal end of democracy will be despotism and decadence after a series of social struggles, of which the

horrors committed in Paris, in 1871, may serve as a foretaste."

The soul of popular states is equality. This is the ethics of the advanced thought of to-day,—no romance but realistic,—stepping out from the dim light of the student's lamp into the broad sunlight seeking actualization among the people. Co-operation is the new social form. Practicalists may sneer at it as a dream. The dream of to-day becomes the deed of to-morrow. It is the gospel of the true crusade of competition against monopoly, of industrial freedom against commercial vassalage, of social order against impending anarchy. Its apostles are preaching it in every land. Its spread is heralded with joy by the most eminent thinkers and wisest publicists of the day. Practical applications of its humane principles have been, and are being, made in many small communities, and with most beneficent results. The common good of the many is of paramount importance to the individual interests of the privileged few. In a recognition of this truth as the basic principle of our political and industrial economy lies the solution of those social problems which are now vexing the nations of the world, our own not less, but rather more, than any other.

Nowhere can the efficacy of this principle, in its practical workings, be as fully observed as in the Canton of Glaris, Switzerland. There we have an agrarian organization of a most remote period, combined with the conditions of modern industry, which, supplemented by the right of occupation in the common mark, has wrought a priceless improvement in the condition of the common workmen in the great factories. Glaris is one of those districts in Europe where the much larger number of the laborers are employed in industrial occupation. Over one-third of the inhabitants (thirty thousand) live directly by such occupations, and nearly all the others indirectly. The workmen obtain of right, and without payment, a house in which to live, and a field for the cultivation of fruits and vegetables. They pay little or no taxes. The expenses of the public service are provided for in the revenue of property set apart for the purpose, all the public institutions having their separate *alp*, forest, and arable, the yield from which is sufficient for their maintenance. How marked the contrast between the condition of the Pittsburg mechanic and that of the workman of Glaris! The former breathing an atmosphere befouled with smoke, with a hovel in some narrow and crowded street as the only abiding-place for himself and family, and the corner saloon as the only resort open to him where he can forget his life and drudgery. The latter breathes the fresh, pure air of his mountain-girdled valley, and is under the generous influence of sublime natural surroundings. He dwells in his own home, tills his own field,—his by right, natural and inalienable. He raises much of the food necessary to supply his family, and thus grows firmly attached to the soil which he owns and uses, to the community in which he is recognized as an active factor, feeling himself bound with the bond of common ownership, and by the common exercise of the same rights to his neighbors and fellow-citizens. His manhood is developed in power to do and in capacity to enjoy. The consciousness of his own entity, being an acknowledged force and factor, imbues his life with a purpose and a power, which, in combination with the same agency dominating the lives of his fellow-members, brings steadiness of pursuit, a healthy progress, and restful happiness to the entire community.

The forbidding conditions of the American workman breed in his mind an enmity of social order, a hatred of his employer and of capital, a feeling of unrest and bitter discontent that ripens into revolt. The Swiss commoner, contented in the enjoyment of all the natural rights of man, thinks not—the thought would do violence to his own nature—of conspiring against a system which provides him such bounteous benefits, and which his own vote helps to perpetuate. Liberty, fraternity, equality to him are not merely the empty shibboleth of the demagogue or the meaningless label of a public document. His personal liberty is complete, and comes down to him clothed in the sanctity of ages; equality is a fact admitted and upheld in all his laws; fraternity is more than a sentiment, it is embodied in social and economic systems which recognize the people of the same community as members of a common family, sharing equally in the heritage bequeathed from sire to son.

CHAPTER V.

PULLMAN AS AN IDEAL INDUSTRIAL COMMUNITY.

In contrast with the *Allemand* system, so admirable in operation and so beneficent in results, let us sketch outlines of the most extensive experiment of any thing approaching this character that we have in the United States. We refer to that social experimentation known as Pullman, Ill., the vastness of the scale upon which it is operated constituting its only significance. And for this reason it compels examination and discussion at this day, when dynamite is the terror of thrones, when the murmurings of discontent are swelling into imprecations that threaten to become the battle-cries of a revolution, and when the earnest, honest friends of humanity, feeling an eager interest in social and economic conditions, are searching for a solution of these industrial problems independent of the dogmas and teachings of a superfine political economy. Pullman is a town of ten thousand *dwellers*, ten miles south of Chicago, founded by the Pullman Palace Car Company—*i.e.*, George M. Pullman—seven years ago. It was to be at once a centre of industry and a home for the employés of the company and such other laborers as might be drawn hither by other opportunities for employment. Its growth has been rapid, owing to the many manufactories established there, all of which, however, are directly or indirectly operated or dominated by the one central power,—the

Pullman Palace Car Company. Between five and six thousand men are employed, four-fifths of whom are in the employ of the Pullman Company. The value of their products can only be measured by millions of dollars. Its success as a manufacturing centre is unquestioned. With this phase of its existence we are not concerned. The question is, Is Pullman a success from the stand-point of the employé? Has it furnished a satisfactory solution of the industrial problem of to-day? While filling the coffers of its projector, is it elevating and enriching the lives wearing away in toil in its shops and factories? To answer these questions aright one must measure Pullman by an ideal standard, for it was the boast of its founder that he would give a practical existence to ideal conditions in the building and maintaining of his new community. There is but one test to be applied to any social system; if it fails to meet the requirements of that test, it has been weighed in the balance and found wanting. That test is, Does it so place each individual that he can share in and enjoy to the extent of his natural capacity the privileges and advantages of the existing civilization?

In Pullman, perhaps to a greater extent than elsewhere in this country, unstinted provision has been made for the material comfort of the dwellers therein. The employés occupy houses that are, as a rule, tasteful in construction and models in neatness; the streets are kept in perfect condition, with a row of shade-trees on each side, giving them a pleasant and picturesque appearance; simple but ingenious designs secure a striking variety of architecture in the houses, which are built in groups of two or more or in blocks. Public squares, hotels, arcades, markets, miniature lakes, a stretch of meadow or a cluster of trees are most happily distributed to relieve the monotony of long rows of buildings. Rents are moderate. There is a public library,—not a free one. Three dollars a year pays for the privilege of reading such of its eight thousand volumes as the artisan may select. The public-school system is permitted to give educational facilities for the children of the employés, provided the trustees rent a building of the Pullman Company to be used as a school-house,—the only instance in the United States where a corporation nullifies that (or any other) provision of the public-school law which requires the trustees to erect suitable buildings in which schools shall be taught. The Pullman Company owns and controls everything. The livery stables, the hotel, the theatre, the fire department, all are the property of the company. No private person can own a foot of ground or a single building. The oligarchy will not even permit the erection of a church ; religious organizations desiring to hold meetings must do so in rented quarters. There is no Lord's acre here.* Every municipal act is the act of a corporation. It is a village within the village of Hyde Park, and the latter seeks to exercise no authority over its territory. Members of the various Pullmanized corporations fill many of the principal

---

* Recently a church society succeeded in purchasing from this corporation ground upon which to erect a church-edifice, but this building-site is located *outside* the town.

offices of Hyde Park village, including that of school trustee.

We have here millions of dollars expended in surrounding wage-workers with beauty and comfort. But every dollar is so invested as to return a handsome profit to its owners. There is naught philanthropic in the entire experiment. Everything is conceived in a business spirit, conducted upon purely business principles, and made a source of revenue to the projectors. The wages paid are the ruling prices for such labor. Steady employment and prompt pay are always assured. Faithful and skilful hands are specially cared for. Employés who chance to suffer loss of limb or any other physical misfortune are provided with such tasks as they can perform. In many ways thus are the physical wants and conditions provided for and satisfied. Every device that the ingenuity of man can invent or suggest is employed by the owners to so completely meet the demands for material comfort and attractive surroundings that their employés, with their physical senses cloyed, will feel no stirring impulse within for social, moral, or mental growth that might breed discontent. But while this scrupulous attention to material details which so strongly combine to enhance the physical comfort of man is most admirable in conception and perfect in execution, yet there are phases of Pullman life that must be admitted are not only unpleasant, but which unfit a man to fully understand the obligations, perform the duties, and share the responsibilities of American citizenship.

CHAPTER VI.

THE PULLMAN ARTISAN A TENANT AT WILL.

THERE is frequent change of men and of officers, and each new incumbent has his chosen friends to reward. Favoritism should have no place in an ideal community. The evils incident to such a condition necessarily exist here, such as petty jealousies, displacement and discouragement of superior capacity, constant changing of residents, and a general feeling of insecurity. The idea of home—that idea the incarnation of which, in man's life, is essential to his true development and happiness —finds no association with the name of Pullman. The people dwell in houses not their own, and their tenure subject to termination at ten days' notice, a condition embodied in the lease, the corporation reserving the right to cancel that lease even though the rent may have been paid in advance for a longer period than the time of notice stipulated. Is not this in contravention of the law fixing and maintaining the relative rights of landlord and tenant? The rent may be paid in the forenoon of the first day of the month, in the afternoon the decree is promulgated that notices be issued to the tenants to vacate in ten days. In this connection we must not forget that about eighty per cent. of the laborers are in the employ of the corporation in control of this petty kingdom, and all the others are employed in establishments which are under its influence. Such an

absolute extinction of individuality and such an utter
absorption of that individuality by a capitalistic organization is without approach or parallel in the history of
any other modern civilized community.   In many respects the power of the Russian Czar pales into utter in-
significance in comparison with the power of the close
corporation which rules at Pullman.   Can it be said that
that power is always rightfully exercised ?   Man is not
perfect, though his coffers be filled with shekels and
he be knighted by the king of Italy.   That power is
there ; the only escape from it is emigration.   Within
the limits of this ideal (?), social, and industrial realm escape from the all-pervading influence of the corporation
is impossible.

Many grievances exist, many acts of injustice occur,
but no one dare utter a cry for help or redress.   The
laborers at Pullman believe that "spotters"—paid
eavesdroppers of the company—mingle with them to
catch and report to their masters any sign or word ex-
pressive of disapproval or criticism of the actions of the
authorities.

Pullman is the only community of ten thousand people in the United States that has not a newspaper pub-
lished within its limits.   The freedom of the press here
would be limited to the promulgation and approval of
the decrees and dogmas of the powers that be.

What a spectacle !   Ten thousand people in utter
subjection to the avaricious cupidity and limitless power
of a dozen men organized and co-operating together as
one man, who own a pseudo-city, exempt from municipal burdens and responsibilities.   Not a single man

of all that ten thousand dare express an opinion about the affairs of the community in which he dwells. These conditions of existence beget a servility little less than slavery, a dependence that is moral weakness and mental degradation. There is a culpable lack of attention in the meagre provisions for religious instruction. The seating capacity of the halls is insufficient for the accommodation of the people, and the rental demanded is so high that it is with great difficulty any religious denomination can pay it. The company, with an eye single to its own selfish purposes, provides shelter and meat for the body, but maketh no provision for manna for the soul. The soul cannot forge a bolt or line a boiler.

No public meetings are ever held in which the citizens could discuss local affairs, and give expression to that responsibility for things done and not done which constitute a practical education in the duties of citizenship, and give opportunity for the development of a capacity equal to the higher conditions and greater trusts,—that is, the practical culture which develops the desire and capacity for self-government is unknown. The individual is environed with restraints and restrictions, unable to do anything for his own material, social, or political advancement, and thus his very entity as an integral part of that community suffers extinction.

The one desire that is dearer to an American citizen than all others, the desire to have and hold a home, finds no expression at Pullman. The industry and economy so necessary to the acquisition of that home become the corner-stones of a career of peace and plenty. Besides, the owner of a home is a guardian of the safety and perpetuity of the community in which he lives. Home-owners are never malcontents. They are a safeguard against social disturbances and industrial revolts. Everything in Pullman must belong to and be a part of the corporation.

The power of the capitalists who conceived and control this community is limitless, and the wrong-burdened history of the world has long ago taught, with all the unction of the divine decree, that no class of men are fit to be trusted with unlimited and irresponsible authority. In the exercise of such power man is prone to yield to the temptation to abuse it. Moreover, the subject of such absolute authority becomes servile and degraded, and he who wields it corrupt and shameless.

In Pullman we find a condition which establishes, in fact, only under a new form, the degrading relation of lord and vassal, which is utterly abhorrent to the advanced humanity of the age, and utterly subversive of every correct principle of true manhood and true womanhood. This relationship should be abolished, and in its stead a co-operation of some kind or another established, which will conduce to the growth and development of the mental and moral nature of man as well as the physical.

Compare,—nay, there is no comparison,—but the contrast is striking and suggestive between the spiritless, propertyless dependent, toiling in the workshops at Pullman, and the fearless and independent commoner of the Swiss Canton. The one will breed a race of slaves, the other beget a nation of heroes.

If the founders of Pullman, with minds imbued with the teachings of a true political philosophy and a conscience quickened by the desire to ameliorate and elevate the condition of their workmen, had, in the organization of their industrial experiment, subordinated the physical comfort of the laborer to his social improvement and moral development, the evils, which we find inherent and active, and which will eventually work its destruction or the enslavement of the laborer, could have had no existence in this community. Provision ought to have been made (1) that the workman could have the opportunity of buying the house which he now rents, and the sum which he pays as rental each month been taken as a partial payment upon the purchase-price. Attached to each house should have been at least one acre of ground upon which the laborer could have grown fruit and vegetables for his family. (2) That he could look forward to promotion in the line of his work as an incentive to and a just reward of fixed terms of faithful service : each promotion bringing an increase of wages. (3) That he could share in the net profits arising from the combination of his labor with the capital of the corporation.

A recognition of the natural right of man to own property, to work out his own elevation, and to share in the products of his own labor is vital to the safety and perpetuity of any industrial or political system.

CHAPTER VII.

ACTION DEMANDED. WHAT SHALL IT BE?

No system of legislation, the enforcement of which would compulsorily deprive the individual of his proprietary rights, can be devised that will not meet with opposition. But since it is admitted on all hands that deep-seated grievances exist among the masses of the people,—whether justly or unjustly it matters not,— arising from the unequal distribution of wealth and from the accumulation of property in the hands of the few, and when it is also admitted that these grievances are growing to such an extent that, if something is not done to remedy them, serious disturbances, destructive of property and detrimental to the well-being of society, may ensue, it is time for men of wealth and property to pause and wisely consider what means to adopt to avert these impending calamities. The grievances existing among the laboring people must be remedied in some reasonable way. They cannot be remedied by brute force. That was resorted to in France, but when the critical moment arrived, the clergy and nobility discovered to their sorrow that the military, who were of the people, sympathized with the people. A handful of armed detectives, or the militia, may succeed for a time in overawing and bringing to terms a few striking factory or railroad hands, but this agitation and unrest among the people will not down. Applying brute force only adds fuel to the fire. The tears of women and appeals of children who are suffering from exposure and famishing from hunger cannot be silenced or appeased with bludgeons and shot-guns. They can be appeased and silenced only by bread and clothes. Will men of wealth and property afford them the means of acquiring these simple necessaries, or wait until they take them? Remember that want and suffering and hunger are elements more dangerous to toy with or handle than gunpowder, Greek fire, or dynamite. Remember the lesson of the French revolution. Remember that it is much safer to render it possible for the deserving poor to earn and enjoy a little from your abundance than, in the withholding from them this chance of living, drive them into the ranks of the viciously idle, who look upon property as the pauper's prey, and thus imperil your all. How shall these deep-seated grievances of the people be remedied without at the same time doing great injustice to the rights of property? Henry George says, Abolish private property in land. Herr Most would throttle the law, destroy the government, and divide the spoils. These are extreme measures, and while both are rapidly gaining many adherents, the capitalists remain *passive* and *inactive*, without turning a hand or suggesting a measure to off-set these dangerous doctrines.

Men who write books or write for the press or who make political speeches—the men who influence and create public opinion—are, as a rule, men of comparatively limited means, with but little experience in the

I   n   17

practical affairs of life. Aware of this fact, the writer addressed letters of inquiry to men of eminence and experience in railroad and manufacturing circles, hoping to elicit from them practical information which he might use to advantage in the preparation of this work, but the usual answer was, " I have no time to consider the subject-matter of your inquiry." So that the same complaint which is made against our wealthiest citizens who do not take sufficient interest in the government to vote on election day may be urged against the capitalists who refuse to impart practical information to men who devote time and who give their best thought to the development of economic and legislative subjects calculated to benefit society. A man who knows nothing about railroading or the relative duties and obligations of the company and its hands cannot be expected to suggest an economic measure or law which would be as beneficial for all concerned in that branch of industry as the late T. J. Potter, who was probably the most thoroughly equipped railroad man of this generation. A man who has had no experience in manufacturing cannot be expected to suggest a measure or to propose a law which would be as far-reaching and beneficial in its effects in regard to the relative rights and duties of manufacturers and their employés as Andrew J. Carnegie. The man of practical experience, who deals honestly and fairly with the subject, should be able to suggest measures or devise and formulate a system of laws of eminent utility, while the man lacking such experience can only deal with the subject as he sees it from a study of the philosophy of the effects produced. If the latter does not meet the full measure of expectations, he should not be blamed or censured on that account. As we cannot look for perfection in human laws or institutions, any system proposed looking to radical changes in the existing order of things must necessarily encounter opposition. The most that any writer can hope for or expect is that the ideas which he advances and the suggestions which he makes, however objectionable they may seem in the concrete, possess elements which, when subjected to the test of practical common sense, may lead society to advance a step in the accomplishment of good results. The great and lasting effects which have proved most beneficial to mankind were not produced by sudden or spasmodic efforts, but by slow, gradual, and successive steps sanctioned by experience and justified by results.

It is universally conceded, because attested by the experience of ages, that the stability and durability of government and the happiness and well-being of society are best secured when the great bulk of the property is in the hands of peasant proprietors,—owned and controlled by the subordinate holders of power; and any economic measure or system of laws which will accomplish the distribution of property among the people without doing great injustice to its present owners must be regarded as one step in advance, looking to a happy medium between the extremes of the socialistic theory and the existing system. I am not unmindful of the fact that any common laborer may pull down an old building, but that it requires a skilful artisan to reconstruct it. In the suggestions which I advance in these pages, I trust the thoughtful reader will credit me with at least furnishing the materials for building a system better than that which I would destroy.

CHAPTER VIII.

THE STATE HAS WROUGHT THE RUIN.   LET HER SUPPLY THE REMEDY.

THE remedy for the grievances of which the laboring classes now so justly complain can be found only in legislation.   The greater number of our Western railways were built by means of subsidies in lands and bonds given to them by States and municipalities,— subsidies which, whether used as securities or converted into cash, were not only sufficient to build and equip the road, but, in addition, to furnish a princely fortune for division among the projectors.   But though so richly dowered at the public expense in the very inception of their enterprise, their insatiate greed for gain prompted the organization of construction companies, composed of the officers of the railway company and a few outside speculators, to whom the contract was let for building the road.   A corporation within a corporation,—nominally and legally (?) distinct, yet actually and morally the same.   These alter-egos of the railroad companies stood as the middlemen between them and the laborers who built the road, relieving the former of all legal liability, while they robbed the latter of their hard-earned wages.

The State is largely responsible for the frauds perpetrated upon the unsuspecting public by speculators and confidence-men in enabling them to issue corporate stocks, bearing, so to speak, the great seal of a sovereign State, which, when thus used, was a badge of fraud, as the stocks were, in fact, worthless. The State is responsible, partially at least, if not wholly, for the manner in which many of these corporations have passed from the hands of the stockholders into the exclusive control or possession of a Gould or a Vanderbilt. The State, through a receiver appointed by its courts, has not only taken possession, but undertook to operate these roads in the interest of a few bondholders and wreckers, who, by means of foreclosure-proceedings, secured all the property. These spoliators, operating under corporate authority and protected by perverted laws, are the moneyed barons of to-day, who, through the pernicious power inherent in their colossal wealth, endanger the perpetuity of the republic. The State is responsible for the legalized rapine by which the people have been despoiled of their heritage—the public domain—in giving it to corporations and selling it to speculators. Unfortunately, too often judges, jurors, and other court officials are bought and sold like sheep in the shambles; the foul imprint of bribery is stamped upon many a corporate act of legislation; all subservient tools in inflicting the most gigantic wrongs and perpetrating the most unblushing frauds upon the people. The State is responsible for the whiskey trusts, tobacco trusts, coffee trusts, sugar trusts, bread trusts, oil trusts, coal trusts, and gas trusts, which are combinations most foul to monopolize trade, regulate production, increase values, and crush unorganized competition. The organization of these trusts, being hostile to the best interests of society, ought to be prevented by making it a felony for individuals or the officers of corporations to enter into any such combination. The State is responsible for laws which make it possible for schemers and sharpers to drive out of business old and respected citizens who, through long years of honest industry and fair dealing, had built up a lucrative trade and gained the confidence of their creditors and neighbors. Honest business men cannot compete with the unscrupulous who sell their wares twenty-five per cent. below cost, and who, after placing the proceeds of their rascality beyond the reach of creditors, go into bankruptcy or make a sham assignment, and in a few days thereafter resume business as agents of their wives or mothers-in-law. It is the fault of the State that the wheels of traffic are now blocked, that business is demoralized, that thousands of men are out of work, and millions of dollars lost through the obstinacy of a railroad magnate on the one hand, or of a labor boss on the other. The State is responsible for the existence of all social and political conditions which work injury to the great body politic when it is within the power of the State, by legislation, to render such existence impossible, or to punish the conspirators who combine to bring about such conditions. The conditions referred

to, with many others of a kindred nature, are the true
causes of the direful discontent and dangerous unrest
now pervading the masses, and it behooves the State, if
it would save itself, to at once set about the removal
of these causes by a wise, yet radical and far-reaching,
system of legislation.

CHAPTER IX.

COMPENSATE EMPLOYÉS INJURED BY DEFECTIVE MACHINERY.

THE daily calendar of injuries and deaths occasioned
by defective machinery in the great trade-centres, and
the record of the law's vexatious delays when it is invoked to secure reparation, even in the most merito-
rious cases, are most condemnatory exposures of criminal
negligence of employers of labor, fostered and relieved
by the iniquitous tardiness of justice,—a stigma and a
shame to our boasted civilization. Paramount to all
ethical considerations, however, there are at the very
root of these pernicious conditions grave questions of
State polity and State economy which deserve and
demand serious thought and earnest action. It is
safe to assume that three-fourths of the persons injured
by defective machinery are the stay and support of
others,—wives, children, younger sisters and brothers,
or aged and infirm parents. It is equally true that the
same proportion of those injured are unable, financially,

to provide that care and attention at their own home
necessary for their comfort and recovery, and must
therefore be sent to the county hospital and cared for
at the public expense, thus taxing the people to pay for
the consequences of the employer's negligence. When
those hands, perforce, are idle whose toil brought food,
raiment, and shelter to others, what fate befalls the
helpless dependents? Call the rolls of the houses of
correction, the poor-houses, the asylums, and the county
jails, and you will find full answer,—an answer fraught
with reproach and rebuke to justice and humanity.
The many and marvellous mechanical combinations
wrought by the inventive genius of to-day, in the form
of labor-saving machinery, compelling rapid construction and frequent changes, render these accidents almost
inevitable, unless the utmost skill and most vigilant
care are exercised in making and maintaining each and
every part of such machinery. Courts of justice, instead of laying down a just and equitable principle of
law for the determination of these cases, which would
stimulate the men who employ dangerous machinery in
operating their business to an exercise of constant and
critical vigilance in avoiding danger, and providing
safety for their employés, have formulated a rule which
encourages their indifference, and places a premium
upon negligence,—that is, the law, as interpreted by the
courts, relieves the employer from liability for injuries
received by his employé while working with or about
defective machinery if the employé knows the machinery is defective ; and if he continues his work without being induced by his master to believe that a change

will be made, he is held to have assumed the risk. Under this rule, the injustice of which is equalled only by its absurdity, the more defective and worthless the machinery the less liable is the employer for injuries inflicted upon the employé.* Many an honest workman, compelled to earn a livelihood for those dependent upon him by his daily toil, with an unselfishness that is heroic, recks not the hazard to his own life, in performing his allotted task, when its abandonment would deprive his family of the necessaries of life. Is it right, is it just, is it humane, to drive the toiler with the lash of necessity to a task fraught with peril, and because, forsooth, he knows the danger, deny him compensation for injuries thereby received, which disable him perchance for life?

The labor which he performs is for the benefit of a private enterprise, instituted and operated for individual gain. The employers, not the public, profit by the services, yet, perforce, through the rulings of our courts, the public must bear the burden of supporting his family and himself when his inability to supply that support is occasioned by negligence of his employer. Why should the public, having received no revenue from the services of the laborer, relieve the employer, who has

---

* During the last two sessions of the Illinois Legislature, the author prepared bills providing for the abrogation of this heinous rule, and the enactment of just and humane procedure for such cases. These bills were sent to members, who admitted the necessity of some such legislation, yet, so far as the writer is advised, they were never considered by that body nor any of a like character.

profited by his toil, of the expensive consequences resulting from that employer's negligence? Why should not the workman have and receive adequate compensation for injuries inflicted? And why should he not receive that compensation immediately upon the occurrence of the accident, for it is then when his necessities require it as much, if not more, than ten years afterwards? Does he get it? No: the State seems to be the father of the employer, and the foster-father of the employé. All the machinery of the courts is put in motion and resort had to the many evasions and delays of the law to hinder and hamper the latter in his efforts to obtain simple justice. Able lawyers, schooled in craft and bristling with technicalities,—those resorts of conscious wrong when seeking to elude the clutches of the law,—are employed by the year upon princely salaries to defend the case. Shrewd and unscrupulous detectives, many of them ex-convicts or fugitives from justice, are hired to hunt up and suborn witnesses for the defence, to intimidate or buy off witnesses for the plaintiff, and to bribe impecunious or dishonest jurors. Continuance after continuance is prayed for and granted upon one pretext or another. After the cause is tried, a verdict rendered, and judgment entered, the defendant appeals to the higher courts. The trial judge omitted to dot an *i* or cross a *t* in his instructions to the jury, and for some technical error of this kind the cause is reversed and remanded. When the remandant order is filed a motion may be made to transfer the case to the Federal court in order to gain more time. An order of transfer is had, and the defendant's attorney has about six months to file the record in the latter court. Thereafter a motion is made to remand the case to the State court, which is granted, as a matter of course, because the application for the transfer was a fraud on the court in the first place. Six months more are consumed before the case comes on for trial. By that time the witnesses of plaintiff are probably spirited away, or the plaintiff takes a change of venue to a court where wicked railroad lawyers are unknown, where detectives and jury-bribers shall enter not therein.

The writer has a case in mind, which is not by any means exceptional, where an employé of a railroad lost his arm in an accident, and it was thirteen years from date of the accident to the time the last opinion of the supreme court sustaining the judgment which he recovered was filed. Hundreds of similar cases might be cited in support of the proposition that the remedy afforded in this class of cases is in effect no remedy at all.

CHAPTER X.

THE REMEDY; ITS ECONOMY AND BENEFICENCE.

ANY thinking man who will take upon himself the trouble of investigating this matter must be convinced that if railway companies, and all other corporations and individuals who employ men at and around dangerous machinery, were compelled by law to pay every employé injured in their employment a fixed sum based upon the nature and extent of the injury, that it would cost them little more than it now does to pay lawyers, detectives, witnesses, and court costs. This is leaving out of view altogether the amount which comes out of the pockets of tax-payers to furnish and maintain a hospital for the care and treatment of the injured, and a poor-house for the support of their dependants.

In the official proceedings of the Board of Supervisors of Cook County, making appropriations to meet the expenditures for the year 1888, I find the following items :

For Salaries, county agent's office	$8,000
" Supplies, rent and transportation	12,000
" Salaries, poor-house	20,000
" Supplies and repairs	95,000
" Salaries, county hospital	50,000
" Supplies and repairs	125,000
" Out-door relief, county towns	25,000
	$335,000

making a total of $335,000 to be expended in feeding the poor and in the treatment and care of the sick of Cook County. I find also that $545,910 is appropriated to meet the expenses of the different courts of record of Cook County, including the sheriff's office, but not including the probate or county court or salaries of the county clerks. Any one having the time and inclination to ascertain the number of days in the year that are spent in the trial of personal injury cases, the number of this class of patients received at the hospital, and the number of poor people relieved by the county agent or housed at the county poor-house, will be able to demonstrate to a mathematical certainty, if such demonstration be deemed necessary, that it would be wisdom on the part of the State as a public measure to pass a law compelling speedy and adequate compensation to be made to employés who are injured in the line of their employment. The State makes laws punishing usury. Is it more of an offence for a money-shark to charge five or ten per cent. a month than it is for a corporation to maim and kill its employés by the use of rotten or defective machinery? No one would pay the brazen usurer five or ten per cent. a month for the use of money unless driven to do so from dire necessity. No workman would risk his life at or about machinery which he knew to be defective unless driven to do so from absolute need. It should be, and it is supposed to be, the object of the law to protect those who are unable to protect themselves, but the rule is reversed in regard to employés injured from defective machinery. The remedy which I should adopt would at once compensate the person injured, decrease litigation in our courts, relieve the tax-payer, and convert the blood-money now wasted in employing lawyers, paying detectives, suborning witnesses, and bribing jurors into bread-money. It is this: When an employé is injured by machinery while at work in the line of his duty, let the fact of the injury be taken as *prima facie* evidence that the machinery was defective, and compel the employer to pay $2000 for the loss of one hand or foot, $4000 for the loss of both hands, both feet, or one hand and one foot, $1500 for the loss of an eye, $4000 for the loss of both eyes, $12 a week for disabling injuries of a temporary nature, $5000 for a permanent injury, and $5000 to the widow or next of kin in the event of his death.*

It may be urged that legislation similar to that here proposed would have a tendency to make men careless, and even induce some to intentionally inflict injury upon themselves, but such contention is a pitiable plea in avoidance. No sane man would inflict injury upon himself in order to obtain the pecuniary consideration provided for the loss and suffering he would sustain any more than the man who is insured will commit suicide to secure the insurance. The fact that a few have taken their own life, declaring beforehand their purpose to compel the insurance company to pay their life insurance, even if true, is not a controlling argument against the adoption of the plan proposed.

The act of suicide is the act of insanity. Could we trace the lineage or have revealed to us the inner life of every suicide, we would find proof strong as the confirmation of holy writ of their insanity inherited from some ancestor of clouded brain, or wrought by some carking care or sorrow grim, borne in shadow and silence until it drove them to their death.

If injury be voluntarily or intentionally inflicted, no

---

* The respective sums suggested may be deemed far below the true measure of damages. The author's plan of procedure contemplates immediate payment without suit, hence the employé or his representative would not have to pay costs of court or lawyer's fees, and the net amount realized by him would equal, if not exceed, that which he now recovers at suit under most favorable conditions.

compensation should be paid ; in such case let the burden of proof rest upon the defendant, and if his plea is not well-founded, compel him to pay attorney's fees and expenses sufficient to compensate the plaintiff for time lost and money expended in litigation.* The employer may easily protect himself by insuring his employés against accident in accident insurance companies, at the trifling cost of about fifteen dollars a year for each employé, or by the creation of a fund, where such is practicable, for the purpose.

CHAPTER XI.

ENFORCE THE PROMPT PAYMENT OF WAGES.

WHEN one contemplates the cost and delay of justice, he is inclined to commend the wisdom of Solon in promulgating a law which declared all debtors discharged and acquitted of all their debts.   To gain some definite idea of the number of civil cases commenced and the cost of litigation in the justices' courts of Chicago, the writer ascertained the number of civil cases commenced in the year 1887 before one justice in each

---

* No plan can be adopted which will wholly do away with litigation.   The method suggested will materially diminish the number of suits for damages arising from personal injuries as the burden of proof is cast upon the employer, or, in other words, he is held to the responsibility of an insurer, and if he fails in the suit he is liable for all costs and expenses incident thereto.

division of the city. The number commenced before
the South Side justice was 2645, and as there are seven
justices in this division, by taking 2000 as the average,
the total number would be 14,000 cases. The number
commenced before the West Side justice was 1953, and
as there are six justices in this division, by taking 1500
as the average, the total number would be 9000 cases.
The number commenced before the North Side justice
was 1200, and as there are five justices in this division,
by taking this number as the average, the total would
be 6000 cases, making the total for the entire city
29,000. The average cost in these cases, including
constables' fees, is not less than $3.00 a case, which
would make a total cost of $87,000. Out of every
thousand of these, there are about thirty appeals to the
higher courts, at an average cost, including the appearance fee of the defendant, of $9.50, to which may be added
an average attorney's fee of $10.00, making a total sum
of $16,695. Estimating the amount paid attorneys
in justices' courts at an average of $1.00 per case,
which is a minimum price, certainly for professional
skill, and calculating the money-value of the time lost
to litigants and their witnesses, which would not be less
than $3.00 a case, the aggregate cost of this petty
litigation exceeds $200,000 annually. At least sev-
enty-five per cent. of the above litigation was occasioned by suits for the collection of petty accounts
and for wages justly due. Of the former class, it
may be truly said that they seldom serve any other
purpose than to increase the indebtedness of the poor;
and of the latter class, that even when successful, the

laborer finds the cost of collection but little less than the earnings of his toil. Would not the community be the gainer if all actions of debt, except for wages, were abolished?

Honest men, however poor, experience little difficulty in obtaining credit from their grocers, bakers, and butchers, and if actions for debt were abolished, to obtain credit would not only be an incentive to honesty, but honesty would become a necessity. Should a man wish to change his residence from one city to another, he would provide himself with credentials for honesty, attested by the signatures of his grocer, baker, and butcher. What better or more honorable letters of credit could a man have? True, if such were the law, lawyers, judges, justices of the peace, and town constables would be at a discount. But matters would soon adjust themselves in such a way that the supernumeraries in these professions would find some other visible means of support, which would contribute to, instead of detract from, the peace and prosperity of the community.

One of the justices who furnished the above statistics called attention to two judgments of three dollars each, one procured by a chambermaid and the other by a washer-woman, and both judgments had been appealed to the higher court by the defendants. While the amounts of these judgments were exceptionally small, it not unfrequently happens that appeals are prosecuted in this class of cases in order to defeat justice or to gratify petty malice. Poor men and women are not able to hire lawyers to prosecute their cases in the higher courts, and as a consequence they are compelled, in many instances, to lose their just claims. Indeed, it is cheaper for one to abandon his claim than to follow his case to any higher court to which it has been appealed, unless the amount involved is considerable, for when he pays his attorney and counts his loss of time, even if successful, he has but won a barren victory.

The legislature should provide for the payment of attorneys' fees and adequate damages to compensate the plaintiff for all time lost by him in the prosecution of this class of cases. That it has the power to do so is unquestioned; that it has so long delayed the exercise of that power is a shame.

Manufacturing and railway companies usually pay their men monthly or fortnightly, and if a man is discharged from service between two pay-days he must wait until the pay-day succeeding his discharge for his wages. It is only those persons who have witnessed the inconveniences arising from a system of discharging men without paying them who can fully appreciate its rank injustice to those directly affected thereby. The days of worthless construction companies have doubtless in a great measure disappeared, but in order to prevent a repetition of the wrongs which they perpetrated by any other corporation or individual, the law should provide that upon the discharge of any person from employment, his employer shall pay him the amount of wages to which he is entitled. As it might be impossible to pay cash under all circumstances, the law should provide that in such cases the employer or his representative shall forthwith issue a time-check to the discharged workman showing the number of days which he has worked, the day of his discharge counting as one full day, and the amount per day to which he is entitled. These time-checks should constitute evidence of the indebtedness payable upon demand,—a demand upon any agent or officer to suffice. Failure or neglect of the employer or his representative to pay such wages in cash, or to issue a time-check to the party entitled thereto as herein provided, shall render him liable to a penalty of one hundred dollars, to be recovered in an action of debt for the use of the school-fund in any court of record of the county, and shall also render him liable in the sum of five dollars a day for each and every day he shall fail or neglect to make such cash payment or to issue such time-check; the latter sum to be recovered by the employé in a summary proceeding before any justice of the peace of the county.

When the time-check herein provided for shall have been issued, fifty per cent. shall be added to the face value thereof, and the sum thus made shall bear interest at the rate of ten per cent. per annum until paid. Such time-checks shall pass by assignment and delivery, and shall be freed from all defences, the same as commercial paper purchased for a valuable consideration before maturity, and the owner and holder of any such check shall be entitled to maintain an action upon the same, and to recover judgment in his own name against the individual or corporation issuing the same. All actions upon such time-checks shall have precedence over other civil suits, and all checks owned and held by the party at the time the action was commenced shall be united in one suit. In addition to the amount recovered in any such action, not less than five nor more than fifty dollars attorney's fee shall be allowed by the court, such attorney's fee to be taxed as costs of the action. In enforcing the payment of such judgment no property belonging to the corporation or individual shall be exempt from execution.

In many of the States imprisonment for debt has been abolished by constitutional provisions, so that the only way of compelling the prompt cash payment of wages is to make a refusal to pay it so onerous that an employer will provide for paying the same before discharging his employé. There is no controlling reason why a penalty of the nature suggested should not be as applicable in the case of non-payment of wages as in the case of the non-payment of taxes. There is no provision in any of the State constitutions with which such a law would conflict. The penalty which attaches to the non-payment of taxes is upheld from considerations of public policy. Similar considerations may legitimately be appealed to in support of the law proposed.

I am well aware of the fact that such suggestions will hardly receive serious consideration when official position has largely become a matter of barter and sale. But if the wage-workers of the country demand that some legislative measure be adopted whereby prompt payment of wages shall be enforced, policy may impel one or other of the leading political parties to pledge itself to support such a measure.

BOOK V.

CHAPTER I.

UNEARNED INCREMENT.

It is conceded that no radical changes can be adopted
affecting the title or right of property in the hands of
its present holders so as to deprive them thereof without
just compensation. This is the guarantee of the Constitution of the United States as it is written and ordinarily understood, but by the construction placed upon that
instrument by the Supreme Court of the United States
in the recent Kansas brewery cases, it would seem that
any legislation which has for its apparent object the correction of abuses detrimental to society may be upheld,
provided the persons directly affected thereby shall not
be absolutely deprived of their property. Since I cannot sanction laws nor approve decisions, no matter by
what court rendered, which, in the spirit if not in the
letter, violate the great fundamental principles of the
constitution, I should not suggest a system of laws
which I thought would contravene it. Hence, when I
speak of legislation, I do not in all cases mean a

legislative act, but the adoption of a constitutional amendment, when necessary, enabling Congress and the legislatures of the respective States to carry out and enforce its provisions. In a government founded upon a written constitution, there is no security to life or property but in obeying the mandates of the constitution. If any thing should be wanting or any change should be made in that instrument, let the people, not the courts or legislatures, supply the want or make the change. It is better for society to move slowly within the law than it is for courts to render the law uncertain by a too liberal construction of constitutional provisions through a process of judicial refinement.

A man who invests his capital in building or improving vacant property ought, in justice, to reap the benefit of the increase in value given that property by the investment. But a part of the increase in the value which attaches to surrounding property from the establishment of manufactories and the development of all kinds of business enterprises might be given to the public without doing great injustice to its owners. This latter increase in the value of property is what is known to writers on economic subjects as the "unearned increment." A man who purchased a quarter of a section of land in the city of Chicago twenty or thirty years ago, and held it until the city grew up around it, finds himself rich without any effort of his own. Other men invested in property situated some fifty or one hundred miles from Chicago and still retain possession of it, yet are little better off to-day than when they purchased. Hence the man who is made independently rich without

any effort of his own, and simply because he was fortunate enough to invest in property which from its location and its surroundings has become of great value,
should have little grounds for complaint if not permitted
to retain the whole benefit to himself. The opening
of streets, the construction of sewers and other improvements, paid for, directly or indirectly, by the public, the
increase of population, and the investment of capital in
improving the adjacent territory, have materially contributed towards enhancing the value of his property,
and while the foresight of such a man in making the
purchase, his good fortune or business qualities or whatever you may call it, ought to receive its just reward,
it would not be an act of great injustice to him if compelled to share his profits with the public who were in-
strumental in making them. How can this division of
profits be made between the individual and the public?
In this way: From and after the year A.D. 1900,
whoever owns property in or adjacent to any city, which
he wishes to subdivide into lots, or when the public
interests of the city require that such a subdivision
should be made, the owner of the property subdivided
shall be entitled to hold as his absolutely one-half
thereof, and the municipality the other half, the lots or
blocks to be allotted alternately so as to prevent any
advantage being taken by the one party over the other.

The sale of the property thus subdivided may be accomplished in this manner: Whoever wishes to buy a
lot for the purpose of a homestead, or with a view to
permanent improvement, may agree upon the purchase-
price with the owner or with the municipality, as the

case may be, and in case of failure so to agree, the lot or
parcel of land which the party may desire to purchase
shall be sold at public auction by the public official
charged with such duty, after due notice, to the highest
bidder for cash or on time.   If sold on time, the deferred payments are to be made in a manner similar to
the regulation provided for the redemption of debentures in the legislation of Germany or Russia, alluded
to in former chapters of this volume.   Purchases for
the purpose of speculation shall be by private bargain
and sale.   Thereafter it shall be unlawful for the owner
or purchaser of any vacant lot to place an improvement
thereon of less value than two thousand dollars unless
for the purpose of occupying the same as a homestead,
and if, after making such improvement, he sells or dis-
poses of the same, any other improvement made by him,
whether as a homestead or otherwise, upon any other
vacant lot he may own, shall not be of less value than
two thousand dollars, the intention being to prevent the
owners of property evading the law by making temporary improvements so as to hold vacant property for the
purpose of speculation.   That from and after the year
1900, whoever owns more than two vacant lots not held
by him as part of his homestead in any city or addition
thereto shall convey one-half the number of lots so
owned or held by him to the city and the other half
shall be owned by him absolutely, subject to the foregoing provision relating to the sale of lots.   That from
and after the division of property between the owner
and municipality as herein provided such property shall
be exempt from taxation the same as school property,

but when improved by the owner, or a sale is made of any lot or lots, whether by the individual or by the municipality, such shall be subject to taxation the same as other property.

The exact number of acres which may be properly held by farmers for farming purposes, by stockmen for stock ranches, and by lumbermen for the promotion of forestry and the supply of lumber, are matters upon which no one man is fully capable of determining. Indeed, the views of any one person upon any of the subjects suggested must necessarily be but limited, and therefore imperfect in many particulars. The essential point to be considered in connection with these matters is: Are the suggestions proposed of such a practical nature that they are capable of being put into execution? If the answer is in the affirmative, the mode and manner of executing them are matters of detail merely.

It is highly important to bear in mind the fact that the advocates of any change in party measures or State polity are apt to go to the other extreme. Great care should be taken therefore, when formulating a constitutional amendment which is intended to correct abuses, not to open too wide a door for other abuses which may become more serious than those sought to be eradicated. For example, there is a certain amount of injustice in compelling the individual to give up one-half of his vacant lots to the municipality, and the adoption of a constitutional amendment as a means of accomplishing that end does not in a strictly ethical sense lessen the injustice or sanctify the wrong. Yet it must be conceded that there is some consideration which the indi-

vidual has received in return for what he loses which
in a political sense may justify it.   Even under the
existing order of things it is said to be the law that the
rights of the individual may be sacrificed for the public
weal.   This is neither right nor just in an ethical sense.
So that the affairs of government are not enforced from
the stand-point of natural justice, but from considerations
of expediency and political justice.   As natural justice
ought to be the aim of governments as well as individuals, after the individual has satisfied the claims of expediency and political justice by giving up half his
vacant property, his right to hold, enjoy, and dispose of
the other half should be scrupulously guarded and protected.   In other words, the grievances incident to a
land monopoly may be remedied in the manner suggested without otherwise rendering the title to property
less secure than it is under existing laws.

It may be asked why the owners of vacant lots should
be required to give up half without exacting a like sacrifice from owners of improved property?   There are
several reasons why this distinction should be made, but
to mention one or two will suffice.   First, the object is
to destroy the monopoly in land by placing it beyond
the power of the owner to withhold it from any one
who is anxious and willing to improve and pay a fair
price for it; and second, provision can be made for the
occupants of tenements or farms, as the case may be, to
become owners of the premises held by them either by
private contract or by fixing a stipulated price to be
paid in cash or in interest-bearing bonds based upon the
rental value of the premises for a certain number of

years, similar to the mode provided in the legislation of
Germany or Russia, already mentioned. There is no
reason why legislation of this nature should be confined
to agricultural property. If just for the landlord of a
rural tenantry, it should be just for a landlord of an
urban tenantry. Besides these considerations, it may be
suggested that the owner of improved property usually
holds it as an investment, and not as a speculation. He
has paid his share of the public burdens in the way of
street and other improvements. He pays a larger proportion of the public taxes than the owner of vacant
property, and his income may be reached, should it exceed a certain amount, by the enforcement of an income
tax.

CHAPTER II.

THE GREED OF WEALTH IMPERILS ITS OWN SAFETY.

THERE is something radically wrong in any system
of government wherein an individual in the brief space
of a lifetime may amass a fortune of one or two hundred millions of dollars. Look around and behold the
number of men who are railroad magnates and merchant princes, owning residences fit for kings, and mammoth, costly, and well-appointed business structures not
inferior to the Bank of England, while around them
are poverty and beggary and squalid nakedness and idleness and hunger. It was the gravity of this condition

of affairs and the depressing influence and the dire effects thereby produced which prompted the attack made upon corporate property in the inaugural address of the present governor of the conservative State of Iowa, instigated the legislation restricting and controlling corporations proposed by the last legislature of that State, and which inspired the pen of a close thinker and thoughtful writer, a well-known journalist of that State, Hon. S. M. Clark, to say: "Here is an Iowa legislature attacking railroad property in the spirit and with the morals of a highway robber. . . . The invincible reason for every upright person to oppose what the present legislature was doing was that that body is menacing free government and civilization by corrupting the people into a belief that dishonesty and theft can be legalized by the legislature. On such an issue there was nothing left for honest people and people who want to see our present form of government endure but to resist and oppose the legislature and the spirit of the anarchist and the communist that pervaded it. And just then the railways began to rob their stockholders by a cut-rate war. It is an act of spoliation and theft, and no casuistry or argument can make it any thing else. . . . The act is characteristic of that fatuity of insolence which has made the railroad managers the Ishmaelites of to-day: their hand against every man's and every man's hand against them. They are the robber barons of these times. Intrenched in the strongholds of millions of dollars of consolidated capital, nearly every dollar of which has been stolen from the men who built the roads, they ravage the land with the remorselessness of Middle-Age feudal chiefs, respecting neither the government above them nor the people whom they trample beneath them in the wanton insolence of their power. They demoralized the American people, who were trained by long generations of respect for private property; they corrupted them and made such a legislature as that in Iowa to-day possible by their own flagrant disregard of all property rights."

Similar complaints may be urged with respect to merchants and manufacturers who have grown enormously wealthy by pursuing methods which are hardly consistent with straightforward business principles. True, they did not rob their stockholders by a "cut-rate war," but they cheated either the public or their employés,—the public, by charging too high a price for the commodities which they were compelled to purchase, or their employés by not paying them adequate compensation for their labor. Every yard of calico or flannel worn by the poor, every pound of tea, coffee, or sugar used in the family, every nail driven in the floor, knob or lock placed on the door, bedstead, spring, or mattress, stove, dishes, knife, fork, spoon, or other household article or utensil, has been sold at too costly a price, or the mechanic, clerk, and salesman who produced these articles and put them on the market have not been sufficiently rewarded for their skill and labor.

One fact must not be lost sight of in the discussion of these and kindred subjects; it is, that all men have the right to live, and unless afforded the opportunity of acquiring the means whereby to sustain and enjoy life, the naked right to exist is but a barren ideality. Whenever, therefore, the business of an individual or of a number of individuals assumes such vast proportions, or is conducted in such a manner that it demoralizes trade and crushes competition, some means should be devised to limit its vastness and control its power.

There is in the city of Chicago one dry-goods house which, it is said, does a business of $35,000,000 annually. This mammoth concern, not content with monopolizing the wholesale trade of well-nigh one-fourth of a continent, prompted by a greed insatiate and conscienceless, offers the innumerable commodities it carries in stock, for sale at retail, at the very door of the small dealer, at nearly the same price that it has charged him for the same articles at wholesale. It induces the small tradesman, by all the arts known to the trade, to invest his limited capital in a stock of goods, and then renders it impossible for him to dispose of those goods by enticing those who would be his patrons to come and buy of it at prices which the humble merchant cannot duplicate.

In its almost illimitable retail establishment, it not only offers for sale such remnants and unseasonable goods as naturally accumulate in the course of trade, in its special line, but keeps a full stock of every article of merchandise required to satisfy the wants and gratify the pleasure of the innumerable army of purchasers. Buying these in immense quantities, it can undersell all others of limited capital, and thus grocers, druggists, jewellers, boot and shoe dealers, other dry-goods merchants, and all vendors with moderate means, are at the

mercy of this commercial octopus, which is ever extending its remorseless tentacles not only to draw into its
rapacious maw all the gold of traffic, but to crush and
kill even the humblest who seek a single shekel of that
wealth which it arrogates as its own.

This Chicago concern, unfortunately, is not the only
one of its kind in this country. Each of the great
metropolitan cities has similar establishments operating
in the same way and with the same disastrous effects.
And this absorption of business and crushing of the
feebler ones engaged therein is not confined to the mer-
cantile, but finds lamentable exemplification in every
department of trade and traffic. The concentration
of capital in gigantic manufacturing enterprises has
quenched the fires in the forge, silenced the wheel, and
closed the shops of thousands of artisans throughout this
land, and thus forced them to seek in other lines and
mid other scenes the ways and means of earning a
livelihood; and ofttimes failing, they have been driven
into the ranks of the legions of dishonored industry
from which are recruited the ever-increasing hosts of
idleness marshalled by want while begging for work,
tramping over the country, goaded by hunger and hardened by suffering, to victory—the victory which death
brings to misery and woe.

These men, driven by the direful force of pitiless
circumstances—seldom of their own making—out into
the world, away from the restraints and virtuous influences of a home, knowing naught of the saving love
of a devoted wife nor the inspiring sweetness of a child's
caress, save as a memory fraught with agony,—these

men, ostracized by society, spurned from every door, denied the favors given even to a homeless dog,—can it be wondered at that in time they should drift into drunkenness, vagabondage, and crime?

These are facts, not theories; facts which confront us on the streets of every city, on the lanes and highways of the country, in the wards of the hospital, in the recesses of the poor-house, and in the cells of the prison; facts which the men of millions will do well not to ignore, and serious contemplation of which may conduce to their personal safety and the security of their much-worshipped wealth. The flippant and cynical, the two classes most worshipful at the shrine of mammon, are wont to stigmatize as shiftless vagabonds and drunken loafers that great number of men who daily loiter upon our street-corners or drag their weary length along the dusty roads from farm-house to farm-house; but in simple truth this is a vicious and cowardly libel, a conception of sordid selfishness, and the voicing of venal inhumanity. It may be true, and doubtless is, that some among them may be drunkards by choice and idlers by preference, but the great majority of them are men who would rather toil than beg, and would welcome as a blessing the fate which would enable them to exchange the life they are leading for one of severest drudgery.

It is a fact, which no man can gainsay, that the great majority of our wealthier men pay no regard to the wants of the poor. This is forcibly true of our rapid-transit aristocracy, so numerous to-day, whose bank accounts constitute their tickets of admission to the society of the upper-tendom, in which he of the plethoric purse out-ranks the manly man of moderate means and modest worth. These gilded parvenus, adapting themselves to their new environments, thrust out of their little minds and still more diminutive hearts all thought and feeling of the wants and rights of those with whom they were wont to associate in other days when "boiling soap" or "shoveling dirt." Consideration for the poor, except in making a donation for the benefit of some charity where it was certain the names of the donors would be heralded to the world through the press, would be social heresy in their circle.

CHAPTER III.

INEQUALITY OF CONDITIONS HUMANITY'S WRONG.

It is but the old story of the toiling millions against the scheming few that has been told and retold in the history of every nation,—the former battling for the privilege of living, the latter grasping for power and pelf; and in this conflict the plutocrat enriches himself by robbing and enslaving the proletariat until the latter turns and, in vicious violence, despoils the former of his ill-gotten gains. In our own country the number of dependents and houseless wanderers is increasing daily. The laborer and mechanic seek in vain for employment that will yield a living for wife and children.

P

While labor begs for work the various industries are closed, owing to the refusal of capital to set the wheels in motion. Safety-deposit vaults and bank-coffers are filled to overflowing with millions of dollars, while thousands of men in every city are clamoring for a chance to earn food and shelter for themselves and families. It is no glittering assertion, but a glaring fact, that the rich are growing richer, and that the poor are growing poorer and more numerous. He who looks through the meretricious coloring of our much-vaunted material progress can but realize this painful truth. With these conditions existing, the poor are confronted with the alternatives of bartering their birthright to the money barons in consideration of their support and protection, or by a united, determined exercise of the modicum of political freedom they still retain, bring about a legal, civil, and social revolution which will establish and perpetuate an equitable equalization of industrial and social conditions. The great majority of the people are virtually propertyless, and with them life is a battle for bread, while the favored few possess the soil and enjoy every comfort and pleasure that opulence can suggest or supply. The last and only resort for those to whom a change is a necessity is the ballot, which in the hands of the mendicant or wage-worker is as potent as when cast by the millionaire. The penniless tramp, the industrious toiler, the struggling tenant, the small landholder, the tradesman of limited means, all who have felt the grinding power of the tyranny of greed, have a common interest in working for a reformation, radical and far-reaching, that will bring to each relief of present burdens and opportunity for future efforts and success. These subordinate holders of power, acting in self-defence, should unite in solid phalanx, and break not ranks until they have engrafted such alterations and amendments upon constitutions and laws, fixing and regulating the title to land, as will work just division of property and consequent equitable distribution of wealth, securing to him who toils full fruitage of his labors.

It is no less significant than lamentable that every effort heretofore made by the masses for their own amelioration has proved comparatively abortive. The failure cannot be ascribed to the weakness of their cause, but the rather must be in a great measure attributed to a want of unity of action and a fatal lack of intelligent conception of proper and effective means and methods requisite to employ in accomplishing the object in view. Another cause which militates against the success of such movements made in behalf of the common people is found in the proneness of men who, through a vigorous championship of their interests, secure the legislative and executive offices to forget ante-election pledges, and, that thrift may follow fawning, crook the pliant hinges of the knee to capital, ever seeking and securing proselytes among judges, governors, and legislators. Another cause, perhaps more potent than all others, that works discomfiture and demoralization in these reformatory movements, is found in the fact that the greater number of those actually interested in the success of such movements are so absorbed in the struggle for existence, and so burdened with the cark-

ing cares which crowd the life of toil, that they can
give neither time nor thought to that which does not
offer immediate relief to their necessities; and hence
they are readily duped by the designing, or all too ready
to clutch the paltry price proffered for their votes. Men
of wealth must be wofully, wilfully blind, if they cannot read in the corruption of the franchise and the bartering of ballots the culmination of the crisis now impending. The day of reckoning may be deferred by
such desperate methods, but at last, when patience is
exhausted by promises broken, the conscience of the
people perverted by those who have profited by its
abasement, stung to madness by sin and suffering, will
seek expiation for the one and revenge for the other in
the destruction of the authors of their degradation and
servitude.

Labor may submit to the exactions and endure the
oppression of organized capital for a long period, but
its permanent enslavement is not possible in a country
where the common school is a fixed and fruitful factor
of individual development.

This antagonism between the rich and the poor, ripen-
ing into revolt on the one hand and rapine on the other,
wrought the overthrow of the democracies of other times,
and while it may not destroy our institutions, it threatens
to dismember the union, unless the causes which provoke
and aggravate it are removed, and their recurrence rendered impossible by the adoption of constitutional provisions and legal enactments inspired by equity, tem-
pered by justice, as demanded by right and reason.

History has made immortal the record of the virtues

and glories that characterized the golden age of Greece, when her sages and statesmen gave full recognition and application to that fundamental maxim that liberty and democracy cannot coexist without equality of conditions, and when this was forgotten or ignored, special privileges and powers were granted to or usurped by the favored few, entailing of necessity that inequality of conditions that at length exhausted itself in the disintegration and downfall of the grandest political structure ever conceived and reared by the brain and hand of man.

The past and present of the United States are but repetitions of the rise and progress of the nations who have gone before. Shall the future record our failure to profit by their example, and witness our decay and destruction from that same cause that worked the overthrow and ruin of others?

We have reached that stage in national development where the common weal is subordinated to individual privilege, and the wants of the many are lost in the exactions of the few. On every hand we have indubitable evidence of positive hardship and rank injustice as resultants of the inequality of conditions which obtains through the amassing of wealth and absorption of property by a meagre minority. It is hardly half a century ago when a man could count the millionaires of the United States on the fingers of one hand, but now they are numbered by thousands. Labor produced these millions, and if labor had received a fair share of its profits, and the employers of labor had taken sufficient interest in the welfare of their operatives to in-

struct them how to husband and judiciously invest their
earnings, the mercenary plutocrats might now enjoy
their millions in comparative safety, as a great majority
of those now stigmatized as vagrant tramps would be
loyal and industrious citizens, living with their families
in their own homes,—" every man under his own vine
and under his fig-tree."

New York City numbers among its millions of inhabitants the richest man in America, if not in the
world, who can expend two million dollars upon a palatial pleasure-yacht, and own a residence and grounds
on Fifth Avenue which cost as much more, and yet
there are thousands of men within the corporate limits
of that city who are without house or home. This man
inherited a princely fortune on the death of his father,
and by shrewd management and skilful manipulation
of stocks, it is said, he has augmented that inheritance
until he is now the possessor of two hundred millions
of dollars. Why should one human being possess so
much wealth and enjoy all the luxury which it affords,
while so many of his countrymen are huddled together in the tenements of that great city, suffering from
sickness, hunger, and privation? May we not ascribe
much of their wretchedness and misery to the ruin
wrought through the fluctuations in the value of stocks,
in the gilded gambling dens of Wall Street, by the
power of his millions; stocks in which the public were
induced to invest their means by allurements far more
captivating than those by which the bunko-steerer of
Chicago captivates the Western stockman? How many
of the haggard, famine-stricken faces daily seen in the

back streets and alleys of that city may not trace the origin of their downfall to the first investment made in Wall Street securities? How many of our Western farmers have been rendered homeless and purposeless through the same cause? Yet this high-handed species of gaming is tolerated under the nose of a supersensitive class of moralists who would arrest a man for laying a wager on a horse-race.

A little Miss, a very child, in Philadelphia, the reputed possessor of seven millions, fondles her dolls arrayed in costly fabrics from across the seas, while thousands of little girls in the city of brotherly love, half-clad and hungry, can be found in the basements and tenements where herd the poor. These two painful but forcible illustrations of the inequality of conditions existing in this country certainly suggest the need of action—positive, heroic action—that will make it impossible for such things to be. It is not sentiment that calls for this action: sense suggests, justice demands, and humanity commands it.

CHAPTER IV.

WEALTH SHOULD BEAR THE BURDEN OF TAXATION.

SINCE the imposition of a tax upon income is one of the means by which the inequality existing between the capitalist and the consumer can be even partially equalized, the question arises, how should this tax be imposed and enforced? It must be imposed in such a manner as not to cripple or necessarily impair individual exertions. The parables of the talents and the ten wise and the ten foolish virgins apply to every condition of life. Some men will make money and accumulate wealth where other men, given the same opportunities and advantages, would starve. So that in adjusting matters for the general good care must be taken not to set a premium on idleness, sloth, or extravagance. Whatever condition of things may be devised, we cannot equalize natural inequalities. Some men are endowed by nature with greater facilities than others, and to that extent are capable of putting forth greater exertions and of accomplishing greater possibilities. How many railroad men have had as good opportunities and advantages as the late T. J. Potter; yet how few were his equals! Utopia is an imaginary state,—a figment of the fancy; government is a practical reality, an existing fact. In utopia men are made for laws as they are; in government laws are made for men as we find them. We will always have the idle, the thriftless, the poor, and the lawless, because it seems to be so ordained. How to deal with these classes, to benefit humanity, to preserve society, and to do justice to all should be the ultimate end of all government. The man who has a net income of one thousand dollars a year should be truly thankful that dame fortune has dealt so kindly by him, and not grumble if required to contribute one per cent. of it to the support of a government under whose laws he may enjoy life and pursue happiness in safety and peace. He whose income is two thousand dollars annually, instead of one, ought to consider himself doubly fortunate, and should willingly part with two per cent. thereof in order to lighten the burden of taxation which would otherwise rest heavily on that portion of the community who are not so fortunate as he is and less able to bear it. The rate per cent. might be increased after his income has reached, say, ten thousand dollars a year, or the same rate could be continued on each additional one thousand dollars until the rate reached twenty-five per centum of his entire income. When this point was reached I should in no event require him to pay more, because to do so would have a tendency to materially chill the ardor and repress the ambition of men to acquire wealth and fortune. The desire to make money and to become wealthy is highly laudable when honorable and legitimate means are employed to accomplish these ends. The object of an income-tax is not to check a laudable ambition or to stifle the efforts of the individual to " gather gear by ev'ry wile that's justified by honor," but to render it impossible for any one man to become an unwieldy cormorant,—a hoarder of millions.

By a fiction of the law, personal property is said to follow the person of the owner, so that a resident of Boston, who owns one million dollars of stock in an Iowa or Illinois corporation, would be compelled to pay taxes on this amount at his place of residence, if he made an honest return of it to the Boston assessor, although the property which gives value to this stock is situated in the foreign State. This is unfair and unjust to the people of the State in which the property that the stock represents is situated. In order to obviate this injustice and to prevent any favoritism on the one hand or discriminations on the other, the United States Collector of Internal Revenue should collect this income-tax, and when collected, it should be apportioned to the different States upon a basis of the taxable value of their property. It may be urged that the collection of such a tax would be impracticable, that men of wealth would evade the law by making false returns. Whatever else may be urged against Federal officers, it must be admitted that they do not often connive at crime or make common cause with criminals. The criminal law is pretty strictly and expeditiously executed in Uncle Sam's courts. If a law was passed making it a penitentiary offence and forfeiture of property to render a false return to the Collector of Internal Revenue, and also making malfeasance in office punishable for life or for a term not less than ten years in the penitentiary, there could be little cause for apprehending that such a law would be evaded or disobeyed.

In the cantons of Switzerland, the villager who has supported cattle through the winter may send a certain number to pasture in the common called the alp. A general assembly of villagers is held in spring, before the herds go up to the mountain pastures, and every villager declares on oath the number of cattle he has kept through the winter. The slightest attempt at fraud is punished by a heavy fine or by suspension of the right of common. In many villages, in order to restore greater equality, they have imposed a tax on each head of large cattle, the amount of which is distributed among those who have no cattle. Now, if this rule produces a "greater equality" in regard to large cattle sent to pasture on the alp, why should it not be productive of good results when applied to individuals in a country where some have grown so fat and unwieldy from devouring the good things of the earth that there is nothing left but crumbs for the lean and hungry to feed upon? While inequality of conditions may be attributed largely to natural causes, to mental and physical inequalities in the human species, if you please, yet it never was ordained by an All-wise Being that one man should live in luxury and extravagance, wasting and squandering sufficient to feed a thousand, while the thousand must look on and starve. It is not natural justice that he should; it is not legal justice; it is not political justice. Tax the large and fatted human cattle, and distribute the amount of the tax among the lean and hungry.

CHAPTER V.

TRUSTS—CAPITAL'S CONSPIRACY AGAINST THE RIGHT TO LIVE.

FOR months the public press has been filled with the details of the formation of new combinations having as the moving cause of their existence the purpose to throttle competition in those lines of industry whose products are necessary for the living and doing of the people. Conspiracies have sprung into being in every department of trade and traffic. Men schooled in the

greed and grasp of monopoly have reached out for and
secured the control of the gas and fuel supplies and
transportation systems in well-nigh all the towns and
cities of our land. The quantity of whiskey distilled
is determined by a trust. Cabals of manufacturers
have been organized to destroy competition in many
fields of productions. The formation of pools, trusts,
and alliances goes on undisturbed or at least with only
a spasmodic effort now and then, here and there, to
retard and embarrass the perfection of the conspiracies.
Although the nefarious schemes by which insatiable
greed is destroying industrial freedom and crushing
honest competition are known to all intelligent observers, and the woful wrongs wrought by their successful operation are seen and admitted on all hands, yet no
positive, tangible action is taken by those who are the
chosen guardians of the rights and well-being of the
people to stay the hands of the despoilers and save
their victims from oppression and plunder. The people
are beginning to clamor for relief, and it is the part of
wisdom for our statesmen to heed and act. It is true,
bills for investigation and suppression of trusts and
conspiracies have been introduced in the national Congress and in some of the State legislatures, but the
suppressions "died a bornin'," and the investigations
have proven profitless because the conditions revealed
have not been removed nor their recurrence rendered
impossible by legislation. I present below a few facts
and suggestions touching upon this crusade of monopoly
against competition. It should be remembered that one
of the most pernicious results of these combinations, and

one of the strongest motives that instigates the conspirators, is the exacting of greater profits from consumers than could be possibly obtained so long as competition exists. The law of supply and demand is powerless to fix the value of products in a market dominated by a trust. Our commercial system cannot survive such violent abuse by arbitrary oppressions of consumers, which would not be tolerated in any other civilized country in the world. The people have their remedy,— that remedy is legislation. The time to apply that remedy is now. The way to secure its application is to elect men to our legislative bodies who have positive and intelligent convictions as to what is right and what is wrong, and the moral courage to leave the imprint of those convictions upon the measures which they advocate and adopt for the righting of the wrongs which corporate conspiracies are now inflicting upon the industrial and commercial system of our country,— wrongs which are destructive to personal liberty and a menace to the perpetuity of the republic. A president of a railroad, in defence of his company for having joined the combination of coal companies to avert the calamity of "too much coal," plead that there are fifty trades or more engaged in the same thing. To justify his own iniquity, he urged the wrong-doing of others. He said, "Every pound of rope we buy for our vessels or our mines is bought at a price fixed by a committee of the rope manufacturers of the United States. Every keg of nails, every paper of tacks, all our screws and wrenches and hinges, the boiler flues for our locomotives, are never bought except at the price fixed by the representatives of the mills that manufacture them. Iron beams for our houses or our bridges can be had only at the price agreed upon by a combination of those who produce them. Fire-brick, gas-pipe, terra-cotta, pipe for drainage, every keg of powder we buy to blast coal, are purchased under the same arrangement. Every pane of glass in the windows of our houses was bought at a scale of prices established exactly in the same manner. White lead, galvanized sheet-iron, hose and belting, and files are bought and sold at a rate determined in the same way."

More than a century ago one of England's wisest economists said, "People of the same trade hardly meet together even for merriment or diversion, but the conversation ends in a conspiracy against the public, or in some contrivance to raise prices." The forceful truth of these words has gathered voice and volume each succeeding year since their utterance. This is verified unto all men in the reports of proceedings of meetings of the various associations of producers, dealers, and manufacturers which are held almost daily. They never fail, by "Whereas" and "Re-solves," to increase prices, determine production, and fix wages, and round up their convention with a sump-tuous feast, for which the people pay.

THE SUGAR TRUST.—The demand for sugar in this country is supplied by the refiners in whose factories the raw sugars imported from abroad, and those fur-nished from the Louisiana plantations, are prepared for use. These refiners have organized a trust which vir-tually places under the control of fifteen men in New

York and Boston the entire consumption of raw sugar and productions of refined sugar in the United States. This trust is governed by ten trustees, who, sitting in council, can, by one vote, raise the price of sugar for sixty millions of people. Only a motion, followed by a second, a calling of the roll, and sending notice to trust agents, and the market-price goes up. Sixty millions of freemen subject to the greed of ten gilded plutocrats! As the law now stands, the people are powerless. They must pay the price these Shylocks demand or do without sugar. A few figures may be interesting. Over three billion pounds of sugar were consumed in this country in 1887. A raise of one-half a cent on the pound gives $15,000,000; one cent, $30,000,000; two cents brings $60,000,000. The trust not only raises the price of refined sugars, but it lowers at will the price of raw sugars. A cargo of raw sugar is brought to New York or Boston; it is offered for sale; there is but one bidder and one buyer,—that bidder and buyer is the trust. It thus fixes the price it will pay for what it buys, as well as determines the price for which it will sell. The trust buys the raw sugar, and sells the refined. It had enjoyed a monopoly of the sugar trade but four months when it had made a profit of twelve per cent. on its capital stock (watered until it was swollen to $60,000,000), or forty-eight per cent. upon the true value of the property actually put into the ring,—$7,200,000 profit in four months on an investment of $15,000,000! Comment is unnecessary. The rapacity of these sugar Shylocks does not exhaust itself in reducing the price of the raw

sugar it buys, and raising that of the refined sugar it
sells, but it determines the supply.   Since it began
operation, nine refineries have closed, in the face of
the positive assurance of the organizers of the combination that they would shut down no refineries, nor
put up the price of sugar.

———————

CHAPTER VI.

OTHER TRUSTS.

CASTOR-OIL.—Nothing escapes the mercenary clutch
of these trusts.   There are but five large mills in this
country making castor-oil, and the owners have formed
a pool, through the power of which they limit production, and sell their product at $1.20 per gallon, while
foreign producers sell the same oil at forty cents.

LINSEED OIL.—The combination which controls
this production advanced the price from thirty-eight to
fifty-two cents (over thirty-six per cent.) last year, and
in the space of four months the advance was thirteen
cents.   There is no legal limit bounding the exactions
of this trust.   The people *must* pay its demands, or
make it impossible for the producers to control production or fix prices.

STEEL RAILS.—During the great season of railroad
building in the West, last year, the combine controlling
steel rails forced the companies to pay $40.00 a ton.   The

railway companies protested against such extortion, and at length determined that they would cease extensions unless $30.00 a ton was accepted. The combine protested that to sell under $32.00 or $33.00 would entail a serious loss to makers, yet they finally consented to sell for $31.50. That is, the trust agreed with the companies to furnish them rails at an actual loss to the makers! Further, when the combine was forced by the railroad companies to accept $31.50, the board of control fixed the output under this agreement at 800,000 tons, assigning a certain number to each maker, and when these were furnished no more orders could be filled.* The board of control regulates the output, distributes the work, and fixes the price. At the time of organizing this trust the price was $25.50 per ton. The cost of production has not increased more than ten per cent. Allowing for that, and assuming there was a fair profit at $25.50, the rate of $36.00 (which was the average price last year) yielded an additional profit of $8.00 a ton. Upon the year's production (2,050,000 tons) this profit was $16,400,000. The profit at $25.50 was $6,000,000 or $8,000,000 more. These enormous sums the people have to pay. The railways only advance the money. They who travel, and who ship their merchandise and produce over the railroads, in the end pay this immense profit which the trust exacts.

---

* The Vulcan Mill, at St. Louis, stood idle for years, its owners, however, receiving $400,000 annually from the combine for not making rails, but its locked-out employés received no share of this bonus.

IRON ORE.—There has been also a consolidation effected of the different iron-mining companies in each region, which is the initial step to the organization of a great combine, which will control the output and fix the price of this ore, which is the staff of every industry.

STEEL.—We have two associations of steel manufactures, not competitors, but working with a singleness of purpose "to remedy irregularities in prices,"—that is, to force all makers to sell at the same price, and that price, the highest.

PLOUGHS.—A manufacturer was paying four and one-half cents a pound for the steel parts of ploughs, a price satisfactory to the mills. The formation of the steel trust was followed by an advance of ten and one-half cents. The plough-makers at once formed a combination and raised the price of ploughs. One plough-maker refused to enter the combine. Those in the trust prevailed upon the steel-makers to make him pay two cents a pound more than the members of the association were required to pay. He was thus forced to enter the conspiracy or be driven out of business. Thus one combine begets another, and the people pay tribute to them all.

THRESHERS.—One-half of the manufacturers of threshing-machines have organized a trust for "mutual protection and harmony of interests," which is fully provided for by passing on the farmer the taxes exacted by the steel and iron trusts.

REAPERS, MOWERS, AND BINDERS.—Nineteen of the twenty-one manufacturers of these machines have combined to "curtail production and fix a system of uniform prices," the full purport of which those who are compelled to use these implements will understand in having to pay the increase in price.

BEAMS.—There are but seven companies making iron and steel beams in the United States. They have organized a pool to destroy competition by establishing and maintaining a common price, which for two years has been $73.92 per ton. The actual cost of making beams is but little in excess of that of making rails, and rails selling at $31.50 per ton yield large profits.

NAILS.—A majority of the nail manufacturers have also entered into a close combination to limit production and increase prices.

STOVES.—The three hundred and fifteen stove manufacturers have, in association assembled, declared "that the fundamental law of commerce and the dictates of reason" compel the adoption of the trust plan, which means the restriction of production and regulation of prices.

SCHOOL-SLATES AND SCHOOL-BOOKS.—A tribute of seventeen and one-half per cent. was levied upon the patrons of schools last year by the "combine" that controls the manufacture of slates. Nineteen of the leading publishers of school books met in solemn conclave and resolved against "dishonest competition," and organized a combination by which they are bound to obey the orders of an executive committee as to prices and other matters. This is one of those incidental aids to free schools which lightens the purse if it does not the heart of those parents who, by stint and toil, strive to bestow upon their children the only heritage within their power, a common-school education.

NATIONAL BURIAL-CASE ASSOCIATION.—Even the dead do not escape the merciless greed of organized capital. The makers of shrouds and coffins have formed a close corporation under the above title, and lest mortality should be discouraged and Death himself dismayed, their scheme to keep up prices and limit the number of winding-sheets and caskets is kept a secret. As a fitting finale to successfully "cornering" the habiliments of the dead, they close their grave deliberations with a round of festivities.

CHAPTER VII.

THE HYDRA TRUST AND QUINTET OF THE SHAMBLES.

STANDARD OIL TRUST.—Kerosene is the people's light the world over. In the United States upwards of three hundred and fifty thousand gallons of petroleum are used annually. It is exported to Europe and the far East. The demand for it in the Orient is growing faster than anywhere else. It illumines the ruins of Babylon and lights the devastation of Tyre; in the isles of the Pacific and far Cathay, in Turkestan, India, and China, the bronzed millions slave and dream, smoke opium and chew hashish, woo and win, decline and die, under the gentle light of this marvellous product of our inexhaustible caverns.

In the United States, in town and country, it is the common illuminator. We light more lamps than we read Bibles. The crude material of this universal light is obtained in a limited area, commencing in Cattaraugus County, New York, and extending about one hundred and sixty miles southwesterly, covering ten counties in Western Pennsylvania, the width of the belt being about twenty miles. Here the bulk is obtained; an unimportant yield being obtained in West Virginia, Tennessee, Kentucky, and Ohio. But comparatively few of the sixty millions of people in our country who nightly burn kerosene are aware that its production, manufacture, and sale are all under the absolute control of a single corporation,—the most gigantic monopoly of this age of monopolies,—the Standard Oil Company. It has a capital of ninety millions of dollars, upon which it declares dividends of millions every year and divides among its stockholders. It tolerates no rival. It does not hesitate to draw its check for one million dollars to suppress a competitor if he cannot be quieted in any other way. It buys the crude oil at a price fixed by itself, and transports over thirty million barrels a year over the railroads under contracts of its own making. In the plenitude of its power it has partitioned the globe among its members. One controls Japan and China, another the countries of Europe, another the East India trade, and another that of the United States.

This company has driven into financial ruin, or compelled to go out of business, or forced into surrender, all of the other coal-oil refineries, with but few exceptions, and these are engaged in a struggle for existence, —the struggle which means extinction. It dictates rates of transportation for its own freight to railroad companies, and at its behest these companies refuse to transport the products of other refineries or demand such a freight rate that its payment would entail bankruptcy.

In towns and cities where gas and electric light supersede the use of kerosene, in the companies organized to supply the former, representatives of the Standard Company are active controlling factors, making their presence and power felt in the exorbitant rates charged for these advanced illuminators. Although seemingly gorged with its ill-gotten gain, its greed still insatiate cries for more, and henceforth it will convey its products by pipe-lines from the wells to the refineries located in the trade-centres, thus dispensing with all outlay for transportation by rail.

Every person who uses kerosene pays a tax to the Standard Oil Trust upon each gallon of oil many times greater than its original cost to the company. Each family pays a tribute of about twenty-five dollars a year to this trust if they use but a quart a day. It is estimated—that the estimate is low is conceded—that the people thus pay into the coffers of this mammoth monopoly twenty-five million dollars each year besides the millions received from the railroads in freight rebates. These have amounted in a single year to fifteen million dollars. With these figures before us, we can understand how it may be true that the Standard pays one and a half millions in monthly dividends.

It can easily divide this amount of its ill-gotten gain among its stockholders and have millions left with which to influence legislation and elect to office, ay, even to the Senate of the United States, one of its master spirits.

THE CATTLE SYNDICATE.—On the floor of the United States Senate, a few days ago, it was charged that five men in the city of Chicago regulate the daily price of cattle. That these men, through their pitiless sagacity and the power of their millions, destroy competition and render it impossible for cattle men to procure a higher price than that agreed upon by this cattle cabal. A Western stockman finds from the market quotations that cattle are three and a half cents a pound. He ships his cattle to market, and when they arrive here a representative of the trust is sent to view them. The owner is informed that he can get two cents and a half a pound. He seeks another purchaser and another, but each gives him the same answer. He cannot store them; he cannot afford to ship them home; they are losing every day in weight and deteriorating in quality; and thus he has no other alternative than to sell at the price dictated by the buyers, who practically confiscate the cattle man's property, as if they had the right to take it from his farm without paying for it. The decrease in price of one cent per pound was not caused by a natural change of conditions in the market, but by the grasping machinations of the five men who control that market. Under the operations of this trust the prices of cattle have been increased without reason, and ruinously. It is estimated that the stockmen of Kansas alone have lost forty million dollars, and their loss was the syndicate's gain. With the fruits of this *robbery* lining their pockets, a committee of the "stock ring" has the *brazen effrontery* to *pollute* the halls of Congress with their presence, seeking to procure the passage of an act giving them exclusive control of cattle quarantine. This "combine" has formed an alliance offensive and defensive with the railroad managers by giving them an interest in stock-yards and feeding-stations and a share in the profits that gild the way from the Western stall to the Eastern shambles. As the syndicate coerces the stock-raiser into accepting the beggarly price it fixes upon his cattle, so it compels the retail dealer to pay an exorbitant price for the beef which he sells to the consumer, who thus is made the helpless victim of the avarice of the iniquitous quintet that speculates upon one of the necessaries of life.

CHAPTER VIII.

THE COAL CONSPIRACY.

THE COAL TRUST.—In the summer of 1883, four men owning the largest interests in the coal-lands and coal railroads of the East, held a conference at Saratoga Springs to adopt some plan for the control of the coal trade. They agreed upon a scale of prices, and, as the most effective way of preventing an overproduction of coal, decided to suspend work at the mines. An order was issued for half-time work during the first quarter of the ensuing year, and for an increase in prices. This was the inception of what has since grown into the crowning combination of avarice and brutality of this age of greed. The companies composing this "combine" mine, transport, and sell their own coal. Our annual consumption of anthracite is over thirty-five million tons, of which about one-fifth is consumed in the West. The mine-owner who refuses to join the combination or disregards its orders is soon obliterated. It avails him nothing to operate his mine, for the railroads refuse to transport its productions. The retailer has become simply the agent of the trust, for if he dares sell at any other than the price fixed by the board of control his supply is cut off, and he is driven out of business. The primal purpose of the combination is solely to determine the output, and thus have a plausible pretext to advance the price. Repression of production necessitates the throwing of thousands of employés out of work. An increase in price of from one dollar to one dollar and a half a ton is no unusual thing. This means from thirty-five to fifty millions more of blood-money for division annually among the members of the "combine." One company owns nearly one-half of the anthracite area of the United States; one-third is divided among five other corporations, and the remaining sixth belongs to individuals and firms, and is "necessarily tributary" to the railroads of the companies that own the five-sixths. Combination has been equally busy and effective in the bituminous coal-fields. A pool controls the annual product and fixes the price of all the soft-coal mines north of the Ohio River, and steps are being taken to extend it to all the bituminous coal districts of the South. Prominent officials of the railroad lines traversing these districts own controlling interests in the coal properties. These combinations thus not only keep the supply down by restricting the output, but, having control of the means of transportation, can withhold that supply from the market. Thus the coal companies and their coparceners in greed—the railroad companies—can bring about a coal famine at their own pleasure. During the summer, when nature gratuitously affords the warmth necessary for our comfort, coal can be bought by the consumer for from $1.25 to $2.00 less per ton than when winter's icy blasts render artificial heat an absolute necessity. The poor,—their name is legion,—unable to take advantage of the low prices of summer and lay in their stock of fuel, become in winter the helpless victims of the pitiless cupidity of the coal barons. The variations of the temperature determine the fluctuations of the coal market. The lower the mercury descends the higher rises the price of fuel. The frozen necessities of the poor are made the fruitful opportunities of the rich. Nature, ever gracious and generous, has provided inexhaustible supplies of the raw material of warmth in her storehouse, but this trust, with its impious hand, bolts and bars the door, and exacts from the people tribute thrice before suffering them to partake of what is their own. He who is pinched with cold, his wife and children freezing, answerable to no law but the law of necessity, should force the door and enter and take that which is his own for the comfort and warmth of his family and himself. The so-called legal rights of such property should not be respected, for they are conceived in rapacity and brought forth in corruption. Man's right to live embraces the right to use and enjoy whatever is necessary as provided by nature for his existence. They who conspire to deprive him of that right are guilty of a sacrilege which proclaims their own outlawry. Let the coal barons beware!

The combinations noted above are but a few of the many conspiracies organized and operating in our country against industrial freedom and individual competition. There is scarce a product of hand or wheel which enters largely into the comforts or necessities of life but what the makers have banded together to absolutely crush out all competition, limit the supply, and control the price. And all this is done, if not with the sanction, at least by the sufferance of our courts. The legislation of State and nation is but the formulating, in legal phrase and prescribed form, the nefarious plottings of corporation conspirators. These conditions should not exist. They and our republican institutions cannot, in their true force and virtue, coexist. The day is rapidly approaching when all these trusts, having perfected each its own system, may and probably will, in furtherance of their respective interests, unite in one grand combination to take absolute advantage of the public. Confronting this emergency, we perforce must choose between two alternatives,

—either let the State control the trusts, or let the trusts control the State. It is patent to the intelligent observer of events that our civilization is finding its highest commercial expression in these trusts, which, endowed with certain legal privileges, dictate terms to labor, fix the value of the necessaries of life, and determine production. These trusts are but the harbingers of a mighty commercial coalition which threatens to take absolute possession of our whole industrial and financial system, creating, in fact, a commercial feudalism. These trusts are inimical to the peace and safety of social and industrial order, for they provoke outbreaks and instigate oppressions which will demoralize and disrupt our whole political system. This condition is nearer at hand than we wot of, and is all the more easily brought about because no apparent apprehension seems to be felt. If the State does not take and hold control, the combines will soon crystallize into one universal monopoly. These trusts, then, operating in conjunction, will reduce the middle and laboring classes to a condition of commercial serfdom, and, through the power of united action, absolutely control the productive industry of our nation. Then will exist a feudalism, based on commercial leagues, in purpose and power more sweeping and autocratic than the baronial leagues of the Middle Ages. Everything is tending to bring about this condition. The State is not only permitting but promoting the establishment of this commercial feudalism. Is it not time to call a halt—to provide legislative checks and restraints which will prevent the destruction of our entire social and political system?

CHAPTER IX.

WHAT SHALL WE DO WITH THEM?

THE corporation is a creature of the State. The creator is above the creature. The right to control and, if need be, to destroy is an attribute of the sovereign power which begets. The State brought these corporations into life and being, and the State alone must see to it that they do not become ruinous to society. When labor appeals to the national government for protection or redress of its grievances it but forges the chains of its own slavery. These corporations were not created by any act of national legislation, and the Federal government has no jurisdiction over them. When the general government under the sanction of a petition from the people attempts to exercise any authority over matters belonging exclusively to the State, it is a step towards the obliteration of State lines, which, if repeated, becomes a stride towards centralization. A government so far removed from the people is *not* a government of the people, by the people, for the people. The functions of the government of the United States are grand and beneficent when properly understood and exercised. We should only appeal to this government when life, liberty, or property is imperiled by the arbitrary and illegal action of the State. When the State has authority to act and to remedy, aid invoked from the general government is

22

pregnant with danger. Power acting within constitutional limits is most salutary, but when it transcends those limits it becomes subversive of liberty. Inter-State commerce, strange to say, has become a shibboleth of the laborer, but the day may come when a minion of power, under the mandate of a district judge of the United States, will, in conflicts between labor and capital, coerce into submissive obedience the laborers along a thousand miles of railroad.

The Inter-State Commerce Bill is a national enactment of doubtful Federal authority, and under it the courts of the Federal government will gradually assume and imperceptibly absorb all jurisdiction of causes arising between railways, and between railways and their employés. The Supreme Court of the United States will doubtless uphold it, because capital inspired its adoption and labor has unwittingly ratified it. The legislature of the State has the constitutional right to provide that any railway corporation doing business within its borders, whether chartered under the laws of a foreign State or its own, shall make and maintain a uniform tariff throughout its entire length, and any discrimination in favor of the citizens of any foreign State as against its own citizens shall involve the loss of its business connections or work the forfeiture of its charter.

The legislatures of Pennsylvania and Ohio, which States are the foster-mothers of the coal and oil trusts, have the undoubted right to control and, if need be, crush them, and it is their bounden duty to do so. They may provide the number of acres of mineral lands which any individual or corporation shall own or operate within the State, and, further, that no individual or corporation shall be directly or indirectly interested in the ownership or operation of the coal property of any other individual or corporation, and that if any such individual, or the agents or officers of such corporation, shall agree or confederate with another to limit the output or fix the prices, the person or persons so offending shall be deemed guilty of a felony. A law embracing similar provisions could be framed and enacted which would reach and effectually prevent all trusts and combinations. Not only so, but the legislature may also provide that the violation of any of the provisions of such law by the officers of any corporation now existing shall work a forfeiture of its charter.

I should not wittingly invade the sacred right of property, but would provide that, after the year 1895, no person or corporation shall own or control to exceed one hundred and sixty acres of coal-lands, except in the manner herein provided. That on the first day of January, 1895, every person owning or controlling such lands shall report to the Secretary of State the number of acres so owned and controlled, giving a full description thereof, and specifying in such report the one hundred and sixty acres which the person or corporation wishes to retain for mining purposes; that thereafter, all lands so reported, other than the one hundred and sixty acre tracts so selected, may be purchased at private or public sale in the manner hereinbefore provided for the disposal of city lots; provided, that in no case shall the owner, or agent of such owner, or person or corporation owning, leasing, or being interested in coal lands, whether as stockholder or otherwise, bid at any such sale or become owner of such property. That a failure or neglect on the part of any individual or corporation to make report to the Secretary of State, as herein provided, shall subject the party offending to a penalty of one hundred dollars a day, and any person bidding at the sale herein contemplated who has not the legal right to do so shall be deemed guilty of a misdemeanor, and liable to a fine of one thousand dollars and imprisonment in the county jail not exceeding three months.

It may be urged that the State has not the constitutional right to divest the owner of property of his title thereto in this manner; that such a law would be in contravention of the national constitution. I should avoid any such objection by simply saying: Amend the constitution to the effect that any State shall have the right to fix the maximum number of acres of agricultural, mineral, grazing, and timber lands which any person may own, and also the number of lots which any person may own in towns or cities; and to provide for the disposal of any surplus in such manner as its legislature may determine.

CHAPTER X.

CRUSH TRUSTS BY LEGISLATION.

As will be observed, the writer has suggested such legislation as is necessary to prevent the formation of trusts in the future and to break up those already existing. The laws requisite to compass the former it is within the province of the legislatures to frame and adopt at once, as nothing is proposed not fully sanctioned by the constitutions of the respective States. As to the latter, which effects what is termed the vested rights of property, requiring, as it does, in the author's judgment, the adoption of an amendment to the Constitution of the United States, sufficient time is given for all the preliminary proceedings necessary to the presenting, discussion, and passage of such amendment, and also giving the holders of properties affected thereby ample opportunity to voluntarily dispose of the same. In this day, when the highest judicial tribunal in the land seems so inclined to strained constructions of constitutional law, it ought not be held, at least by those who sanction such decrees, revolutionary or conflicting with " vested rights," if the author had proposed immediate legislation limiting ownership already acquired of the properties referred to in preceding chapters. For if the State is vested with the authority under the constitution (as the United States Supreme Court has decided in the Kansas brewery cases) to carry the exercise of its police power to abate nuisances so far as to compel a citizen to wholly quit a business in which he has invested hundreds of thousands of dollars under the sanction of the law because, as claimed, the carrying on of that business offended the moral sentiment and worked the abasement of the community in which it was operated, then does it not follow, by a parity of reasoning, that the State is equally empowered by proper legislation to say to these trusts, whose work is the work of robbery and ruin of the people, " Cease your operations,—dissolve your unholy combinations, —the public good demands it." It might be urged that the plan suggested contemplates a virtual confiscation of the citizen's property. What more ruthless sequestration can be cited than that practically resulting from the decree of the court above referred to? The buildings, machinery, and all the appliances used by the brewer, of the peculiar character and construction required in operating his business, are comparatively utterly valueless except when devoted to the use for which they were intended. What doth it avail a man to leave him in possession of property and at the same time forbid him to use it? Is not this confiscation in the concrete, although observing right of possession of property in the abstract? Will the people without the means to buy food suffer any more from hunger than he who is forbidden to buy food though his pockets be lined with silver? And, besides, the plans suggested for reducing the possessions of present owners of property neither involves the taking of the same without any compensation nor the rendering of it unproductive.

There can be no question as to the power of the State to condemn and subject to sale the property affected by the legislation proposed, but such condemnation would involve an appraisement of the property and the payment of its ascertained value to the owner by the State. This would open the door to collusion between the owners of the properties and State officials, which would result in the placing of fanciful values and a consequent misappropriation of thousands of dollars of the people's money.

Let the wrong be as grievous as it may, no remedy should ever be resorted to save one that embraces a strict observance of the rights of all concerned; and where force and virtue are denied from the highest source of justice and of right, the expressed will of the people, adopt an amendment to the Constitution of the United States in order that existing trusts may be dissolved and forever destroyed. It is foreign to the purpose of the author to seek to change or abolish present forms or institutions without suggesting what he believes to be something better in their stead, and he is equally solicitous that, in effecting all the transitions so imperatively demanded, we keep within the unwavering parallels of right and equity. "The mere time of the reform is by no means worth the sacrifice of a principle of law. Individuals pass like shadows, but the commonwealth is fixed and stable. The difference, therefore, of to-day and to-morrow, which to private people is immense, to the State is nothing. At any rate, it is better, if possible, to reconcile our economy with our laws than to set them at variance,—a quarrel which in the end must be destructive of both."

BOOK VI.

DISTRIBUTION OF POPULATION AND DIVISION OF PROPERTY.

CHAPTER I.

THOSE THAT WANT AND THOSE THAT HAVE.

THIS fair land of ours was not made to be a workhouse in which the spirit of its people must be broken and suppressed by servile toil. Wealth is on every hand, and princely provision for every need, comfort, and pleasure felt by man. Every measure is supplied for the growth and development of humanity. Why in this land of plenty does want so much exist? Why such a multitude, born to equal heirship of nature's rich heritage, forced to the bondage of unrequited labor, to exhaust their energy and be despoiled of their better natures in the bitter strife for sheer existence? Why so much private woe in the midst of so much public pomp? Why a squalid hut within the shadow of every splendid mansion? Why the homeless and starving mendicant tramping along the highway where roll the glittering equipages of the pampered millionaire? Why all this ignorance festering so near the thresholds of our temples of learning? Why in a

260

land so richly dowered are there so many thousands who want? Resounding above the clamor of traffic, the clangor of machinery, the deafening din of the madding strife for gain, the echoes of a million voices can be heard, "Why do I want while others have?"

It will not suffice to seek to prove this cry a delusion by presenting a dazzling array of figures and statistics evidencing our marvellous progress and almost incredible increase of national wealth. Nothing is more misleading than figures, and statistics are often naught but illusive generalizations. It would be suicidal folly to endeavor to silence these voices with a policeman's club or a Gatling-gun.

Conditions exist which give just cause for complaint. In a country where the lower millions own nothing and the upper tens own millions there cannot but exist inequality which, perforce, must breed hardship and suffering. The concentration of capital in the hands of a few is rendered possible only through the robbery of the many. Colossal fortunes proclaim the abject misery of the laborer. Pitiful squalor follows in the wake of excessive opulence,—a spectre of its own creation that will not down. These extremes should not exist,—they must not. The condition of the wageworkers should be the primal and most serious object of the government's concern. That they are at present in a most unhappy and deteriorating state cannot be successfully denied, and most certainly in a land of such vast and varied wealth and resources this condition can only be attributable to defective organization or maladministration.

The true object of popular government, such as ours is claimed to be, does not consist in solely enriching and peopling a country, but in the enactment and administration of a code based upon a recognition of the fact that morality is the only true basis of life and law, that the growth and well-being of the individual are the foundation of productive power and of wealth secure, adhering to this course unfalteringly until the line which divides utilitarianism from humanitarianism is obliterated. Such modes of life and such avocations should be encouraged which are most conducive to wise living and virtuous growth.

As it is now, not only the tendency of the times, but the purposed endeavors of the government, are promoting the accumulation of enormous fortunes, establishing a landed monopoly, and helping to build up populous industrial centres, which become necessarily hot-beds of seditious revolt, mental degeneracy, and moral degradation, the only patent product of all which is an increase of mendicants and millionaires.

Immense private fortunes are hostile to democratic institutions, begetting envy, unrest, and pauperism on the one hand, and sordid tyranny and political debauchery on the other, presaging anarchy and despotism.

To corporations have been donated tracts of the public domain in range and resources rivalling the realm of a king of the Middle Ages, and individuals permitted to buy and hold thousands of acres to await the growth of the country before using or selling; and thus have the people, despoiled of their patrimony, been forced to become tenants and hirelings. The history of the world contains the bloody recital of agrarian revolts instigated by a frenzied desire to regain the people's birthright in the soil and equalize more nearly the conditions of men.

The building up of great manufacturing centres fosters the concentration of wealth and encourages the congregating of thousands in cities, where they are housed in crowded and comfortless quarters, depending upon employment which is ever uncertain, being subject to the fluctuations of the market and the caprices of capital. The house in which a laborer lives has much to do in moulding his character, and he can but endure bitter self-humiliation when he sees his employer's horses better housed than his own family. Switzerland is the poorest country in Europe, and the United States boasts of being the richest in the world, yet the Swiss artisan would turn with contempt from such houses as his fellow-craftsmen occupy in this country.

The home is the initial point of every ennobling element of civilization, and its ownership should always be vested in its occupant; then it would become the centre of loyalty, the abiding-place of love and beauty. In all well-organized communities the ownership of property is indispensable to the enjoyment of freedom, and in all stages of civilization the possession of a home is a condition requisite to the exaltation of humanity. If life is a natural right of the individual, home is equally a natural right of the family. It is urged against any method proposed for a restoration of comparative equality of conditions and for the general betterment of the common people, that its practical application involves a violation of the right of property. The right of property itself is subordinate to the general welfare, and that welfare is not conserved by any system of political economy which permits or sanctions the acquisition of princely wealth by a few and dooms the toiling millions, the producers of that wealth, to a life of despairing drudgery or abject pauperism. The elevation of the poor does not involve the humiliation of the rich. A proper and salutary adjustment of social and industrial conditions, which justice demands and wisdom dictates, can be effected without a single member of society having any right infringed or any privilege impaired which he is justly entitled to enjoy.

An equitable division of property and a judicious and timely distribution of population, provided for and enforced through legislative enactments, the writer believes, would effectuate and preserve the harmonious adjustment of all the parts of our individual and national economy. I have suggested in preceding chapters the legislation necessary for a just and reasonable division of property and limitation of ownership therein, and now proceed to treat of the distribution of population, its necessity, and the best way in which to accomplish it.

CHAPTER II.

AN EQUITABLE DIVISION OF PROPERTY DEMANDED.

A DISTRIBUTION of population would be impracticable without a division of property, and before inquiring into the necessity of the former it may be well to further consider the justice of the latter. Necessity makes that lawful which is otherwise unlawful, and, were there no other justification that could be pleaded in favor of an allotment of the property of a country among its people, this necessity would suffice. But, in truth, there are other tenable grounds upon which this can be rightfully urged, within whose limits arise many of the inhibitions at present imposed upon owners in the use and enjoyment of their property,—inhibitions to prevent that use and enjoyment from being perverted into abuse or from working injury to others. It should not be understood that by a division of property we mean that an equal portion should be assigned to each individual, but that, in addition to the means suggested in other parts of this work for preventing a land monopoly and promoting a fair division of the joint profits of labor and capital, something practical should be done to relieve the strained conditions now existing between labor and capital, so as to place the greater number of those who are a burden upon both in a position where they may become self-supporting. Every man has the right to live.

M 23

It is moral murder if we admit this right and yet make its exercise impossible. The earth was made for man, not man for the earth, and when conditions interdict his enjoyment of his rightful portion he is robbed of his birthright; and it matters not whether that robbery be perpetrated in the name of the law or by the lawless, it is robbery still. But we are told that what a man acquires is his and that what is his cannot be taken from him without his consent. Yet it will be admitted that that consent is not necessary when a national emergency requires the sacrifice of the property of the individual. The nation is but the individual in the aggregate. That which is conceded to national necessity should not be denied to individual need.

It is a common saying, accepted as true by the unthinking, "that a man has a right to do as he pleases with his own," and yet there is none more untrue. He is forbidden by the law to maltreat the animals which he may own or to inflict injury and torture upon any living thing. If he sets fire to his own house, thereby endangering the person or property of others, he is guilty of arson. A man's right in the use and enjoyment of his own property is determined by the common conscience of the community of which he is a part. Why should the law be so sensitive about the harming of a brute and so callous as to the hungering of the human? Why punish a man for destroying his own house, yet permit him to make it impossible for another to have a home? Right in the absolute is fixed and changeless, yet the standard of right rises

with the advancement of humanity, and may not this
ascending change soon impel the public to determine
how far individual vandalism against nature shall extend and where the rights of the common people shall
begin? The law forbidding the mangling unto death
of slaves by wild beasts that Rome might have a holi-
day was denounced as infamous by the money barons
of the imperial city; they declared it to be a ruthless
spoliation of vested property-rights and unwarranted
interference with the pleasurable pastimes of the people.
The cry of "vested rights" is the "stop thief" of him
whose purse has grown plethoric by the impoverish-
ment of others when he is ordered to disgorge his ill-
gotten gains. The right of property in human beings
was once a vested right in this country, created by
common consent, guaranteed by the constitution, and
consecrated by a century's legislation; yet the quicken-
ing conscience of the nineteenth century, beholding in
this vested right the world's crowning crime, revolted,
and the rebellion which followed wrought the extirpa-
tion of the "vested right" as the lightning of heaven
with its electric flash calcines the poisons in the atmosphere. It was a triumph of the nobler sentiments,—
the higher law of enlightened conscience overthrew
these legislative enactments, and in their destruction
branded the vested right of yesterday as the venal
wrong of to-day. Men of thought, men of conscience,
have no patience with the civilization which permits
one man to acquire a hundred million dollars while a
hundred thousand of his fellow-men starve.

Absolute ownership of property unrestricted by any

regard for the rights and well-being of the present and
coming generations finds no warrant in right or reason
or any parity in law or nature, and clearly has it been
shown by the world's best thinkers that that social
economy which finds no analogy in the economy of nature
is false in inception and vicious in results. These
things are all admitted to be correct in theory, but are
said to be wrong in practice. That which is true in
the abstract cannot be false in the concrete. Man,
however, does not, save when prompted by selfish motives and controlled by avarice, commend that in others
which he refuses to do himself, and resist all attempts
to prevail upon him to perform an act which in others
meets his own approval. The giving away of large
tracts of land or large sums of money embalms the
names of the donors in the memory of mankind, and
those are loudest in their praise who, though rich,
stint dependants and see, unmoved, penury and want all
around them. Is not this but an acknowledgment of
the correctness and justice of the principle that men
should share their wealth with their less fortunate
fellow-men, offer them a helping hand, and provide
for their material comforts and their mental, moral,
and social elevation? But as sordid wealth takes no
note of such matters, it is the duty of the State to look
after the welfare of all her children, and, through wise
and salutary laws, compel the hoarder of millions to
contribute to the doing of that which he should have
done voluntarily. Can that which as a charity is
right be wrong as a duty? Is it consistent to praise
others for doing that which we deny the right of the

State to make us do? Does the compelling constitute the wrong? Men should be consistent. Whatever their conscience approves in others they should be willing to do themselves, and if they have not the manhood to discharge a duty while it is only a moral obligation, they should be willing for that moral obligation to be made a legal duty. The division of property in view would neither impoverish nor enrich the parties affected, and the legislation proposed does not contemplate the taking of an individual's possessions without fair compensation. The one prime object is to supply a home to every family, secure to them the means of making a living, and elevate them into the highest and best citizenship.

The stability and progress of a country must depend upon the character of its peasantry, and whether the character of that peasantry will be debased or elevated will depend upon the relation they sustain to the land of their country. Ownership of property is the true condition of liberty. He who is dependent upon another for the land he cultivates cannot be free and independent. In England and Belgium, in truth wherever in Europe the liberty of voting is secured, the introduction of the ballot was necessary and hedging it about with many legal precautions lest the landlords should know how their tenants voted. In Switzerland every one can exercise the right of suffrage, but every one can likewise enjoy the right of property. The highway of nations is strewn with the ruins of the democracies of the past. Their decline and fall can be truthfully ascribed to the defect in their polity, which, while recognizing and protecting political equality, failed to establish an equality of conditions such as would have prevented the conflicts between the rich and the poor which grew into the revolution that resulted in despotism. After the common people have wrested their liberty from the ruthless hands of an oligarchy or despot, and secured the establishment of political equality, there remains a strife which will be coexistent with the life of the republic : it is the struggle between the rich and the poor, between those who own property and those who are propertyless. To-day the peril is admitted by all intelligent observers, and recent events in our own country declare this to be the vital defect in democratic institutions.

Permitting all to share in the collective prosperity would prevent excessive inequality opening a chasm between the higher and the lower classes across which bitter warfare will rage until the former are enslaved by the latter. To prevent this is a consummation devoutly to be prayed for.

CHAPTER III.

THE GREAT CITY A FRUITFUL SOURCE OF NATIONAL PERIL.

It may well be doubted whether there is another source from which the industrial interests and political peace of our country are so imperilled as from the concentration of capital and congregation of people which make up the mighty cities of our land. To the student of history it is clearly apparent that we are rapidly approaching that period in national existence which was attained by Rome when the empire was transformed into one grand organization of municipalities that absorbed every element of industry, save the agricultural, and that soon became servilely dependent. Then arose those dissensions, tumults, and social convulsions which worked the decline and final destruction of the world's greatest empire. The lessons of the recent strikes, referred to in a former chapter, can be studied to an advantage in this connection.

The report referred to of the Bureau of Labor shows that in the five States of Illinois, Massachusetts, Ohio, New York, and Pennsylvania, occurred 74.84 per cent. of the strikes and 89.48 per cent. of the lock-outs happening during the term covered by the report, and also that these States contain 49 per cent. of the manufacturing establishments in the country and 58 per cent. of the capital invested in that industry. These States contained by the census of 1880 about one-third of the population, and less than 6 per cent. of the area, of the United States, and within their borders these disastrous, social, and industrial disturbances which are growing more frequent and violent each succeeding year, exceeded three times the number happening in all other States and Territories. Is not the bare statement of this fact sufficient to excite the anxious inquiry as to the reason why it exists? It is certainly suggestive of the existence of forces, violent and vicious, at work in that limited portion of our national domain, embraced

within these States which can find comparatively no
encouragement in the vast expanse of territory included
in the remaining nineteen-twentieths of the Union.

The five States named, with a total population in
round numbers of 17,000,000, had, in 1880, an urban
population of over 7,500,000, or nearly one-half of the
citizens of these States dwelt in the towns and cities.
Within their territory we find those great industrial
centres, New York City, Philadelphia, Chicago, Boston, Pittsburg, Cleveland, Cincinnati, supplemented by
large mining districts, where thousands of men are
herded together without any diversion but drudgery,
and without any association or connection with the
prosperity or property of the section they inhabit.
The most violent and consequently the most disastrous
of these industrial outbreaks we find occurring in these
great manufacturing and mining centres.

In Illinois the urban population forms one-third of
the entire population of the State; in Massachusetts,
two-thirds; in Ohio, nearly one-half; in Pennsylvania,
over one-half; and in New York, over three-fifths.
In the States of Alabama, Georgia, Iowa, Kentucky,
Michigan, Mississippi, North Carolina, Tennessee,
Texas, Virginia, and Wisconsin, having a total population equal to that of the five States named, the urban
population constituted less than one-fifth of the total,
and within their borders occurred only 5.93 of the
strikes and 2.48 of the lock-outs, although containing
13 per cent. of the manufacturing establishments and
21 per cent. of the capital invested in those industries
in the Union.

A further comparison of the economic conditions existing in these two respective groups of States shows that in the first group there were 93,000 lunatics, imbeciles, mutes, and others classed as "defective;" 52,200 paupers, and 25,000 prisoners in jails and penitentiaries, while in the latter group there were but 75,000 defectives, 23,000 paupers, and 18,000 prisoners. This excess of insanity, pauperism, and crime existing among 17,000,000 people in one section of the country as compared with that existing among the same number of people in another section of the same country should prompt earnest inquiry that would grow into searching investigation as to the cause and conditions that contribute to and aggravate its existence. Such an investigation would disclose the fact that the cities furnish the far greater proportion of the unfortunate classes referred to who are a burden and a menace to the progress and permanency of society. An examination of statistics would also show that the increase of the urban population in the United States each successive year is much greater than the increase of population in the country. This "congestion to the metropolis," so characteristic of modern times, seems inevitably incident to civilization; yet it goes without question that the advantages gained by it in material progress and wealth are overbalanced by the evils it occasions in the social and moral life of society.

It has been truly said the city is the grave of humanity, for while the artificial advancement of the favored minority is evidenced in the grandeur of its structures and the splendor of their appointments, in the lavish display of luxury and sumptuous living that glitters and glows along its boulevards, yet back of this dazzle and glare, away from the marble mansions and the gold-coining mart, the great majority are herding in hovels and fighting for life mid environments and associates that render escape impossible and existence a curse. To see and know the truth of city-life we must go not upon the wide, well-paved thoroughfares, where dwell the rich and prosperous in commodious homes, but where the poor and unfortunate burrow in crowded houses and crawl through narrow and dingy streets and alleys.

CHAPTER IV.

THE HOVELS WHERE HOMELESS THOUSANDS DWELL.

THE "lower million" in every city exist close to the "upper ten," yet their presence, though near, in fact, is deemed but the figment of a disordered fancy, and but little thought and less care is given to them in any direction that would lead to their discovery and consequent betterment. A visit to a region of poverty, degradation, and crime, where hope and thrift are unknown, may not be without its lesson. It is a strange anomaly in human life that within an area of one hundred blocks forming a portion of what is known as the South Side in Chicago can be found the owners of colossal fortunes and human beings in the most abject poverty,—palaces filled with plenty and luxury and huts ever haunted with hunger and want,—troops of children sporting on shaded lawn or making frescoed halls ring with joyous laughter, while a few blocks away boys and girls, with pinched features and laughless lips, crouch in the shadow of grimy walls or search for food from garbage-box and gutter. In this locality —which has its prototype in every other large city in the land—the palatial homes of the rich, their churches and schools, and broad streets and boulevards, border the shores of the beautiful, far-spreading lake, while just across a single street the hovel-homes of the poor are huddled together on narrow, noisome, and smoke-clouded streets running to or along the slimy river. Here the rich and poor are together, yet as far apart as though separated by many a league. Within the limits occupied by the poor it is estimated there are 35,000 souls, and of these not 3000 dwell in decent houses ; long stretches of unpaved streets, covered many feet deep with the offal of an unclean populace, who, unrestrained, cast out whatever they will, and it is left to breed contagion and disease. The summer sun converts much of it into pest-breeding dust, which is blown by careless winds across the border-line and into the homes of the rich, whose owners have never seen the source whence it comes. .

Along these filthy streets are rickety, rambling buildings, almost overlapping each other, with roofs and sides awry and reeking with filth and swarming with vermin, the latter disporting themselves with all the freedom of ownership in the broad light of day. But few of these wretched tenements are for rent, and all up and down the length and breadth of this plague-spot each demoralized dwelling is seen to be crowded to its utmost capacity. Although the houses and their occupants at first impress one as though here was no sense of shame or desire to better their lot, it is not so, for the excuses they offer for the untoward condition of things in general, and the genuine gratitude for a few words of cheer or kindness which finds expression from these battered wrecks of manhood and woman-hood, show that they yet possess the ability to respond to better things, and are painfully conscious of their own degradation and seemingly hopeless of escape from it. As must needs be, the vicious and criminal are at home here, but it is also the enforced abiding-place of industrious poverty.

Here is the opportunity to study social and humane problems from the very actuality of human destitution and degradation, and here the evils, born of the ine-quality of conditions, can be traced to their rightful origin with a distinctness that must perforce bring conviction that the readjustment and reformation of our social and political economy .is a necessity demanded by justice and humanity. In this quarter, devoted to human demoralization and degradation, there are from six to ten members to a family, and these are stowed away in three or four small rooms, often wholly under ground. A few of the many children go to school, but the greater number, not having the necessary clothes or books, spend their days in aimless idleness upon the streets, taking their first lessons in that vagabondism which, as the years go by, generates vice and crime. Inertia is the one potent evil here. This, to the unthinking, would seem inexcusable and indicative of an innate worthlessness that would render abortive any effort at their elevation. But it is not so. Look deeper. How can bricks be made without straw, and when the feet are once set upon the tread-mill and there is no hope of ever being lifted therefrom, where is he who would tread faster than he must? Courage, energy, and industry are active only when incited by hope, and when hope dieth their impelling force is gone. The stoutest energy will quail and sink, and utterly die out in the constant presence of filthy housing, vile companionship, foul air, and forbidding sights and sounds.

From these the actually poor have no escape,—no hope of escape as things are now ordered; for one of the things which is most difficult, nay, almost impossible, to find in any large city are clean, wholesome, and decently-appointed tenements, near the laborer's work, which can be rented at a price he can afford to pay. It cannot be otherwise that here the causes which work the ruin of manhood are untouched and ever active, breeding indefinitely limitless broods of evil and woe, and until homes are provided for the poor, where it is possible for them to live at least decently upon their own industry, this social problem will fail of solution. In this quarter more than 30,000 people are living as no human being should be obliged to live. Surely there is a field in all our cities for broad basic endeavor, for social and industrial reform, and they who have the mind and means to pursue this endeavor should apply themselves to its accomplishment as a matter of personal safety and public good. Why such localities as the one here briefly described should be permitted to exist is a painful commentary upon the selfishness and greed of those who could if they would render its existence impossible.

The rental collected from the wretched habitants of the section referred to brings the owners an income of ten per cent., while the property a few blocks away on the wealthiest residence street in the city nets its owners only about four per cent. or five per cent., which is regarded a satisfactory return, and here we have the poorest of the poor paying ten per cent., while the man who is able to pay one thousand dollars a year for a home pays less than half as much interest to the investor as does the pauper. In this do we find one reason for the continued existence of such disgraceful localities?

Something ought to be done to relieve the cities of this great surplus, suffering population. What shall it be? In the densely populated countries of Europe emigration has proven the true remedy for over-population. With us migration can be made a great national fact and social blessing. There are millions of acres of fertile lands, with fat harvests sleeping in their unwrought and unbroken soils, awaiting the awakening touch of human hands. These lands should be peopled with the thousands now crowding the cities. Many would go upon them from choice had they the means; to such let the means be given. Those who would not go willingly, make their going and occupancy compulsory. Divide the land which is the people's heritage among the people for use and occupancy, and make ownership a condition of certain wise provisions well fulfilled. How this may be done we will show in the succeeding chapter.

CHAPTER V.

LAND-HOMES FOR THE HOMELESS.

MR. GLADSTONE, the world's Great Commoner, in referring to our landed area and its marvellous resources, said, "The United States have a natural base for the greatest continuous empire ever established by man." We need but build aright upon this base, made to endure as long as time shall last, to construct an empire the material greatness of which would be exceeded only by its moral grandeur, both wrought and crowned by the divine forces of Justice and Equality. The resources of this great empire are ample for the support in plenty and peace of a population equal to that of the entire world. The area of the United States, excluding Alaska, is 2,970,000 square miles. An estimate, admitted to be too small, places the arable area at 1,500,000 square miles. China, which contains over 400,000,000 people, has a total area of 1,348,870 square miles, not equalling one-half of ours. The Chinese are an agricultural people, and that vast multitude obtains its support from the soil. The mountains and barren plains of China occupy over 300,000 square miles, so that it is seen that our arable lands at the lowest estimate exceed those of China by one-half. The fact, therefore, that hundreds of millions of Chinese, with the rudest of implements, with no incentive to lift themselves out of the rut of ages, with a positive indisposition to adopt new and better methods, are supported by the agriculture of their country, ought certainly to be suggestive of the grand possibilities of America. Our agricultural resources alone fully developed would feed a billion of people, and uniting with these the great employing and sustaining resources of our mineral wealth and manufacturing industries, it is perfectly reasonable to assert that the United States can sustain with every comfort that should be sought and with every luxury that should not be shunned such a population. And yet in this land, as we have seen, are thousands who hunger and struggle with poverty until they die in penury. Why? Is it not because we fail to utilize the means provided by the bounteous Benefactor for their support? That the means are given is not denied. That they are not used is attested by the thousands of untilled acres found in every State of the Union.

Labor should lay tribute upon these lands. The people should occupy them,—use them. This occupancy and use means industry, which builds homes and fills them with comfort and content,—homes which become the chapels of patriotism, the bulwarks of the nation, the temples of a common humanity.

Of the 960,000,000 acres of arable area of the United States there were but 536,000,000 acres comprised in farms, and of these nearly one-half was unimproved, a very large part of which belonged to farms containing more than 1000 acres. Thus we see that nearly three-fourths of our tillable acreage is unused, while thousands are deprived of that support which they themselves could secure from the possession and cultivation of the soil. These unused lands may be divided into four classes: (1) government lands, State and national; (2) railroad lands; (3) vast tracts belonging to individuals and syndicates (home and foreign); (4) the surplusage in farms exceeding 1000 acres. That the government (either State or national) has the right to give the lands included in the first class to the people for settlement and use will not be questioned, and that there should be a rigid enforcement of the contract by which the corporations were given the lands of the second class must be admitted as a matter of simple justice, and in every instance where the conditions have not been fully complied with in letter and spirit forfeitures should be declared which would add a vast and desirable acreage to the territory covered by the first class. Speculators and syndicates, whether home or foreign, should be compelled to relinquish all but a limited quantity of their immense holdings, and also those farmers or planters who own to exceed 1000 acres, which can be done without impoverishing the few and yet enrich the many, by some such plan of procedure as the author suggests in a foregoing chapter. Upon these broad, fertile acres should live and labor the great and ever-increasing surplus population of the towns and cities.

It will be urged that every one can, under the homestead law, now secure a home and become a land-owner in this country, and the fact that any one does not is proof conclusive that he does not desire to. A canvass of a half-dozen families in any of the poor quarters of any city will expose the fallacy of such an assumption by revealing the fact that there are many who would avail themselves of the benefits of the homestead act had they but the necessary means. The entry fee required, it is true, is but a very small sum, and yet this pittance, as it seems to those who have plenty, to those who have nothing is a chance of life. This fee provided for, then comes the expense of removal and the means to erect and furnish a house, provide food until a crop can be harvested, and purchase the necessary stock and implements for farming. All these are beyond the reach of the poor, and, although willing and anxious to have them, they are forced to forego them, for their scanty earnings scarce provide the absolute necessaries of living as the days come and go. Doubtless there are those in our towns and cities who have become so enervated and almost dehumanized by idleness, want, and wickedness that they would be loth to leave their haunts of wretchedness, and would shrink from a life and conditions involving effort and industry. To the credit of humanity, even in its lowest conditions, be it said that there are but few of these, when compared with the multitude, who would be voluntary workers if opportunity offered. To provide both classes with homes, with the necessary instruments of industry, and to see that by the faithful use of the latter they deserve and improve the former is clearly within the province of the government in the exercise of its most beneficent function in promoting the general welfare of the nation.

By special enactment it should be provided that all male persons over twenty-one years of age, whether heads of families or not, who are not able to furnish the necessary comforts of life for themselves and families, either through inability to obtain work or an indisposition to work, remove from the place in which they are residing and locate upon a tract of public land, the size of which shall be regulated according to the number constituting the family. In the event of any one being unable to pay the entry-fee required, the cost of removal, and any other expenses incident to the occupancy and use of the land, then the government shall suspend the payment of the fee and provide for all the other outlay from the public treasury. Transportation, erection of a suitable house, stabling for stock, provisions for twelve months, necessary household furniture, farming implements, stock, and insurance would constitute the bill of expenditure. The settler should not only be compelled to reside upon and cultivate continuously for the term of five years the tract allotted him before receiving a patent therefor, but he should not be permitted to abandon the same during that time, and at no time within twenty-five years of its entry should the land be permitted to pass out of the possession of the family (or its descendants) to whom it was originally granted.

The settler should be required to pay in three annual instalments, beginning with the end of the third year of his occupancy of the land, to the government the amount expended by it in his behalf. A punishment of a penal nature should be provided for a failure on the part of the settler to make full payment of the annual instalment when due, to a suspension of which, of course, he would be entitled in the event of such inability having been caused by sickness, death, or failure of crops through some untoward action of the elements. If at the expiration of five years any annual instalment should be wholly or partly unpaid, the patent should not issue until the same is paid in full. Before the issuance of the patent the settler should not be permitted to sell, mortgage, exchange, or dispose of, in any way, any of the personal property furnished him by the government, and personal property of the same kind to the same amount must be always kept on the place free from mortgage or any incumbrance. No mortgage shall be valid upon all or any part of the original grant.

The expenses of settlement on United States lands incurred might be divided between the national government and the State from which the settler removes, as the latter could well afford to bear part of the burden, as it would be relieved in many instances of positive or possible paupers and offenders, who would, should they remain, become costly charges or dangerous disturbers.

CHAPTER VI.

USE THE TREASURY SURPLUS TO PAY THE COST, THE HOME OWNER WILL PAY THE PROFIT.

In this metallic age, " Will it pay ?" is the crucial question that promptly confronts the suggestion of any action, whether it involves a feast or a funeral, a business venture or a pleasure parade, a material enterprise or a moral reformation. A negative answer buries it beyond resurrection, an affirmative vivifies it with a virile vigor and electric energy that compel success. The plan proposed for relieving towns and cities of their suffering and dangerous classes, and giving work and homes to the unemployed thousands in our country, being in accordance with the dictates of common sense and based upon the principles of equal and exact justice to all men, subjected to the most critical examination of intelligent utilitarianism, will, the writer believes, meet every exaction and conform to every condition imposed and required to insure national benefit and pecuniary profit.

Various colonization societies have been and are engaged in locating families upon lands in the Western States and Territories. These societies have reduced colonization to a science, and from their reports we are able not merely to approximate, but to actually ascertain, the outlay necessary for homing a family and putting it in the way of becoming not only self-supporting but of contributing to the wealth and power of the State. The land is owned by the government through its purchase or procurement by the people, so that in giving to any member of the national family a portion of the public domain the government but gives the donee that which belongs to him.

In the matter of transportation figures cannot be given, as the cost would be determined by distance and number of persons composing the family. The same rates should be secured by legislation, if necessary, of the railway companies for the transportation of settlers under the plan proposed as these companies give to persons buying and locating upon lands tributary to their respective roads. This would not be placing a hardship upon the railroads, as they would, in the settlement, greatly profit through the consequent increase in travel and traffic, and in the end be far more than compensated for the reduction enforced.

The land being free, transportation reduced to a minimum, the following bill of costs presents a full and correct estimate of locating a family of five children and parents on a farm :

Buildings :
    House $250.00
    Stabling for stock.. ....   50.00
Furniture :
    No. 9 cook-stove, with outfit...   22.00
    Washing utensils, tubs, pails, etc.......... ....   3.50
    Crockery and cutlery.................................. ....   5.00
    Three beds, three tables, chairs, etc 10.00
    Bedclothes...   15.00
    Sundries...... ....   5.00

Implements and farm tools:

One wagon..	$50.00
One 12-inch break-plough	16.00
One 14-inch stubble-plough	12.00
One yoke and chain	4.00
One 5-feet break-harrow...	7.00
Small tools (spade, 90 cents ; shovel, $1.00)................	1.90
Hay-fork, manure-fork, two rakes..............................	1.65
Scythe and stone and snath, $1.75; hammer, 50 cents.	2.25
Monkey-wrench, cold chisel, brace............................	1.25
Three bits ($\frac{1}{4}$, $\frac{1}{2}$, and 1 inch) ; screw-driver, saw	3.00
Square, $1.25 ; sundries, $3.75..................................	5.00

Food and fuel for one year:

Three half-barrels pork...	30.00
Eighteen hundred pounds flour..................................	45.00
Groceries, tea, sugar, coffee, etc..............................	30.00
Potatoes to begin season (three months)......................	10.00
Five cords fire-wood...	32 50
Sundries, soap, lights, salt, etc..................................	25.00

Seeds (all will grow on first breaking):

Ten bushels flax.................	15.00
Two " corn..	1.00
Six " potatoes...	4.00

Live-stock :

One yoke of heavy oxen	125.00
One cow..	25.00
Two hogs (young)...	5.00
Feed for stock..	20.00
Insurance on buildings and live stock for one year..........	2.50
Total.............. ....$	$834.55

For less than one thousand dollars a family has been provided with a home and placed upon the line of industrious living, and the community in which they lived has been relieved of an actual or possible burden. Human hands fettered by enforced idleness or enervated by sloth have been unshackled and invigorated. The willing have been given a chance, the unwilling subjected to the necessity of working, which is health and happiness and wealth. It has been said that every industrious and thrifty settler is worth one thousand dollars a year to the State. In a single year he pays back the expenditure required to secure for the State the benefits of his industry and thrift.

According to the reports of the Commissioners of Poor Houses and Prisons in Massachussetts, the average yearly cost to the State of each prisoner is eighty-three dollars, and that of the poor one hundred and nine dollars and forty-five cents each. With the list of the criminal and poor growing each year, the expense of protection against the one and of support for the other increases. So in computing the actual cost of locating a family one must not fail to deduct the amount which it is possible the State would have to expend upon them if they were compelled to continue in the condition from which the plan proposed would rescue them.

The abode of poverty is the recruiting-station of pauperism and crime. Transfer its inmates to a home with pleasant surroundings, where the procurement of the necessaries of life is not only a possibility but a pleasure, and you transform them into good and independent citizens.

In the national treasury there are over one hundred and eighty million dollars idle and unproductive. This vast sum belongs to the people from whom it has been exacted as taxes, and it should be used for the benefit and protection of those to whom it belongs. Taking one thousand dollars as the cost of locating a family, the surplus in the national treasury would house and help to become self-helping 180,000 families, an aggregate of 1,260,000 persons,—a population almost equal to that of Maine and Connecticut. Is it possible to conceive of any better use to which the unexpended millions of national wealth could be applied? Is it not patent to all that the outlay would not only be returned a hundredfold, and that as a matter of State and national economy the plan proposed should be adopted and applied, but that personal good and public safety, human advancement and national existence, demand it?

That the necessity exists for the introduction and incorporation of a new and better economic system into our national polity which will provide, among other things, for the relief of our over-populated cities and the legions of the unemployed swarming all over the land is not only admitted but contemplated with alarm by all who consider conditions and investigate causes in the great world of humanity.

The troubles and dangers that confront us as a nation must be met and conquered within our own borders. There is no other possible escape. Emigration has been the safety and salvation of Eastern lands. There can be no emigration from America. This is the Mecca of the human race, the final resting-place of unresting humanity.

Earth's imperial people have ever moved westward as if impelled by a resistless power divine, and parallel with their migrations civilization and sovereignty moved. The world's sceptre has made the circuit of the earth : first raised and wielded in Egypt, it passed to Greece, from Greece to Rome, from Rome to France, from France to England, and from England it is passing unto America ; here to remain, for the Orient is just beyond us,—the land where it first arose. By the logic of causes that know no change the solution of the problems, mighty and grave, which confront us as a people must be reached through agencies of our own, and that solution not only involves the life of the nation, but it comprehends the future of the world.

CHAPTER VII.

NATIONAL PERILS AND PROBLEMS OF TO-DAY.

THE institutions of a country are inevitably moulded by its laws defining and determining the ownership and disposition of property in land. They who own the land are the rulers, and democracy to endure must be grounded in the soil. Individual freedom cannot be exercised under a government which permits the land through purchase or gift to pass into the hands of a few. A landed monopoly is destructive of democracy, and establishes upon its ruins an aristocracy whose rule is most galling and oppressive. With it a bold peasantry, a country's strength and pride, cannot exist, and its very presence is a relentless warfare against the normal life of the family. It engenders ignorance, penury, and crime, and brings the toiling millions into debasing subjection to the privileged few. Equality among the people can only be maintained through a great and permanent subdivision of the land, in the disposition of which the government should give no thought to immediate revenue, but its chief concern should be the homing of its people and the consequent building up of a true yeomanry that will insure its advancement and elevation in social and political virtue, keeping pace with its growth and progress in material development and wealth. Unfortunately, the founders of the republic, and those who have moulded its legislation and shaped its policy in each successive generation down to the present, considered the public domain as so much bullion, out of which must be coined the money to defray the expenses of government, or as the basis of mighty enterprises for material development of the country. Ignoring the great political truth that democratic equality finds its germ and growth in the soil itself, they took no " bond of fate" to secure the well-being of the generations to come, but prepared the way and created the conditions for large monopolies which have continued to increase in number and size until now their magnitude is colossal and their might is masterful. Such is the legitimate result of selling vast tracts to speculators and companies, giving to railway corporations nearly 300,000,000 acres, enabling land-sharks to seize upon great bodies of land withheld from the people as Indian reservations through as pernicious a system of legislation as ever blotted a national statute, and, by legislation equally harmful and inexcusable, placing it within the power of speculators and monopolists to obtain possession of thousands of acres under the guise of swamp-lands and by means of school, military, and Indian scrip. The present Homestead Law, which could not find a place in our land-system until for three-fourths of a century the public domain had been given up to the spoliation of speculators and sharpers, was hailed as the harbinger of a new and better era, yet it failed to work the emancipation of land from the grasping greed of monopolists. With the rulings of the Department of the Interior in the interest of corporations and the State and Federal courts under the domination of the landed monopoly, the rights of actual settlers meet oftener with " breach than observance." To such an extent has this vicious system of land legislation and adjudication obtained that not more than one head of a family out of every five is a home-owner in this great republic. The curse of the land monopoly rests as a withering blight upon the prosperity of every State from the Alleghanies to the Pacific slope, and beneath its baleful shadow is multiplying a race of crouching and servile tenants. These facts are pregnant with fateful meaning. The system which is responsible for their existence must be destroyed, or the child is now living who will witness the overthrow of American democracy. Republican institutions cannot endure among a dishomed people.

Subsidiary to the crime against the republic perpetrated in the establishment of a landed monopoly is the evil which threatens the peace and perpetuity of our institutions, generated and intensified in the growth and domination of great cities. As we have shown, they are the abiding-places rather of frightful poverty than of enviable wealth, and in them are breeding the Goths and Vandals of modern civilization, threatening, true to their teachings and environments, to play the part in our own fair land which their prototypes, swarming from jungles and forests, played in Europe in the fourth, fifth, and sixth centuries. The government of great cities is as yet an unknown art, and its discovery, to say nothing of its perfection, by the wisest publicists is deemed almost an impossibility through democratic methods. Our own experience is wholly in support of this view. Popular government in the United States outside of the cities is a success unquestioned and unquestionable; within them the record of the last score years proves it wellnigh an utter and ignominious failure. In the rural districts life and property is safe, education is generally diffused, social progress touches every one alike, equality of condition begets and fosters the spirit of fraternity and justice, the law is obeyed, and the registry of the ballot is the voice of the people. In the cities the public treasury is but a place for official pilfering, elective positions are articles of merchandise, legislatures are bartered for shekels, courts are bought by gilded rascals, and great numbers of men steeped in ignorance, penury, and drunkenness are made the dupes of reckless schemers and shameless demagogues who seek political preferment that they may gorge themselves from the public flesh-pots. The picture is not overdrawn, but the

rather a faint outline of that which is practically illus-
trated in the life of not only one, but all the metropolitan cities of the Union. Is not the apprehension
well grounded, that, unless something is done to arrest
the growth and elevate the character of the denizens of
our cities, the American republic will find in them
its decay and dissolution? Consideration of these
facts may well excite a profound concern for the future
of our people. The tillers of the soil have ever been
the hope and strength of a country. In the United
States men are seeking to escape from agricultural pursuits and yearning for the impassioned strife of city
life. Can the Union endure the depletion of the farming class and increasing unhealthful mastery of the
hurtful elements which dominate the cities? Through
the centralization of her population in the capital,
which wrought the enslavement of her peasantry, Rome
lost the sceptre of the world. History ever repeats
itself.

Another impending peril which confronts us is the
expanding and absorbing power of mighty corporations,
—the privileged creations of legislative invidiousness.
To clothe private enterprises with corporate power is
the prostitution of sovereignty through legislative
license to the lust of official avarice. It fastens the
till of dishonesty with the bar of knavery, and enables
worthless sharpers to float inflated enterprises by securing some wealthy deacon for their decoy-duck and
figure-head. Modern legislation enabling corporations
to issue wild-cat securities ought to be wiped from the
statute-books of every State in the Union. Corpora-

tions should be the servants of the people, established
for their convenience or necessity. When they cease
to fill their true functions and seek to exercise a mastery, as they are doing, of those who created them,
then the power that gave them existence should assert
its prerogative of control over its own creation. The
most formidable of all these are the railway corporations, with an aggregate capital of ten billion dollars,
their vast network of over one hundred thousand
miles of track extending and ramifying over and
through a continent, gathering into their coffers a billion dollars every year, having in their service—a
service characterized by a discipline as exacting and
emasculating as that which transforms a soldier into
a machine—over a quarter of a million of men, including the shrewdest and most unscrupulous financiers
and the most learned and skilful legal talent of the
nation, and securing the aid of every influence that
consolidated wealth can buy or coerce. And this vast
aggregation of ever-active agencies has no limit to its
existence. Corporations never die. They are endowed
with a greater power than the feudal barons of mediæval
Europe, and their very existence portends the ultimate
subjugation of the people. The one inspiring principle of democracy is that which involves an absolute
denial of the divine right of kings and the unqualified
demand for equal rights for all. Yet in the growth
and presence of the corporation we have a new and
most dangerous form of the one-man power and a
deadly enemy to human equality. We view with sus-
picion and oppose with every energy an attempt to

exalt one man thrice to the presidency, impelled by a latent fear of a contingent subversion of our political institutions; yet these railway magnates, who often determine the result of a presidential election and control those who make and interpret the laws, virtually hold office for life, and are endowed with the amplest hereditary powers. Here is food for reflection.

Another danger, which in truth includes and is an outgrowth of the others referred to, is found in the burdens and wrongs imposed and inflicted upon labor by capital. A successful solution of the labor problem cannot be attained until in our political economy *man* is acknowledged to be superior to wealth, and as a consequent that the rights of the many are paramount to the privileges of the few. Then will follow the complete emancipation of labor from the practical ownership which now holds it in bondage, and unto it will be given an equitable portion of the wealth it produces in alliance with capital. The rights of labor must be recognized. It must cease to be considered a staple in trade like wheat and houses. The rights of the laborer are the rights of mankind. The full recognition of this truth is demanded by justice and humanity, and until it obtains in full force and practice throughout every workshop in the land, and wherever hands are toiling that minds may build and bodies grow, there will be wrong and poverty and wretchedness leading to rapine, ruin, and death.

How to eradicate the evils enumerated from our national organism is the grand problem which presents itself to American statesmanship to-day, and the deferment of its solution is fraught with danger to the republic.

The writer believes that all the evils pointed out find their origin and increase, either as cause or effect, in the false relations existing between the people and the land and between labor and capital, and that until these relations are established upon the natural and divine principles of man's common property in the land and the right of Toil to share in its fruits these evils will intensify even unto the utter destruction of every vestige of American democracy. The people must assert themselves. There must be conference in counsel and concert in action among the true, the brave, and the faithful friends of humanity in every State. To such the author submits this book, with the confidence that if the measures proposed and legislation suggested are not found equal to the exigencies of the reformation demanded a thoughtful consideration of them will contribute to the devising and perfecting of means and methods whereby the great and good work will be accomplished. This grand work does not find its true scope in the highest advancement of privileged individuals or classes, or the concentration of immense wealth in the hands of a few, but in the uttermost development and paramount well-being of all. It is not the exceptional enlightenment or superior benefit of the minority, but the upbuilding of the lowly and humble multitudes. It will be done. It must be done. There may be seasons of woful waiting and dangerous delays. The insatiate greed of pelf, blind to its interests, unmindful of its own safety, may carry its utter disregard for the rights of humanity to such a point as to drive the people into violence and revolution, but at the great finale the people will be triumphant. All things foreshadow this result. It will be the conflict between right and wrong, with every divine force arrayed in invincible power with the former. Justice and right cannot, will not, be defeated. Whether the triumph shall come through peace or war depends wholly upon the prompt and judicious use of opportunities offered. The time is opportune now for action.

APPENDIX.

CONVICT LABOR.

LEGISLATION PROPOSED.

THE subject of convict labor ought not only to incite the laudable efforts of the humanitarian and philanthropist, but the best and wisest thought of the economist and publicist. Imprisonment as a punishment for the infraction of law is necessary for the protection of society, and as solitary confinement is a relic of barbarism, which would not be tolerated in this age and clime, all considerations looking to a discussion of that phase of the question must be dismissed without comment. Indeed, the practical phase of the question, as to whether the labor and the manufactured articles produced by free men must compete with the prices paid for convict labor and its productions, has, of late years, received serious attention in the discussion of economic subjects.

In February, 1887, the author prepared a bill relating to convict labor, which he forwarded to one of the senators in the Illinois General Assembly, then in session, with a request to introduce it in the Senate, or procure its introduction in the House, in order, if possible, to have the subject-matter thereof discussed by the Assembly; but aside from the mere perfunctory courtesy of introducing the bill it received no attention from that body, sharing the fate which but too commonly befalls all measures presented to legislative bodies not involving partisan dogmas or political jobbery. Subjected to critical examination by men conversant with the needs and schooled in the wisdom of legislation, it is believed this bill, which is here given in substance as hastily prepared, would serve at least as the basis of a judicious and practical solution of this important question:

A BILL FOR AN ACT RELATING TO CONVICT LABOR.

SECTION 1. *Be it enacted, etc.,* There is hereby created a board of convict labor commissioners, composed of three persons to be appointed by the governor of this State, by and with the consent of the Senate, at a salary of three thousand five hundred dollars per year each, whose term of office shall commence on the first day of May, 1887, and continue for two years thereafter, unless sooner removed by the governor, as hereinafter provided.

SEC. 2. It shall be the duty of said board immediately after its appointment to meet at the city of Springfield and consult with the governor, auditor, and secretary of state as to the best and most advisable manner in which to make the purchase of and to maintain in the penitentiaries of this State sufficient and suitable machinery for the manufacture of boots, shoes, hats, caps, and wearing apparel of every kind such as is worn and used by the inmates of the several institutions of this State, and also for the manufacture of furniture, beds, and bedding such as is required in the several institutions of this State.

SEC. 3. It shall be the duty of the auditor of state to procure and complete forthwith, within sixty days from the taking effect of this law, a full statement of all the moneys paid out by the State for the different articles of wearing apparel used by the inmates of State institutions, and for all articles of furniture, beds, and bedding furnished and purchased for the various institutions of this State; and in order to assist the auditor of state to make his said report it is hereby made the duty of the officers of the various institutions, when notified by the auditor of state, to furnish him a detailed statement within thirty days after the receipt of such notification, setting forth therein the cost of all articles purchased for their several institutions during the fiscal year preceding, whether such costs have been paid by the county or out of the State treasury. And for the refusal of any such officer to furnish such report he shall be liable to a penalty of twenty-five dollars a day, to be recovered for the use of and in the name of the People of the State of Illinois.

SEC 4. It shall be the duty of said board of commissioners to assign such a number of convicts as may be required to manufacture each article hereinabove contemplated for the use of all State institutions in this State, and to purchase such tools, appliances, and machinery as in the judgment of said board, after consultation with the governor, auditor, and secretary of state, it will be deemed necessary to carry out the object of this bill.

Sec. 5. Each convict assigned to manufacture said articles shall not be required to work more than eight hours per day of each working-day, and it shall be the duty of said board to see that some competent person, skilled in the manufacture of each particular article so to be furnished, shall give instructions to the convicts in the proper use of tools and machinery used in their respective departments for at least one hour each day, and it shall also be the duty of such board to see that the convicts receive instruction for at least one hour each day in common English branches.

Sec. 6. Every convict who shall comply with all the rules of the institution and who shall not be guilty of any breach of prison discipline shall receive at the expiration of his term of imprisonment the sum of ten cents for each and every day's work performed by him, and in case any convict shall be guilty of a breach of any of the rules of prison discipline, the wardens of the several penitentiaries shall make, keep, and preserve a record of the same, specifying wherein such convict was guilty of such breach of the rules of prison discipline, and every convict so guilty shall not be entitled to receive any compensation for any day of that week in which he has violated said rules.

Sec. 7. When the needs of all the State institutions shall be supplied with articles of furniture, beds, bedding, boots, shoes, and wearing apparel of every kind, if any surplus remain such surplus shall be assigned to the various counties of this State, in proportion to their inhabitants, to be distributed among the deserving poor of such counties in such manner as the board of supervisors of the respective counties may, by resolution, determine.

SEC. 8. The governor may remove any of the commissioners appointed by him as hereinbefore specified for any cause which in his judgment will warrant such removal, and it shall not be necessary for him to specify or state such cause to the person so removed, and it is hereby made the duty of the governor to remove any such commissioner so appointed if in his judgment a person better qualified to carry out the intent and meaning of this bill may be found to take the place of the person so removed; *provided*, the person so removed shall not be entitled to compensation after the date of his removal.

SEC. 9. No article which can be produced by hand shall be manufactured by machinery, nor shall any machinery for the manufacture of such articles be purchased except for the purpose of instructing the convicts in the use of machinery commonly used in the manufacture of articles similar to those manufactured by them in their respective departments.

SEC. 10. There is hereby appropriated out of the State treasury the sum of one hundred thousand dollars for the purpose of carrying out the object and intent of this bill, the same to be paid from time to time on warrants drawn on the auditor of state, which warrants shall be accompanied by a voucher of the person receiving the same, and approved by the board of commissioners, specifying the article of machinery or other object for which such voucher is issued.

A section might be added prohibiting the sale within the State of any article produced by convict labor, whether manufactured within or without the State. In the many attempts of the Supreme Court of the United States to draw the line between the power of the State and the Federal government the soundness of the doctrine has never been questioned, that the State may prohibit convicts, paupers, idiots, lunatics, and persons likely to become a public charge, as well as persons or animals afflicted by contagious diseases, coming within her limits. The right to exclude articles manufactured by convicts in foreign States would necessarily follow as incident to the power to exclude convicts, especially when the State which adopts the law prohibits the sale of the products manufactured by her own convicts.

While I think the candid reader will admit that the plan embodied in the foregoing bill is simple in its provisions, direct in its purpose, and comprehends the entire subject, yet I do not claim absolute perfection for it, or that it should be passed by the legislature without being amended in such manner as the wisdom of that august body may suggest, but I *do* consider it free from all the objections urged against the enforcement of a constitutional amendment prohibiting the hiring out of convict labor as well as that urged against the product of such labor being brought into competition with free labor. I feel perfectly safe in asserting that if a legislature would call for and obtain a statement as to the expenditures by the State and the several counties thereof, for the purchase of the articles for the manufacture of which this bill provides, that it will far exceed the amount of money received by the State from contractors for the service of convicts. Economy, therefore, commends this plan as lightening the burden of the tax-payers, but in dealing with this matter law-makers should be governed by higher motives than those prompted by pecuniary considerations, and when considered from a philanthropic stand-point,—which is the true one,—or from the platform of a wise publicist, it must be admitted that the adoption of such a measure would contribute to the well-being and happiness of humanity by reason of the instruction and elevation of those unfortunate human beings, some of whom are consigned to long years of imprisonment for the commission of petty offences, which they might not have committed had they been able to earn a livelihood by honest industry in the plying of some trade or avocation. These unhappy creatures, oftentimes the victims of circumstances or the products of conditions, thus condemned to servitude, are worse off than were the slaves in the South, for they toiled in the open fields, warmed by the sunlight, breathing the fresh, pure air of heaven, and while driven by the lash of the cruel taskmaster their toils were lightened and their scourging was deprived of half its sting in the hope assured of being supplied with food, raiment, and shelter in their declining years ; but the poor convict, breathing the prison's foul air, filling his body with the germs of disease, drags his lengthening chain of toil unto the end without hope or heart for the future. His term of servitude expires and he is turned adrift into the world. Society will not receive him, that society the perverted conditions of which perchance made his transgression not only possible, but almost inevitable. Every avenue leading to the position he occupied before the commission of the offence which branded him as a felon and every opportunity to re-establish himself in the good graces and esteem of his fellow-men are barred against him. This is neither just nor humane.

The object of all punishment should be reformatory, not retaliatory. If those convicts who are sentenced for long terms—many of them for a first offence—were treated with kindness, instructed in the common English branches, trained in some useful line of industry, taught to believe that every man owes a duty to society from which naught can absolve him, inspired with the assurance that they can regain their place among men, and then, when their imprisonment ends, given sufficient means to enable them to seek new fields and new surroundings, in a short time the penitentiaries would not be overcrowded as now, the State would grow stronger in good citizenship, society gain many useful members, and humanity be greatly and grandly benefited. It is true that some convicts seem to be beyond reclamation, but the true object of government and the purpose of all law are to conserve the public good, and as for those who deserve speedy and condign punishment for repeated offences of a gross and grave character, the habitual criminals' act and others of like import will be found sufficient to protect society against those whose reformation is hopeless. As to the amount of money necessary to carry out the provisions of the bill, it may be urged that one hundred thousand dollars would be inadequate. Let two hundred and fifty thousand dollars be appropriated for this purpose, and it will be found amply sufficient in any State in the Union. The prime object of the bill I propose is to instruct, educate, and reform the convicts, and to make shoemakers, tailors, carpenters, masons; in a word, to make out of them mechanics, and to keep them at work while in prison; and as it is imperative, in order to carry out the full scope and purpose of the measure proposed, that the greater part of their work should be done by hand, the quantity produced being of minor importance, it will be necessary only to purchase costly machinery for the purpose of instructing them in its use. The surplus articles produced under this plan could be distributed to most excellent advantage among those deserving poor in every community who, though reduced to penury, are very loth to become a charge upon the public bounty.

It must be admitted that the adoption of the measure I propose, or one very similar to it, will obviate every serious objection and answer any tenable argument not only against convicts being hired out to contractors, but also against the products of their labor being brought into competition with free labor. All that can be truthfully urged against my plan, under any circumstances, is that its operation implies the withdrawal of the State institutions from the market as purchasers, and to that extent would lessen the consumption of the products of free labor. But this could not be deemed an objection of vital or controlling importance, for the reason, admitted of all fair-minded men, that free labor, labor unions, knights of labor, and all other industrial organizations must, in the spirit of good citizenship, in common with all members of society, make some sacrifices when such sacrifices are necessary for the common weal.

Since preparing the foregoing bill and writing the above suggestions in February, 1887, I have taken occasion to look into the reports of penal institutions and of bureaus of statistics of the several States and of various countries as collected in the Second Annual Report of United States Commissioner Wright, and I find the bill, even in its crude state, meets nearly every requirement of the best and most advanced thought on the subject. Indeed, it contains provisions which obviate many of the difficulties which the learned commissioner of labor encountered in discussing the advantages and disadvantages of the various systems and plans proposed, in that it provides not only for the manufacture of the various articles by hand, but for the *instruction* of the convicts in the use of tools and improved machinery, such as are commonly used for the manufacture of such articles. Thus the convict who spent his term of sentence on hand-made goods, and who, at the same time, was properly instructed in the use of machinery for the manufacture of such goods, would, when discharged, be fully qualified to enter any workshop or factory and earn an honest living. It also provides for the disposal of all surplus articles produced.

Any one who will take the trouble to examine the historical notes presented by the Commissioner of Labor in his most valuable report will be astonished to discover how far we are behind our sister republics of South America in the matter of prison discipline for the reformation of convicts. Indeed, in this respect, to our shame be it said, we have not kept pace with the humanity of the age. In the penitentiary of the State of Boyacá, United States of Columbia, for example, there is in use a progressive system of classification, rewards, etc. In the first grade the prisoner is confined for the most part of the time in a separate cell, going out only to his meals, chapel, and to do small portions of household work. This lasts for from one to four months. In the second grade his style of clothing is changed, his fare is better, he is allowed to talk at meals, and is marked each day for conduct, labor, etc. Gaining six hundred marks, he goes into the last grade; there he finds still greater material comfort, and sleeps no longer in a cell, but in a dormitory with his entire grade. He may talk in the workshops also; may be employed as a guard or in prison offices; may even go outside the gates on errands; and when he has served in this grade the third part of his term of imprisonment, may be recommended for pardon. On leaving the establishment he receives a sum equal to fifteen cents a week for all the time served in this highest grade. Similar rules of discipline and pecuniary compensation is provided for the reformation, reclamation, education, and elevation of convicts in every State of the South American republics. Humanity and public policy alike require that something should be done immediately to check the commission of crime by making provision for housing the poor and reforming the criminal.

THE ENCROACHMENTS OF CONVICT LABOR UPON FREE LABOR.

THE encroachments of convict labor upon free labor are very pertinently presented in that portion of the Second Annual Report of United States Commissioner Wright, of the Bureau of Labor, directed specially to convict labor in the United States. From the figures there given it appears that the total number of prisoners of all grades employed in the penal institutions is 64,349, the males numbering 58,454, and the females 5895. Of this total number, 45,277 are engaged in productive labor of some kind, 15,100 are engaged in prison duties, and 3972 are sick or idle. Of the total number, 14,827 are employed under the public-account system, 15,670 under the contract system, 5676 under the piece-price system, and 9104 under the lease system.

This prison population, in proportion to the population of the United States, as here estimated, is 1 in 930 ; but the proportion to those engaged in mechanical, agricultural, and mining pursuits in the whole country is about 1 convict to every 300 persons so employed.

The summary by States shows that there is a total of 44,512 long-term convicts, 33,661 being employed in productive labor, 8146 in prison duties, 2705 idle and sick, with 233 contractors or lessees. In houses of correction, workhouses, and jails there is a total of 9839 convicts, 5859 being engaged in productive labor, 3205 in prison duties, and 775 idle and sick, the number of contractors or lessees being 30. The number of inmates in industrial and reform schools, and other institutions where short-term prisoners are temporarily employed, is 9998, of which number 5757 are engaged in productive labor, 3749 in prison duties, and 492 idle and sick, while the number of contractors or lessees is 28.

The industry employing the greatest number is that of the manufacture of boots and shoes, in which 7476 males and 133 females, or a total of 7609 prisoners, are engaged. The industry coming next to boots and shoes, so far as persons employed are concerned, is clothing, engaging 5561, while stone employs 4876; then come farming, gardening, etc., with 3569, furniture, employing 3446, and mining, 3273.

The total value of goods made and work done by productive labor in the penal institutions of the whole country was $28,753,999.13. It took 45,277 convicts one year to produce this total value. It would have taken 35,534 free laborers to have produced the same quantity of goods in the same time; or, in other words, a free laborer is equal to 1.27 convict, or to reverse the statement, one convict is equal to .78 of a free laborer. The State producing the largest amount of convict-made goods is New York, the value there being $6,236,-320.98. The next State in rank is Illinois, producing $3,284,267.50 worth of convict-made goods. Indiana comes next with a product of the value of $1,570,-901.37, while Ohio stands next in line with a product of the value of $1,368,122.51 ; then Missouri, $1,342,-020.07; then Pennsylvania, $1,317,265.85. Kansas ranks next, with a product of $1,270,575.77. Tennessee comes after Kansas, with only $1,142,000 ; then Michigan, $1,087,735.62 ; and last of the States producing over a million dollars' worth, New Jersey, $1,019,-608.32. Each of the other States and Territories dropped below the million-dollar point, Dakota coming at the bottom of the list with a product of $11,577.36. It is interesting to examine these values by industries. Boots and shoes lead, the product being $10,100,279.61, or 35.13 per cent. of the whole product of the penal institutions of the country, $28,753,999.13 ; the next largest item being the manufacture of clothing, which is $2,199,634.25, while carriages and wagons are manufactured to the value of $1,989,790. In all other industries the product is less than $2,000,000, the smallest being lumber to the value of $63,890.

The penal institutions of the first class employed 33,661 convicts on productive labor out of the total of 45,277 (or 74.34 per cent.), producing $24,859,810.31 worth of products (or 86.46 per cent. of the whole product). This product would have required 27,912 free laborers to have produced it, considering one free laborer in this class equal to 1.20 convict. The bulk of the goods made, then, in the prisons of the United

States is produced by the long-term prisoners. The convicts in the houses of correction, etc., produced $2,150,959.07 worth of product, or 7.48 per cent. of the whole, while they were in number 5859, or 12.94 per cent. of the whole. These goods might have been produced by 4139 free laborers; that is, in institutions of this class, one free laborer is equal to 1.42 convict. The short-term prisoners produced but $1,743,229.75 worth of goods, being 6.06 per cent. of the total product of all institutions. To produce these goods required 5757 convicts (or 12.72 per cent. of all), and they might have been produced by 3483 free laborers; that is, in this class, one free laborer is equal to 1.65 convict.

Under the public-account system the value of goods made is $4,086,637.87, or 14.21 per cent. of the total product, while under the contract system the value is $18,096,245.74, or 62.94 per cent. of the total product. Under the piece-price system goods are made to the value of $2,379,180.52, being 8.27 per cent. of the total product, and under the lease system the value of goods made is $4,191,935, or 14.58 per cent. of the total product.

Under the contract system, those industries producing the greatest total value are carried on under this system, as, for instance, the total product of boots and shoes in all the prisons of the country is $10,100,-279.61. Of this total, boots and shoes to the value of $8,861,771.91 are produced under the contract system.

Whatever competition with free labor arises from the employment of convicts should be considered from three points of view: First, the competition with all

o   27

the industries of the country ; second, the competition with special industries ; and third, the competition in States or special localities. In regard to the competition with the industries of the whole country à few figures will suffice. The total manufactured products of the United States, according to the tenth census, amounted to $5,369,579,191. The total product of all the penal institutions amounted to $28,753,999, which is $\frac{54}{100}$ of 1 per cent. of the value of the total products of the industries of the country. To produce the products of the industries of the whole country in 1880 there were paid in wages $947,953,795, or $1 in wages to $5.66 in product. The wages paid by contractors and lessees to States and counties for the labor of convicts was $3,512,970, or $1 in convict-labor wages to $8.19 of product of convict labor.

The amount of competition in each of the leading industries and the competition in each State are matters of special interest. Take boots and shoes, for instance : The per-capita product of free labor for the year is $1492 in all the States in which boots and shoes are manufactured in prisons, while the per capita for convict labor is $1327 per annum. The product for all States, whether employing convicts on boots and shoes or not, is $1496. These values show that, so far as boots and shoes are concerned, the convict produces as much per annum as the free laborer, lacking $169 per capita. In boots and shoes alone, in all the States wherein they are made in prison, $1 of prison product is represented by $18.23 of free-labor product. Of the persons employed in their manufacture, there is one convict employed to 16.2 free laborers. In New York, the heaviest boot and shoe State, so far as prisons are concerned, there is one convict employed in this industry to eight free laborers, while in Massachusetts, the largest producing State in boots and shoes, there is one convict employed to 111.7 free laborers.

The total product of all industries of the United States for 1880, as already stated, was $5,369,579,191, produced by 2,732,595 employés, a per-capita production of $1965. The total product of convict labor was $28,753,999, by 45,277 convicts, being a per-capita prison production of $635.

These figures are full of meaning, full of instruction, full of food for intelligent reflection. The products of convict labor ought not to be brought into competition with honest industry. To do so can have no other effect than to cripple manufacturers, reduce the wages of mechanics, and increase pauperism and its concomitant evil, crime. The State has no right to make money at the expense of the well-being and prosperity of her people. She has no right to sell human beings, body and soul, for pelf. To do so is no less criminal than it would be to license houses of ill repute for the purpose of revenue. No one is really benefited from the sale of contract labor but the contractor who is enabled to get rich out of the crimes of others. The State needs not wealth: the people are her stay, support, and safeguard. The people are the State. Less criminal was it to seize and take by force and stealth the untutored savage from the jungles of Africa and sell him into slavery than it is to confine convicts for a term of years in a place where they are driven by the lash of the taskmaster, where every barrier is thrown in the way of their civilization and reformation. Nine out of every ten of those committed to prison or confined in the penitentiary necessarily return and mingle with society, and if their conditions and surroundings during detention have rendered them more hardened, vicious, and brutal than before, our whole theory of penal institutions is a miserable, pitiable failure.

THE END.